HARDY AT HOME

Other books by Desmond Hawkins

Hardy, Novelist and Poet
Hardy's Wessex
The Tess Opera
Concerning Agnes

Cranborne Chase
Avalon and Sedgemoor
Wildlife of the New Forest

When I Was (autobiography)
Hawk among the Sparrows (novel)
Lighter than Day (novel)

HARDY AT HOME

THE PEOPLE AND PLACES
OF HIS WESSEX

A Critical Selection by
DESMOND HAWKINS

BARRIE & JENKINS

LONDON

To Hal Orel and Bob Schweik
whose friendship narrowed my ocean

Introduction and commentaries copyright © Desmond Hawkins 1989

First published in Great Britain by
Barrie & Jenkins Ltd
289 Westbourne Grove
London W11 2QA

British Library Cataloguing in Publication Data

Hawkins, Desmond
　　Hardy at home : the people and places of his Wessex.
　　1. Fiction in English. Hardy, Thomas, 1840-1928 –
　　Critical studies
　　I. Title
　　823'.8

ISBN 0-7126-2034-6

Illustrations by Pip Moon
Design by Gail Engert

Filmset in Linotron Baskerville No. 2
by SX Composing Limited, Rayleigh, Essex

Printed and bound by Richard Clay Ltd, Bungay, Suffolk

CONTENTS

Acknowledgements

For permission to draw on Hardy material I am grateful to the Trustees of Miss E. A. Dugdale and the Trustees of the Thomas Hardy Memorial Collection in the Dorset County Museum.

I am also indebted to James Gibson, whose authoritative knowledge of Hardy texts is always so generously made available to his friends and colleagues; and to the librarians at the county libraries in Dorchester and Blandford, and the University library at Southampton.

My acknowledgements would be incomplete without a grateful reference to my American friends who encouraged me to attempt this study of the 'Englishness' of Hardy, and more particularly the West Country factor in his make-up. And I am grateful also to Malvina Tribe for overcoming the difficulties in converting my manuscript into an immaculate typescript.

It was one of those sequestered spots outside the gates of the world where may usually be found more meditation than action, and more listlessness than meditation; where reasoning proceeds on narrow premisses, and results in inferences wildly imaginative; yet where, from time to time, dramas of a grandeur and unity truly Sophoclean are enacted in the real, by virtue of the concentrated passions and closely-knit interdependence of the lives therein.

The Woodlanders

'I suppose it *is* an advantage to be thoroughly at home in one region, however narrow'.

Thomas Hardy in conversation with William Archer
The Critic

INTRODUCTION

Thomas Hardy could claim that he knew 'every street and alley west of St Paul's like a born Londoner, which he was often supposed to be'. As a young man he lived and worked in London. In middle age he liked to spend part of each year there during the Season. He became a member of the Savile Club and the Athenaeum. Nevertheless it is as the quintessential man of Wessex that he is identified. Towards the end of his life he expressed his conviction that 'it is better for a writer to know a little bit of the world remarkably well than to know a great part of the world remarkably little'. The little bit that he knew remarkably well was what he himself named Wessex, and more particularly the country within about a couple of dozen miles of Dorchester that forms the heartland of his Wessex. It is here that Hardy was always and truly at home. It is from this native heath that he drew his imaginative strength as a novelist and a poet.

The phrase 'native heath' is particularly appropriate. He was born in a heathland cottage on that great waste of heather and gorse east of Dorchester that he named Egdon Heath. His was the third generation of Hardys to live there. Built in 1800 as the first habitation in a new settlement on the heath the cottage was a lonely place; even today it retains an aloof and self-absorbed atmosphere at the end of a lane in what has become Higher Bockhampton within the parish of Stinsford. In such a narrowly enclosed context the matrix of family life must have been all-important, the more so because of the characters of two dominant women, Hardy's mother and his grandmother. They were rich repositories of folk memories, legends, superstitions and the dramatic chronicles of rural life. The convivial and musical nature of his father – and indeed the whole music-making tradition of the older generations – sweetened and mellowed the harsher realities of the second quarter of the nineteenth century in Dorset. The boyhood inheritance of Thomas Hardy was worth a good deal more than its face value.

London was to be his goal, the place to conquer, the scene of such triumphs as a writer can win – the compliments of literary and aristocratic society, a night of acclamation at Covent Garden, the award of the Order of Merit. Beyond that he entered in spirit the larger international world of the intellect in which men of letters communicate across the frontiers of language and creed. His was no narrowly regional outlook. That I must emphasize before going on to claim, nevertheless, that very few writers can have owed so much to their native origins. The gut, bone and sinew of Hardy's work constantly draw on reserves accumulated at home.

It is instructive to consider the locations of his homes during his lifetime, as distinct from the lodgings he occupied occasionally. For his first thirty-four years his only permanent home was his birthplace near Dorchester. He then married, and with his wife Emma set up home in a rather uncertain and transient way which included a three-year period in London but otherwise took them to a succession of towns within about twenty miles of Dorchester – Swanage, Yeovil, Sturminster Newton and Wimborne – before he decided to build at Dorchester in 1885 the house, Max Gate, in which he resided for the rest of his life. In the eighty-eight years of his lifetime his home during seventy-seven of those years was either his birthplace or – two miles away – Max Gate. What might be described as his taproot was uncommonly strong and tenacious.

In the choice of subjects for his stories and poems he had no wish to confine himself to Wessex. He looked to wider horizons and dwelt on a variety of themes reflecting his interest in Napoleon, European travel, the philosophical controversies of his lifetime and broad human issues. After the early success of *Far from the Madding Crowd* he was anxious to avoid being typecast as a portrayer of shepherds and sheep. Even so the magnetic pull of the Wessex heartland cannot be gainsaid. Imagery, rhythm, vocabulary, metaphor, all the constituents of the texture of his writing carry an implicit acknowledgment of their source.

Many of the features of Hardy's personal inheritance are well known to his readers and widely recognized but they are scattered through a formidably massive body of writing. My aim in this book is to identify the chief preoccupations of those generations of Hardys in the cottage at Higher Bockhampton and to draw together their appearances in the work of Thomas the Youngest. To describe him in that dynastic way helps to underscore my intention. It is a distinctive part of Hardy's achievement that what he wrote was so often a making articulate, an epiphany almost, of what already stirred within that potent group of elders.

The music-making and the cider-making; the neighbourly gossip about witches and the hangman's rope; the annual cycle of ceremonies and festivals from the Whitsun club-walks to the carol-singers and mummers at Christmas; the life of the fields and dairies; the little masters of the rural crafts; the fairs and circuses – all these accumulated as a capital on which Hardy drew imaginatively until, in 1911, he could write 'There was quite enough human nature in Wessex for one man's literary purpose'.

To include every word that might claim a place would be to exceed the limits of a single volume. In making my selection I have given preference to what I consider the choicest examples and to excerpts from the less familiar books. If some favourite piece is omitted I hope the reader will nevertheless enjoy meeting Hardy here exclusively on his home ground.

Desmond Hawkins

A note on the text. In making my selection from Hardy's writings my first concern has been to preserve the integrity of his published texts, with only minimal concessions to the need to give clarity to an excerpt. This involves no more than the slightest sub-editing – replacing a pronoun with the appropriate name, for instance. In the presentation of poems I have occasionally not given the entire poem, when a single verse, or several verses but not all, are what are germane to my purpose. Each passage is identified by the title of the book in which it occurs, or – in the case of poems and short stories – by their individual titles.

1

THE NATIVE HEATH
AND BIRTHPLACE

In *The Life of Thomas Hardy* the autobiographical description of the
place of his birth and the scenes of his childhood, as he recalled
them in his later years, forms a continuous, familiar and readily
accessible narrative. To make excerpts from it would be to perform no
useful service. What I shall include in this section is the range of
imaginative creations in verse and prose that he reared like blooms
from those seeds of first experience.

In the poem 'Wessex Heights', written in middle age, Hardy
chooses for his spiritual home the downland of Wessex, from 'Ingpen
Beacon eastward to Wyll's Neck westwardly', and more particularly
Dorset's northern scarp from 'homely Bulbarrow' to 'little Pilsdon
Pen'. Here he could stand apart from 'men with a wintry sneer, and
women with tart disparagings.'

Even so there remains a more elemental and more deeply felt
refuge for at least the darker side of Hardy's imagination Egdon
Heath. It was Egdon that most strongly coloured his childhood. It was
to Egdon that the outcast Michael Henchard went symbolically to die
at the end of *The Mayor of Casterbridge*. It was Egdon that seemed to
match Hardy's image of himself as something of an outsider, a misfit, a
man – like the returning native, Clym Yeobright – out of tune with the
mood of his contemporaries. Nineteenth-century 'improvers' saw the
barrenness of Egdon as a challenge, almost a reproach, but the heath
aborted their progressive plans, frustrated their efforts to cultivate it

and tame it; and Hardy exulted in Egdon's tenacious pristine wilderness. 'Civilisation', he wrote, 'was its enemy'. Of all the Wessex landscapes that he portrayed it is surely Edgon Heath that lingers most vividly in the reader's memory.

To be strictly accurate, though, there is no such place. 'Egdon' is a collective name coined by Hardy for the multiplicity of heaths that extend to the south-east of Dorchester, and this quintessential heath of his is idealized or intensified to emphasize particular attributes. It is the enduring, unchanging face of prehistory that he stresses persistently. It records the beginning of life, as he saw it, the original creation; and it was the context for the beginning of his own life.

In 1800 the owner of the Kingston Maurward estate decided to convert the edge of Piddletown Heath into a settlement to be known as New Bockhampton, in the parish of Stinsford. An estate map marks the course of a new road on the heath beside which the first building plot is marked with the name 'Hardy'. It was Hardy's great-grandfather who acquired the plot, on a lease covering the duration of three lives, and there built for his son what is now known simply as 'Hardy's Cottage'.

In the isolation of its early years the cottage attracted the attention of the smugglers who transported their tubs of brandy across the bleak deserted heaths that ran inland from the coast between Weymouth and Lulworth. For them the Hardys provided a safely obscure storage-place, until the vicinity began to be populated and lost its remoteness. Through the recollections of his grandmother Hardy could envisage the loneliness of her young married life and the whiplash on the window at night as the smugglers rode up. From her he learnt how wild it was 'when first we settled here'.

He was reluctant to admit any dilution of that wildness. Apart from a Roman road and some prehistoric burial mounds the only marks on the landscape, in his view, were 'the very finger-touches of the last geological change'. As for the vegetation, 'ever since the beginning of vegetation its soil had worn the same antique brown dress'. The only stirring of the soil down the ages had been 'the scratching of rabbits'. In 'The Withered Arm' he made some concessions to reality in what might be described as a less poetic and more documentary treatment of Egdon, allowing that Enclosure Acts and agricultural reclamation had made significant changes; but on the whole he preferred not to notice that an alien plant, the rhododendron, was overpowering the indigenous gorse and heather; and that, decade by decade, the area of heathland was contracting. The image of Egdon that he preserved was of the great wilderness outside the walls of the ancestral home, the playground of his earliest years, vast and rich in sight and scent and sound, yet also close and secret under the arching fronds of bracken where he hid and meditated the deep thoughts of childhood.

Egdon was populated with heath-croppers and furze-cutters rather than with sheep and shepherds, and the downs where most of the latter were to be found lay some to the north, some to the west of Egdon.

The Return of the Native

> The outlook, lone and bare,
> The towering hawk and passing raven share,
> And all the upland round is called 'The He'th'.

'By the Barrows'

A Saturday afternoon in November was approaching the time of twilight, and the vast tract of unenclosed wild known as Egdon Heath embrowned itself moment by moment. Overhead the hollow stretch of whitish cloud shutting out the sky was as a tent which had the whole heath for its floor.

The heaven being spread with this pallid screen and the earth with the darkest vegetation, their meeting-line at the horizon was clearly marked. In such contrast the heath wore the appearance of an instalment of night which had taken up its place before its astronomical hour was come: darkness had to a great extent arrived hereon, while day stood distinct in the sky. Looking upwards, a furze-cutter would have been inclined to continue work; looking down, he would have decided to finish his faggot and go home. The distant rims of the world and of the firmament seemed to be a division in time no less than a division in matter. The face of the heath by its mere complexion added half an hour to evening; it could in like manner retard the dawn, sadden noon, anticipate the frowning of storms scarcely generated, and intensify the opacity of a moonless midnight to a cause of shaking and dread.

In fact, precisely at this transitional point of its nightly roll into darkness the great and particular glory of the Egdon waste began, and nobody could be said to understand the heath who had not been there at such a time. It could best be felt when it could not clearly be seen, its complete effect and explanation lying in this and the succeeding hours before the next dawn: then, and only then, did it tell its true tale. The spot was, indeed, a near relation of night, and when night showed itself an apparent tendency to gravitate together could be perceived in its shades and the scene. The sombre stretch of rounds and hollows seemed to rise and meet the evening gloom in pure sympathy, the heath exhaling darkness as rapidly as the heavens precipitated it. And so the obscurity in the air and the obscurity in the land closed together in a black fraternization towards which each advanced half-way.

The place became full of a watchful intentness now; for when other
things sank brooding to sleep the heath appeared slowly to awake and
listen. Every night its Titanic form seemed to await something; but it had
waited thus, unmoved, during so many centuries, through the crises of so
many things, that it could only be imagined to await one last crisis – the
final overthrow.

The Return of the Native

'It seems impossible to do well here, unless one were a wild bird or a
landscape-painter'.

The Return of the Native

He walked along towards home without attending to paths. If any one
knew the heath well it was Clym. He was permeated with its scenes, with
its substance, and with its odours. He might be said to be its product. His
eyes had first opened thereon; with its appearance all the first images of
his memory were mingled; his estimate of life had been coloured by it; his
toys had been the flint knives and arrow-heads which he found there,
wondering why stones should 'grow' to such odd shapes; his flowers, the
purple bells and yellow furze; his animal kingdom, the snakes and
croppers; his society, its human haunters. Take all the varying hates felt
by Eustacia Vye towards the heath, and translate them into loves, and
you have the heart of Clym. He gazed upon the wide prospect as he
walked, and was glad.

To many persons this Egdon was a place which had slipped out of its
century generations ago, to intrude as an uncouth object into this. It was
an obsolete thing, and few cared to study it. How could this be otherwise
in the days of square fields, plashed hedges, and meadows watered on a
plan so rectangular that on a fine day they look like silver gridirons? The
farmer, in his ride, who could smile at artificial grasses, look with
solicitude at the coming corn, and sigh with sadness at the fly-eaten
turnips, bestowed upon the distant upland of heath nothing better than a
frown. But as for Yeobright, when he looked from the heights on his way
he could not help indulging in a barbarous satisfaction at observing that,
in some of the attempts at reclamation from the waste, tillage, after
holding on for a year or two, had receded again in despair, the ferns and
furze-tufts stubbornly reasserting themselves.

The Return of the Native

Though the date was comparatively recent, Egdon was much less
fragmentary in character than now. The attempts – successful and

otherwise at cultivation on the lower slopes, which intrude and break up the original heath into small detached heaths, had not been carried far; Enclosure Acts had not taken effect, and the banks and fences which now exclude the cattle of those villagers who formerly enjoyed rights of commonage thereon, and the carts of those who had turbary privileges which kept them in firing all the year round, were not erected. Gertrude, therefore, rode along with no other obstacles than the prickly furze-bushes, the mats of heather, the white water-courses, and the natural steeps and declivities of the ground.

'The Withered Arm'

The scene before the reddleman's eyes was a gradual series of ascents from the level of the road backward into the heart of the heath. It embraced hillocks, pits, ridges, acclivities, one behind the other, till all was finished by a high hill cutting against the still light sky. The traveller's eye hovered about these things for a time, and finally settled upon one noteworthy object up there. It was a barrow. This bossy projection of earth above its natural level occupied the loftiest ground of the loneliest height that the heath contained. Although from the vale it appeared but as a wart on an Atlantean brow, its actual bulk was great. It formed the pole and axis of this heathery world.

. . .

The first tall flame from Rainbarrow sprang into the sky, attracting all eyes that had been fixed on the distant conflagrations back to their own attempt in the same kind. The cheerful blaze streaked the inner surface of the human circle – now increased by other stragglers, male and female – with its own gold livery, and even overlaid the dark turf around with a lively luminousness, which softened off into obscurity where the barrow rounded downwards out of sight. It showed the barrow to be the segment of a globe, as perfect as on the day when it was thrown up, even the little ditch remaining from which the earth was dug. Not a plough had ever disturbed a grain of that stubborn soil. In the heath's barrenness to the farmer lay its fertility to the historian. There had been no obliteration, because there had been no tending.

The Return of the Native

It faces west, and round the back and sides
High beeches, bending, hang a veil of boughs,
And sweep against the roof. Wild honeysucks
Climb on the walls, and seem to sprout a wish
(If we may fancy wish of trees and plants)
To overtop the apple-trees hard by.

Red roses, lilacs, variegated box
Are there in plenty, and such hardy flowers
As flourish best untrained. Adjoining these
Are herbs and esculents; and farther still
A field; then cottages with trees, and last
The distant hills and sky.

Behind, the scene is wilder. Heath and furze
Are everything that seems to grow and thrive
Upon the uneven ground. A stunted thorn
Stands here and there, indeed; and from a pit
An oak uprises, springing from a seed
Dropped by some bird a hundred years ago.

        In days bygone –
Long gone – my father's mother, who is now
Blest with the blest, would take me out to walk.
At such a time I once inquired of her
How looked the spot when first she settled here.
The answer I remember. 'Fifty years
Have passed since then, my child, and change has marked
The face of all things. Yonder garden-plots
And orchards were uncultivated slopes
O'ergrown with bramble bushes, furze and thorn:
That road a narrow path shut in by ferns,
Which, almost trees, obscured the passer-by.

Our house stood quite alone, and those tall firs
And beeches were not planted. Snakes and efts
Swarmed in the summer days, and nightly bats
Would fly about our bedrooms. Heathcroppers
Lived on the hills, and were our only friends;
So wild it was when first we settled here.'

'Domicilium'

There were no sounds but that of the booming wind upon the stretch of
tawny herbage around them, the crackling wheels, the tread of the men,
and the footsteps of the two shaggy ponies which drew the van. They
were small, hardy animals, of a breed between Galloway and Exmoor,
and were known as 'heath-croppers' here.

The Return of the Native

While superintending the church music from 1801 onwards to about 1805,
my grandfather used to do a little in smuggling, his house being a lonely
one, none of the others in Higher Bockhampton being then built, or only

one other. He sometimes had as many as eighty 'tubs' in a dark closet (afterwards destroyed in altering staircase) each tub containing 4 gallons. The spirits often smelt all over the house, being proof, & had to be lowered for drinking. The tubs, or little elongated barrels, were of thin staves with wooden hoops: I remember one of them which had been turned into a bucket by knocking out one head, & putting a handle. They were brought at night by men on horseback, 'slung,' or in carts. A whiplash across the window pane would awake my grandfather at 2 or 3 in the morning, & he would dress & go down. Not a soul was there, but a heap of tubs loomed up in front of the door. He would set to work & stow them away in the dark closet aforesaid, & nothing more would happen till dusk the following evening, when groups of dark long-bearded fellows would arrive, & carry off the tubs in two & fours slung over their shoulders. The smugglers grew so bold at last that they would come by day, & my grandmother insisted to her husband that he should stop receiving the tubs, which he did about 1805, though not till at a christening of one of their children they 'had a washing pan of pale brandy' left them by the smugglers to make merry with. Moreover the smugglers could not be got to leave off depositing the tubs for some while, but they did so when a second house was built about 100 yards off.

Many years later, indeed, I think in my mother's time, a large woman used to call, & ask if any of 'it' was wanted cheap. Her hugeness was caused by her having bullocks' bladders slung round her hips, in which she carried the spirits. She was known as 'Mother Rogers'.

Personal Notebooks of Thomas Hardy

The Roman Road runs straight and bare
As the pale parting-line in hair
Across the heath. And thoughtful men
Contrast its days of Now and Then,
And delve, and measure, and compare;

Visioning on the vacant air
Helmed legionaries, who proudly rear
The Eagle, as they pace again
                    The Roman Road.

But no tall brass-helmed legionnaire
Haunts it for me. Uprises there
A mother's form upon my ken,
Guiding my infant steps, as when
We walked that ancient thoroughfare,
                    The Roman Road.

'The Roman Road'

I sat one sprinkling day upon the lea,
Where tall-stemmed ferns spread out luxuriantly,
And nothing but those tall ferns sheltered me.

The rain gained strength, and damped each lopping frond,
Ran down their stalks beside me and beyond,
And shaped slow-creeping rivulets as I conned,

With pride, my spray-roofed house. And though anon
Some drops pierced its green rafters, I sat on,
Making pretence I was not rained upon.

The sun then burst, and brought forth a sweet breath
From the limp ferns as they dried underneath:
I said: 'I could live on here thus till death;'

And queried in the green rays as I sate:
'Why should I have to grow to man's estate,
And this afar-noised World perambulate?'

                                        'Childhood Among the Ferns'

2

THE OLDER FOLK

Michael Millgate has described Hardy as 'a child of the oral tradition, and perhaps, in England, that tradition's last and greatest product'. Hardy himself, in the poem 'The Oxen', has left us a vivid thumbnail sketch of the Hardy children sitting 'by the embers in hearthside ease' while they listened to 'an elder' telling them a legend of Christmas Eve. That image of the little family gathering by the fireside, attending to the stored memories of parents and assorted elders, is one that suffuses much of Hardy's writing. He seems to have had little contact with other children, except his sister Mary, and to have focused his interest on the wealth of general lore and parish history, of tragic and comic anecdote and 'rambling old canticle' that was the stuff of adult conversation around him. Much of it would be, as he later described the reminiscences of an old Stinsford worthy, 'neither truth nor lies, but a Not Proven compound which is very relishable'. It is that 'relishable' quality which seized the boy's imagination and comes through so vividly in the writing of his manhood.

Both his grandfathers had died before he was born. His maternal grandmother saw the first seven years of his life, his Hardy grandmother lived with his parents in the Bockhampton cottage until he was approaching manhood. The influence of these immediate family elders was reinforced by uncles and aunts and venerable neighbours, who collectively stimulated the boy's mind with a folk-weave of colourful episodes and traditional themes. The French Revolution, the Industrial Revolution and the Napoleonic Wars, with their social and political consequences, were the portentous forces that progressively revolutionised the small rural world of Hardy's parents and grandparents. Indeed the fifty years preceding Hardy's birth saw as radical a transformation of many aspects of English life as any in our history, but through them there persisted those older threads of custom and folk culture that drew their vitality from earlier centuries. The deep-rooted character of Hardy's genius was grounded in the talk, the music, the laughter and the sorrows of those elders whose portraits he later drew so affectionately – the tranter and his colleagues in the Mellstock choir, Grandfer Cantle with his proud military moments in the Local Defence Volunteers, Robert Creedle with his repertoire of the 'pomps' of ancient days, and many more.

The music-making enthusiasm of the Hardy men, for church music and country dance impartially, passed readily to Hardy from his father, along with anecdotes of the grimmer sort about public executions and whippings in Dorchester. His mother had a remarkable memory for the ballads and stories of her young days, and the Hardy grandmother drew on recollections so remote that she seemed to her grandson like 'one left behind of a band gone distant'. The constant presences of these two powerful women in the childhood home evidently had a spellbinding influence on the future author.

In the foreground of his novels – perhaps surprisingly – it is the young who occupy the centre of the stage, with Michael Henchard as the one striking exception. The older characters have supporting roles; the 'ancients' lurk in the background. Hardy did not see his own ancestors in terms of high dramatic promise. He credited them rather with a stoicism, a 'sturdy muteness' which took from life 'what it grants, without question'. In his celebration of the older folk, therefore, he included the impassive silence that lay between the bursts of spirited conversation. Farmer Cawtree and the nameless hollow-turner in *The Woodlanders* sit like stone figures in a lost civilization playing their interminable game of langterloo. And Hardy remembered also that old age too often meant not a family circle of adoring descendants, but the poor-house or the 'Union'.

> I know not how it may be with others
>   Who sit amid relics of householdry
> That date from the days of their mothers' mothers,
>   But well I know how it is with me
>   Continually.

I see the hands of the generations
    That owned each shiny familiar thing
In play on its knobs and indentations,
    And with its ancient fashioning
      Still dallying:

Hands behind hands, growing paler and paler,
    As in a mirror a candle-flame
Shows images of itself, each frailer
    As it recedes, though the eye may frame
      Its shape the same.

On the clock's dull dial a foggy finger,
    Moving to set the minutes right
With tentative touches that lift and linger
    In the wont of a moth on a summer night,
      Creeps to my sight.

On this old viol, too, fingers are dancing –
    As whilom – just over the strings by the nut,
The tip of a bow receding, advancing
    In airy quivers, as if it would cut
      The plaintive gut.

And I see a face by that box for tinder,
    Glowing forth in fits from the dark,
And fading again, as the linten cinder
    Kindles to red at the flinty spark,
      Or goes out stark.

Well, well. It is best to be up and doing,
    The world has no use for one to-day
Who eyes things thus – no aim pursuing!
    He should not continue in this stay,
      But sink away.

                        'Old Furniture'

Gabriel thought fit to change the subject. 'You must be a very aged man, malter, to have sons growed up so old and ancient,' he remarked.

    'Father's so old that 'a can't mind his age, can ye, Father?' interposed Jacob. 'And he's growed terrible crooked, too, lately,' Jacob continued, surveying his father's figure, which was rather more bowed than his own. 'Really, one may say that Father there is three-double.'

    'Crooked folk will last a long while,' said the maltster, grimly, and not in the best humour.

'Shepherd would like to hear the pedigree of yer life, Father –
wouldn't ye, shepherd?'

'Ay, that I should,' said Gabriel, with the heartiness of a man who
had longed to hear it for several months. 'What may your age be, malter?'

The maltster cleared his throat in an exaggerated form for emphasis,
and elongating his gaze to the remotest point of the ashpit, said, in the
slow speech justifiable when the importance of a subject is so generally
felt that any mannerism must be tolerated in getting at it, 'Well, I don't
mind the year I were born in, but perhaps I can reckon up the places I've
lived at, and so get it that way. I bode at Upper Longpuddle across there'
(nodding to the north) 'till I were eleven. I bode seven at Kingsbere'
(nodding to the east) 'where I took to malting. I went therefrom to
Norcombe, and malted there two-and-twenty-years, and two-and-twenty
years I was there turnip-hoeing and harvesting. Ah, I knowed that old
place, Norcombe, years afore you were thought of, Master Oak' (Oak
smiled sincere belief in the fact). 'Then I malted at Durnover four year,
and four year turnip-hoeing; and I was fourteen times eleven months at
Millpond St Jude's' (nodding north-west-by-north). 'Old Twills
wouldn't hire me for more than eleven months at a time, to keep me from
being chargeable to the parish if so be I was disabled. Then I was three
year at Mellstock, and I've been here one-and-thirty year come
Candlemas. How much is that?'

'Hundred and seventeen,' chuckled another old gentleman, given to
mental arithmetic and little conversation, who had hitherto sat
unobserved in a corner.

'Well, then, that's my age,' said the maltster, emphatically.

'O no, Father!' said Jacob. 'Your turnip-hoeing were in the summer
and your malting in the winter of the same years, and ye don't ought to
count both halves, Father.'

'Chok' it all! I lived through the summers, didn't I? That's my
question. I suppose ye'll say next I be no age at all to speak of?'

'Sure we shan't,' said Gabriel, soothingly.

'Ye be a very old aged person, maltster,' attested Jan Coggan, also
soothingly. 'We all know that, and ye must have a wonderful talented
constitution to be able to live so long, mustn't he, neighbours?'

'True, true; ye must, malter, wonderful,' said the meeting
unanimously.

Far from the Madding Crowd

Supper-time came, and with it the hot-baked meats from the oven, laid
on a snowy cloth fresh from the press, and reticulated with folds as in
Flemish Last Suppers. Creedle and the boy fetched and carried with
amazing alacrity; the latter, to mollify his superior, and make things

pleasant, expressing his admiration of Creedle's cleverness when they were alone.

'I s'pose the time when you learnt all these knowing things, Mr Creedle, was when you was in the militia?'

'Well, yes. I seed the world that year somewhat, certainly, and mastered many arts of strange, dashing life.'

'I s'pose your memory can reach a long way back into history, Mr Creedle?'

'O yes. Ancient days, when there was battles and famines, and hang-fairs, and other pomps, seem to me as yesterday. Ah, many's the patriarch I've seed come and go in this parish! There, he's calling for more plates. Lord, why can't 'em turn their plates bottom upward for pudding, as we bucks used to do in former days!'

The Woodlanders

She told how they used to form for the country dances –
    'The Triumph', 'The New-rigged Ship' –
To the light of the guttering wax in the panelled manses,
    And in cots to the blink of a dip.

She spoke of the wild 'poussetting' and 'allemanding'
    On carpet, on oak, and on sod;
And the two long rows of ladies and gentlemen standing,
    And the figures the couples trod.

She showed us the spot where the maypole was yearly planted,
    And where the bandsmen stood
While breeched and kerchiefed partners whirled, and panted
    To choose each other for good.

She told of that far-back day when they learnt astounded
    Of the death of the King of France:
Of the Terror; and then of Bonaparte's unbounded
    Ambition and arrogance.

Of how his threats woke warlike preparations
    Along the southern strand,
And how each night brought tremors and trepidations
    Lest morning should see him land.

She said she had often heard the gibbet creaking
    As it swayed in the lightning flash,
Had caught from the neighbouring town a small child's shrieking
    At the cart-tail under the lash . . .

With cap-framed face and long gaze into the embers –
    We seated around her knees –
She would dwell on such dead themes, not as one who remembers,
    But rather as one who sees.

She seemed one left behind of a band gone distant
    So far that no tongue could hail:
Past things retold were to her as things existent,
    Things present but as a tale.

'One We Knew'

Mother described to-day the three Hardys as they used to appear passing over the brow of the hill to Stinsford Church on a Sunday morning, three or four years before my birth. They were always hurrying, being rather late, their fiddles and violoncello in green-baize bags under their left arms. They wore top hats, stick-up shirt collars, dark blue coats with great collars and gilt buttons, deep cuffs and black silk 'stocks' or neckerchiefs. Had curly hair, and carried their heads to one side as they walked. My grandfather wore drab cloth breeches and buckled shoes, but his sons wore trousers and Wellington boots.

The Life of Thomas Hardy

Kenfield, the mail-coach guard from London to Dorchester, lived at Higher Bockhampton in the eighteen thirties, the reason probably being that the spot lay near the London Road, so that he could take small packages to London on his own account, by collusion with the coachman. He used to have butter brought to him by old Hedditch the dairyman, also eggs. Also game, which he bought of poachers – old Critchel for one. The provisions were packed into a box, the box into a hamper, & the whole put into the boot of the coach with the letter-bags, the boot being under the guard's seat, & opening behind with a door on wh were 'G.R.', a crown, & 'Royal Mail.'

    He carried 2 pistols, a cutlass, & a blunderbus in a long tin box 'like a candle-box, in front of him; also a ball of tar-twine, & a screw-hammer (in case of a break down). Also 'a little time-piece strapped on to him in a leather pouch,' which when he got home he placed on his mantel piece.

    He kept a pony & gig to drive to Dorchester (2½ miles) to take his seat on the mail coach, putting on his red uniform before starting, & his dog's-hair hat with a gold band round it. He was on the coach two nights out of three.

    Meanwhile John Downton, a youth of the village whom he employed, would carry the packed hamper in the evening about 5 down through the plantation separating Higher Bockhampton from the turnpike road, & knowing the exact time the coach would pass wait at the plantation gate for it, which pulled up for a moment to receive the hamper, & rolled on again.

Although Kenfield went right through to London, there were two or three coachmen to the journey. Whether they all knew of this butter & game business cannot be said. Oliver of Dorchester, who horsed the mailcoach, horsed it only as far as to Blandford, where another contractor took on.

Personal Notebooks of Thomas Hardy

I pace along, the rain-shafts riddling me,
Mile after mile out by the moorland way,
And up the hill, and through the ewe-leaze gray
Into the lane, and round the corner tree;

Where, as my clothing clams me, mire-bestarred,
And the enfeebled light dies out of day,
Leaving the liquid shades to reign, I say,
'This is a hardship to be calendared!'

Yet sires of mine now perished and forgot,
When worse beset, ere roads were shapen here,
And night and storm were foes indeed to fear,
Times numberless have trudged across this spot
In sturdy muteness on their strenuous lot,
And taking all such toils as trifles mere.

'A Wet Night'

When the wasting embers redden the chimney-breast,
And Life's bare pathway looms like a desert track to me,
And from hall and parlour the living have gone to their rest,
My perished people who housed them here come back to me.

They come and seat them around in their mouldy places,
Now and then bending towards me a glance of wistfulness,
A strange upbraiding smile upon all their faces,
And in the bearing of each a passive tristfulness.

'Do you uphold me, lingering and languishing here,
A pale late plant of your once strong stock?' I say to them;
'A thinker of crooked thoughts upon Life in the sere,
And on That which consigns men to night after showing the day
    to them?'

' – O let be the Wherefore! We fevered our years not thus:
Take of Life what it grants, without question!' they answer me
   seemingly.
'Enjoy, suffer, wait: spread the table here freely like us,
And, satisfied, placid, unfretting, watch Time away beamingly!'

'Night in the Old Home'

'Come in, come in,' said Mrs Yeobright; and Clym went forward to welcome them. 'How is it you are so late? Grandfer Cantle has been here ever so long, and we thought you'd have come with him, as you live so near one another.'

'Well, I should have come earlier,' Mr Fairway said, and paused to look along the beam of the ceiling for a nail to hang his hat on; but, finding his accustomed one to be occupied by the mistletoe, and all the nails in the walls to be burdened with bunches of holly, he at last relieved himself of the hat by ticklishly balancing it between the candle-box and the head of the clock-case. 'I should have come earlier, ma'am,' he resumed, with a more composed air, 'but I know what parties be, and how there's none too much room in folks' houses at such times, so I thought I wouldn't come till you'd got settled a bit.'

'And I thought so too, Mrs Yeobright,' said Christian earnestly; 'but father there was so eager that he had no manners at all, and left home almost afore 'twas dark. I told him 'twas barely decent in a' old man to come so oversoon; but words be wind.'

'Klk! I wasn't going to bide waiting about till half the game was over! I'm as light as a kite when anything's going on!' crowed Crandfer Cantle from the chimney-seat.

Fairway had meanwhile concluded a critical gaze at Yeobright. 'Now, you may not believe it,' he said to the rest of the room, 'but I should never have knowed this gentleman if I had met him anywhere off his own he'th: he's altered so much.'

'You too have altered, and for the better, I think, Timothy,' said Yeobright, surveying the firm figure of Fairway.

'Master Yeobright, look me over too. I have altered for the better, haven't I, hey?' said Grandfer Cantle, rising, and placing himself something above half a foot from Clym's eye, to induce the most searching criticism.

'To be sure we will,' said Fairway, taking the candle and moving it over the surface of the Grandfer's countenance, the subject of his scrutiny irradiating himself with light and pleasant smiles, and giving himself jerks of juvenility.

'You haven't changed much,' said Yeobright.

'If there's any difference, Grandfer is younger,' appended Fairway decisively.

'And yet not my own doing, and I feel no pride in it,' said the pleased ancient. 'But I can't be cured of my vagaries; them I plead guilty to. Yes, Master Cantle always was that, as we know. But I am nothing by the side of you, Mister Clym.'

'Nor any o' us,' said Humphrey, in a low rich tone of admiration, not intended to reach anybody's ears.

'Really, there would have been nobody here who could have stood as decent second to him, or even third, if I hadn't been a soldier in the Bang-up Locals (as we was called for our smartness),' said Grandfer Cantle. 'And even as 'tis we all look a little scammish beside him. But in the year four 'twas said there wasn't a finer figure in the whole South Wessex than I, as I looked when dashing past the shop-winders with the rest of our company on the day we ran out o' Budmouth because it was thoughted that Boney had landed round the point. There was I, straight as a young poplar, wi' my firelock, and my bagnet, and my spatterdashes, and my stock sawing my jaws off, and my accoutrements sheening like the seven stars! Yes, neighbours, I was a pretty sight in my soldiering days. You ought to have seen me in 'four!'

The Return of the Native

After supper they sat down to cards; Cawtree and the hollow-turner monopolizing the new packs for an interminable game of langterloo, in which a lump of chalk was incessantly used – a game those two always played wherever they were, taking a solitary candle and going to a private table in a corner with the mien of persons bent on weighty matters. The rest of the company on this account were obliged to put up with old packs for their round game that had been lying by in a drawer ever since the time that Giles's grandmother was alive. Each card had a great stain in the middle of its back, produced by the touch of generations of damp and excited thumbs, now fleshless in the grave; and the kings and queens wore a decayed expression of feature, as if they were rather an impecunious dethroned dynasty hiding in obscure slums than real regal characters. Every now and then the comparatively few remarks of the players at the round game were harshly intruded on by the langterloo jingle of Farmer Cawtree and the hollow-turner from the back of the room:

> And I' will hold' a wa'-ger with you'
> That all' these marks' are thirt'-y two'.

accompanied by rapping strokes with the chalk on the table: then an exclamation, an argument, a dealing of the cards; then the commencement of the rhymes anew.

The Woodlanders

Then there were the Poor-houses, I remember – just at the corner turning down to the dairy. These were the homes of the parish paupers before workhouses were built. In one of them lived an old man who was found one day rolling on the floor, with a lot of pence and halfpence scattered round him. They asked him what was the matter, and he said he had heard of people rolling in money, and he thought that for once in his life he would do it, to see what it was like.

The Life of Thomas Hardy

I thought they'd be strangers aroun' me,
    But she's to be there!
Let me jump out o' waggon and go back and drown me
    At Pummery or Ten-Hatches Weir.

I thought: 'Well, I've come to the Union –
    The workhouse at last –
After honest hard work all the week, and Communion
    O' Zundays, these fifty years past.

''Tis hard; but,' I thought, 'never mind it:
    There's gain in the end:
And when I get used to the place I shall find it
    A home, and may find there a friend.

'Life there will be better than t'other,
    For peace is assured.
The men in one wing and their wives in another
    Is strictly the rule of the Board.'

Just then one young Pa'son arriving
    Steps up out of breath
To the side o' the waggon wherein we were driving
    To Union; and calls out and saith:

'Old folks, that harsh order is altered,
    Be not sick of heart!
The Guardians they poohed and they pished and they paltered
    When urged not to keep you apart.

'"It is wrong," I maintained, "to divide them,
    Near forty years wed."
"Very well, sir. We promise, then, they shall abide them
    In one wing together," they said.'

Then I sank — knew 'twas quite a fearsome thing
    That misery should be
To the end! . . . To get freed of her there was the one thing
    Had made the change welcome to me.

'To go there was ending but badly;
    'Twas shame and 'twas pain;
'But anyhow,' thought I, 'thereby I shall gladly
    Get free of this forty years' chain.'

I thought they'd be strangers aroun' me,
    But she's to be there!
Let me jump out o' waggon and go back and drown me
    At Pummery or Ten-Hatches Weir.

                        'The Curate's Kindness'

3

RURAL LIFE AND RUSTIC SPEECH

In 1886, in a letter to W. H. Rideing, Hardy wrote: 'My life when a boy was singularly uneventful & solitary'. In such circumstances a contemplative and receptive nature would develop readily, taking deep impressions from its immediate surroundings. In Hardy's case the small chronicles of village life and the reminiscences of his elders became the theatre of his imagination. 'Where nothing particular is going on,' he wrote later, in *The Hand of Ethelberta*, 'one incident makes a drama.' He became a great collector of such solitary incidents. 'I hear that – ' and 'Mother tells me' are recurring turns of phrase in his notebooks. Never would he be more 'at home' than in the scenes of his upbringing and among the voices of those who, like Ethelberta's brother Joey, 'talk the Wessex way'. It is from these homely ingredients that he constructed the masterpieces of his maturity. The highest flights of tragic drama gain a down-to-earth authenticity from the accompanying murmur of vernacular speech. We cannot detach Henchard from Abel Whittle, Giles Winterborne from Creedle, Tess from her mother – and they are thereby the richer.

The exact rendering in print of the essential qualities of dialect speech is a virtually insoluble problem. Idiosyncrasies of grammar are easily conveyed, and obscure localized items of vocabulary – such as 'bruckle' and 'chippol', which Hardy uses – can be carried in context or interpreted in a glossary, but intonation and 'flavour' are almost incommunicable. At best they can be suggested, with some degree of approximation. Indeed, to be accepted within the general body of literature, a purist perfection could defeat its own object. The phonetic system of William Barnes and the intensely Scottish idiom of Robert Burns both point in that direction – winning a specially intimate affection from their kindred but not so much appreciation as they merit from the larger readership which finds them difficult to grasp. Hardy's admiration of Barnes was sincere and given ungrudgingly but he had the strength of mind to break away from what might have become a narrowly Dorset school of poets. After an early success with the dialect humour of 'The Bride-Night Fire' he decided to develop his poetry along different lines.

In fiction the rendering of dialect speech tended to derive from established theatrical conventions. Scots, Irish and Welsh forms of English had their traditional stage stereotypes and Cockney would have developed similarly. Dorset, or more broadly 'West Country', is largely a creation of the second half of the nineteenth century and the early decades of the twentieth, pioneered by Barnes, developed by R. D. Blackmore and Hardy, and later by Walter Raymond and A. J. Coles ('Jan Stewer'). It was easily corrupted into a burlesqued form by converting 's' to 'z' and 'is' to 'be', producing a bogus 'Zummerzet' which in turn came to be known in the acting profession as 'Mummerset', where it has been used almost indiscriminately for any old-fashioned English rustic.

Hardy's technique evolved as he went along. In its earliest form, in *Desperate Remedies*, he wrote the normal verb ending *-ing* as *-en* – thus 'schemen', or 'liven'. Some of his coinings were difficult to translate back readily into standard forms. The reader had to recognize that 'I zid' represented 'I seed' and therefore meant 'I saw'. Similarly 'so's' did not instantly yield its meaning as 'souls'. More effective were words and phrases like 'a-coming homealong' which combine instant intelligibility with an undoubted vernacular quality. As his practice developed he tended to simplify and standardize the conventions he needed to convey the forms of rustic speech. To suggest the distinctive sound of a Devonshire voice he concentrated on a single feature, the richly fluted 'u' vowel, which he rendered as 'tew' for 'to', 'dew' for 'do' etc., in 'The Romantic Adventures of a Milkmaid'. In *Jude the Obscure* he took the word 'might' in its Wessex forms of 'mid' and 'med' as the single definitive indicator of Berkshire speech: 'Well ye med ask it', says Jude's great-aunt Drusilla. The heritage of older forms of dialect which were already becoming obsolete was recognized by Hardy in the speech of Grammer Oliver in *The Woodlanders*. Her loyalty to 'Ich woll' as a Saxon form of 'I will' probably echoes a usage that Hardy learnt from his grandmother who preserved such antique habits of speech.

In a letter to the *Athenaeum* in 1878, defending his dialect technique, Hardy made the point that standard speech is not printed phonetically and therefore to do so for rustic speech is to emphasize the grotesque element unduly and exaggerate what should be a point of inferior interest. His method was to retain the general idiom of his rural folk and their characteristic expressions. What gave him his mastery in this form was his remarkable ear for rhythm and timing and cadence. His *mot juste* is the folk word dropped in at precisely the right moment. A few conventions, used sparingly, draw the reader into a conspiracy to hear words with a rural intonation. Writing 'heath' as 'he'th', 'have' as 'hav'' and 'verse' as 've'se' does not really add a useful nuance, in any phonetic sense, to what the reader mentally hears, but it creates an atmosphere of difference.

The influence of Shakespeare is evident, for instance in the use of ''*a*' for the third person pronoun – the Anglo-Saxon *er*. The obvious model is Falstaff's death scene – ''a' babbled of green fields'. And there is an unmistakeably Shakespearean ring about Maryann's enquiry in *Far from the Madding Crowd*,

> 'Do anybody know of a crooked man, or a lame, or any second-hand fellow at all that would do for poor me?' said Maryann. 'A perfect one I don't expect to get at my time of life. If I could hear of such a thing 'twould do me more good than toast and ale'.

One of the perils of dialect-writing is that it may become an end in itself, as part of a glorification of rural life in sentimental terms. No writer was less likely than Hardy to fall into that trap. He was well aware of the narrowness and intolerance of village life, and of the pressures that threatened the settled traditions of earlier times. In 'The Dorsetshire Labourer' he wrote of rural depopulation and the rootlessness of the increasingly nomadic farm-worker. Like Richard Jefferies he deplored the demolition of cottages when leases under the lifehold system expired. Yet he also recognized the necessity of change, acknowledging that the peasantry could not remain at a standstill 'for the benefit of romantic spectators'. The old maltster, Joseph Poorgrass, Haymoss, Creedle, Christian Cantle and their fellows belong to a world that was already falling apart when Hardy portrayed them. Their ultimate survival as we know them is the consequence of their own humanity and Hardy's perception of it.

What is so impressive, and may fairly be described as unique in his dialect-writing at its best, is its emotional range and the total fusion of character and speech idiom. There is a sardonic wryness of humour which is distinctively the peasant's way of surviving the harshness of life. It enables Hardy to open up areas of social satire which would have been impermissible in conventional terms, as – for example – in religious matters. There is a warmth and ebullience in the perennial topic of courtship and marriage, quite alien again to conventional usage. There is a touchingly sensitive handling of the minor

commonplaces of life in Mrs Cuxsom's account of the death of Susan
Henchard – 'all her shining keys will be took from her, and her
cupboards opened; and little things 'a didn't wish seen, anybody will
see'. In the maltster's portrait of Levi Everdene there is a delicious
irony that never quite lacks compassion; and by contrast there is the
patient, dignified testimony of a Greek chorus in Abel Whittle's
account of Henchard's departure from Casterbridge to his death on
Egdon Heath. It is not given to these rustic worthies to move far from
the ultimate simplicities but they enliven them with a wonderful
variety of robust and ingenious turns of phrase in an idiom which
remains inimitably theirs.

To make himself as locally harmonious as possible, Mr Bellston
remarked to his companion on the scene –

'It does one's heart good,' he said, 'to see these simple peasants
enjoying themselves.'

'O Mr Bellston!' exclaimed Christine; 'don't be too sure about that
word "simple"! You little think what they see and meditate! Their
reasonings and emotions are as complicated as ours.'

'The Waiting Supper'

Mother tells me of a woman she knew named Nanny Priddle, who when
she married would never be called by her husband's name 'because she
was too proud,' she said; and to the end of their lives the couple were
spoken of as 'Nanny Priddle and John Cogan'.

The Life of Thomas Hardy

Heard to-day an old country tradition; that if a woman goes off her own
premises before being churched, e.g. crosses a road that forms the
boundary of her residence – she may be made to do penance, or be
excommunicated. I cannot explain this, but it reminds me of what old Mr
Hibbs of Bere Regis told me lately; that a native of that place, now ninety,
says he remembers a young woman doing penance in Bere Church for
singing scandalous songs about 'a great lady'. The girl stood in a white
sheet while she went through 'the service of penance', whatever that was.

The Life of Thomas Hardy

I hear of a girl of Maiden Newton who was shod by contract like a horse,
at so much a year.

The Life of Thomas Hardy

At Lyme they 'met a man who had turned his trousers hind part before, because the knees had worn through.'

On The Cobb they encountered an old man who had undergone an operation for a cataract:

'It was like a red-hot needle in yer eye whilst he was doing it. But he wasn't long about it. Oh no. If he had been long I couldn't ha' beared it. He wasn't a minute more than three-quarters of an hour at the outside. When he had done one eye, 'a said, "Now my man, you must make shift with that one, and be thankful you bain't left wi' narn." So he didn't do the other. And I'm glad 'a didn't. I've saved half-crowns and half-crowns out of number in only wanting one glass to my spectacles. T'other eye would never have paid the expenses of keeping en going.'

The Life of Thomas Hardy

'If I talk the Wessex way 'tisn't for want of knowing better; 'tis because my staunch nater makes me bide faithful to our old ancient institutions. You'd soon own 'twasn't ignorance in me, if you knowed what large quantities of noblemen I gets mixed up with every day.'

Joey in *The Hand of Ethelberta*

Meanwhile, in the empty house from which the guests had just cleared out, the subject of their discourse was walking from room to room surveying the general displacement of furniture with no ecstatic feeling; rather the reverse indeed. At last he entered the bakehouse, and found there Robert Creedle sitting over the embers, also lost in contemplation. Winterborne sat down beside him.

'Well, Robert, you must be tired. You'd better get on to bed.'

'Ay, ay, Giles – what do I call ye? Maister, I would say. But 'tis well to think the day is done, when 'tis done.'

Winterborne had abstractedly taken the poker, and with a wrinkled forehead was ploughing abroad the wood-embers on the wide hearth, till it was like a vast scorching Sahara, with red-hot boulders lying about everywhere. 'Do you think it went off well, Creedle?' he asked.

'The victuals did; that I know. And the drink did; that I steadfastly believe, from the holler sound of the barrels. Good honest drink 'twere, the headiest drink I ever brewed; and the best wine that berries could rise to; and the briskest Horner-and-Cleeves cider ever wrung down, leaving out the spice and sperrits I put into it, while that egg-flip would ha' passed through muslin, so little criddled 'twere. 'Twas good enough to make any king's heart merry – ay, to make his whole carcase smile! Still, I don't deny I'm afeard some things didn't go well with He and his.'

Creedle nodded in a direction which signified where the Melburys lived.

'I'm afraid, too, that it was a failure there.'

'If so, 'twere doomed to be so. Not but what that slug might as well have come upon anybody else's plate as hers.'

'What slug?'

'Well, maister, there was a little small one upon the edge of her plate when I brought it out, and so it must have been in her few leaves of winter-green.'

'How the deuce did a slug get there?'

'That I don't know no more than the dead; but there my gentleman was.'

'But, Robert, of all places, that was where he shouldn't have been!'

'Well, 'twas his native home, come to that; and where else could we expect him to be? I don't care who the man is, slugs and caterpillars always will lurk in close to the stump of cabbages in that tantalizing way.'

'He wasn't alive, I suppose?' said Giles, with a shudder on Grace's account.

'O no. He was well boiled. I warrant him well boiled. God forbid that a live slug should be seed on any plate of victuals that's served by Robert Creedle. . . . But Lord, there; I don't mind 'em myself – them green ones; for they were born on cabbage, and they've lived on cabbage, so they must be made of cabbage. But she, the close-mouthed little lady, she didn't say a word about it; though 'twould have made good small conversation as to the nater of such creatures; especially as wit ran short among us sometimes.'

The Woodlanders

One grievous failing of Elizabeth's was her occasional pretty and picturesque use of dialect words – those terrible marks of the beast to the truly genteel.

The Mayor of Casterbridge

I chance to be (I believe) one of the few living persons having a practical acquaintance with letters who knew familiarly the Dorset dialect when it was spoken as Barnes writes it, or, perhaps, who know it as it is spoken now. Since his death, education in the west of England as elsewhere has gone on with its silent and inevitable effacements, reducing the speech of this country to uniformity, and obliterating every year many a fine old local word. The process is always the same: the word is ridiculed by the newly taught; it gets into disgrace; it is heard in holes and corners only; it dies; and, worst of all, it leaves no synonym.

Preface to Select Poems of William Barnes

He observed that every aim of those who had brought her up had been to get her away mentally as far as possible from her natural and individual life as an inhabitant of a peculiar island: to make her an exact copy of tens of thousands of other people, in whose circumstances there was nothing special, distinctive, or picturesque; to teach her to forget all the experiences of her ancestors; to drown the local ballads by songs purchased at the Budmouth fashionable music-sellers', and the local vocabulary by a governess-tongue of no country at all.

The Well-Beloved

The round-faced country cook floundered in, untying her bonnet as she came, laying it down on a chair, and talking at the same time. 'Such a place as this London is, to be sure!' she exclaimed, turning on the gas till it whistled. 'I wish I was down in Wessex again. Lord-a-mercy, Berta, I didn't see it was you! I thought it was Cornelia. As I was saying, I thought that, after biding in this underground cellar all the week, making up messes for them French folk, and never pleasing 'em, and never shall, because I don't understand that line, I thought I would go out and see father, you know.'

'Is he very well?' said Ethelberta.

'Yes; and he is going to call round when he has time. Well, as I was a-coming home-along I thought, "Please the Lord I'll have some chippols for supper just for a plain trate," and I went round to the late greengrocer's for 'em; and do you know they sweared me down that they hadn't got such things as chippols in the shop, and had never heard of 'em in their lives. At last I said, "Why, how can you tell me such a brazen story? – here they be, heaps of 'em!" It made me so vexed that I came away there and then, and wouldn't have one – no, not at a gift.'

'They call them young onions here,' said Ethelberta quietly; 'you must always remember that.'

The Hand of Ethelberta

For some reason or none, many persons suppose that when anything is penned in the tongue of the countryside, the primary intent is burlesque or ridicule, and this especially if the speech be one in which the sibilant has the rough sound, and is expressed by Z. Indeed, scores of thriving story-tellers and dramatists seem to believe that by transmuting the flattest conversation into a dialect that never existed, and making the talkers say "be" when they would really say "is", a Falstaffian richness is at once imparted to its qualities.

But to a person to whom dialect is native its sounds are as consonant with moods of sorrow as with moods of mirth: there is no grotesqueness in it as such.

Preface to *Select Poems of William Barnes*

A somewhat vexed question is re-opened in your criticism of my story 'The Return of the Native'; namely, the representation in writing of the speech of the peasantry, when that writing is intended to show mainly the character of the speakers, and only to give a general idea of their linguistic peculiarities.

An author may be said to fairly convey the spirit of intelligent peasant talk if he retains the idiom, compass and characteristic expressions, although he may not encumber the page with obsolete pronunciations of the purely English words, and with mispronunciations of those derived from Latin and Greek. In the printing of standard speech, hardly any phonetic principle at all is observed; and if a writer attempts to exhibit on paper the precise accents of a rustic speaker, he disturbs the proper balance of a true representation by unduly insisting upon the grotesque element; thus directing attention to a point of inferior interest and diverting it from the speaker's meaning, which is by far the chief concern where the aim is to depict the men and their natures rather than their dialect forms.

Thomas Hardy

Letter published in the *Athenaeum*, 30 November 1878

'I am come, Grammer, as you wish. Do let us send for the doctor before it gets later'.

''ch woll not have him!' said Grammer Oliver decisively.

The Woodlanders

I heard 'Ich' only last Sunday; but it is dying rapidly. I know nobody under seventy who speaks so.

Letter to Edmund Gosse, 26 October 1888

'The misery of remote country life is that your neighbours have no toleration for difference of opinion and habit. My neighbours think I am an atheist, except those who think I am a Roman Catholic; and when I speak disrespectfully of the weather or the crops they think I am a blasphemer'.

Dr Fitzpiers in *The Woodlanders*

The topic at present handled was a highly popular and frequent one – the personal character of Mrs Charmond, the owner of the surrounding glades and groves.

'My brother-in-law told me, and I have no reason to doubt it,' said Creedle, 'that she'll sit down to her dinner with a gown hardly higher than her elbows. "O, you wicked woman!" he said to hisself when he first see her, "you go to the Table o' Sundays and kneel, as if your kneejints were greased with very saint's anointment, and tell off your hear-us-good-Lords as pat as a business-man counting money; and yet you can eat your victuals a-stript to such a wanton figure as that!" Whether she's a reformed character by this time I can't say; but I don't care who the man is, that's how she went on when my brother-in-law lived there.'

The Woodlanders

Knollsea was a seaside village lying snug within two headlands as between a finger and thumb. Everybody in the parish who was not a boatman was a quarrier, unless he were the gentleman who owned half the property and had been a quarryman, or the other gentleman who owned the other half, and had been to sea.

The knowledge of the inhabitants was of the same special sort as their pursuits. The quarrymen in white fustian understood practical geology, the laws and accidents of dips, faults, and cleavage, far better than the ways of the world and mammon; the seafaring men in Guernsey frocks had a clearer notion of Alexandria, Constantinople, the Cape, and the Indies than of any inland town in their own country. This, for them, consisted of a busy portion, the Channel, where they lived and laboured, and a dull portion, the vague unexplored miles of interior at the back of the ports, which they seldom thought of.

Some wives of the village, it is true, had learned to let lodgings, and others to keep shops. The doors of these latter places were formed of an upper hatch, usually kept open, and a lower hatch, with a bell attached, usually kept shut. Whenever a stranger went in, he would hear a whispering of astonishment from a back room, after which a woman came forward, looking suspiciously at him as an intruder, and advancing slowly enough to allow her mouth to get clear of the meal she was partaking of. Meanwhile the people in the back room would stop their knives and forks in absorbed curiosity as to the reason of the stranger's entry, who by this time feels ashamed of his unwarrantable intrusion into this hermit's cell, and thinks he must take his hat off. The woman is quite alarmed at seeing that he is not one of the fifteen native women and children who patronize her, and nervously puts her hand to the side of her face, which she carries slanting. The visitor finds himself saying what he wants in an apologetic tone, when the woman tells him that they did keep that article once, but do not now; that nobody does, and probably never will again; and as he turns away she looks relieved that the dilemma of having to provide for a stranger has passed off with no worse mishap than disappointing him.

The Hand of Ethelberta

'Well, what was the latest news at Shottsford yesterday, Mr Cawtree?'

'Oh, well, Shottsford is Shottsford still – you can't victual your carcase there unless you've got money; and you can't buy a cup of genuine there, whether or no. . . . But as the saying is, "Go abroad and you'll hear news of home." It seems that our new neighbour, this young Doctor What's-his-name, is a strange, deep, perusing gentleman; and there's good reason for supposing he has sold his soul to the wicked one.'

'I won't praise the doctor's wisdom till I hear what sort of bargain he's made,' said the top-sawyer.

"Tis only an old woman's tale,' said Cawtree. 'But it seems that he wanted certain books on some mysterious black art, and in order that the people hereabout should not know anything about them, he ordered 'em direct from London, and not from the Sherton bookseller. The parcel was delivered by mistake at the pa'son's, and as he wasn't at home, his wife opened it, and went into hysterics when she read 'em, thinking her husband had turned heathen, and 'twould be the ruin of the children. But when he came he knew no more about 'em than she; and found they were this Mr Fitzpiers's property. So he wrote "Beware!" outside, and sent 'em on by the sexton.'

The Woodlanders

The changes which are so increasingly discernible in village life by no means originate entirely with the agricultural unrest. A depopulation is going on which in some quarters is truly alarming. Villages used to contain, in addition to the agricultural inhabitants, an interesting and better-informed class, ranking distinctly above those – the blacksmith, the carpenter, the shoe-maker, the small higgler, the shopkeeper (whose stock-in-trade consisted of a couple of loaves, a pound of candles, a bottle of brandy-balls and lumps of delight, three or four scrubbing-brushes, and a frying-pan), together with nondescript-workers other than farm-labourers, who had remained in the houses where they were born for no especial reason beyond an instinct of association with the spot. Many of these families had been life-holders, who built at their own expense the cottages they occupied, and as the lives dropped, and the property fell in they would have been glad to remain as weekly or monthly tenants of the owner. But the policy of all but some few philanthropic land-owners is to disapprove of these petty tenants who are not in the estate's employ, and to pull down each cottage as it falls in, leaving standing a sufficient number for the use of the farmer's men and no more. The occupants who formed the backbone of the village life have to seek refuge in the borough. This process, which is designated by statisticians as 'the tendency of the rural population towards the large towns', is really the tendency of water to flow uphill when forced.

'The Dorsetshire Labourer'

'Sit down, Shepherd Oak,' continued the ancient man of malt. 'And how was the old place at Norcombe, when ye went for your dog? I should like to see the old familiar spot; but faith, I shouldn't know a soul there now.'

'I suppose you wouldn't. 'Tis altered very much.'

'Is it true that Dicky Hill's wooden cider-house is pulled down?'

'O yes – years ago, and Dicky's cottage just above it.'

'Well, to be sure!'

'Yes; and Tompkins's old apple-tree is rooted that used to bear two hogsheads of cider, and no help from other trees.'

'Rooted? – you don't say it? Ah! stirring times we live in – stirring times.'

Far from the Madding Crowd

When in the midst of the field, a dark spot on an area of brown, there crossed her path a moving figure, whom it was as difficult to distinguish from the earth he trod as the caterpillar from its leaf, by reason of the excellent match between his clothes and the clods. He was one of a dying-out generation who retained the principle, nearly unlearnt now, that a man's habiliments should be in harmony with his environment. Lady Constantine and this figure halted beside each other for some minutes; then they went on their several ways.

The brown person was a labouring man known to the world of Welland as Haymoss (the encrusted form of the word Amos, to adopt the phrase of philologists). The reason of the halt had been some inquiries addressed to him by Lady Constantine.

'Who is that – Amos Fry, I think?' she had asked.

'Yes, my lady,' said Haymoss; 'a homely barley driller, born under the eaves of your ladyship's out-buildings, in a manner of speaking, – though your ladyship was neither born nor 'tempted at that time.'

'Who lives in the old house behind the plantation?'

'Old Grammer Martin, my lady, and her grandson.'

'He has neither father nor mother, then?'

'Not a single one, my lady.'

'Where was he educated?'

'At Warborne, – a place where they draw up young gam'sters' brains like rhubarb under a ninepenny pan, my lady, excusing my common way. They hit so much larning into en that 'a could talk like the day of Pentecost; which is a wonderful thing for a simple boy, and his mother only the plainest ciphering woman in the world. Warborne Grammar School – that's where 'twas 'a went to. His father, the reverent Pa'son St Cleeve, made a terrible bruckle hit in 's marrying, in the sight of the high. He were the curate here, my lady, for a length o' time.'

'Oh, curate,' said Lady Constantine. 'It was before I knew the village.'

'Ay, long and merry ago! And he married Farmer Martin's daughter – Giles Martin, a limberish man, who used to go rather bad upon his lags, if you can mind. I knowed the man well enough; who should know en better! The maid was a poor windling thing, and, though a playward piece o' flesh when he married her, 'a socked and sighed, and went out like a snoff! Yes, my lady. Well, when Pa'son St Cleeve married this homespun woman the toppermost folk wouldn't speak to his wife. Then he dropped a cuss or two, and said he'd no longer get his living by curing their twopenny souls o' such d— nonsense as that (excusing my common way), and he took to farming straightway, and then 'a dropped down dead in a nor'-west thunderstorm; it being said – hee-hee! – that Master God was in tantrums wi' en for leaving his service, – hee-hee! I give the story as I heard it, my lady, but be dazed if I believe in such trumpery about folks in the sky, nor anything else that's said on 'em, good or bad. Well, Swithin, the boy, was sent to the grammar school, as I say for; but what with having two stations of life in his blood he's good for nothing, my lady. He mopes about – sometimes here, and sometimes there; nobody troubles about en.'

Two on a Tower

He had not paused under the prickly foliage more than two minutes when he thought he heard a scream from the other side of the ridge. Fitzpiers wondered what it could mean; but such wind as there was just now blew in an adverse direction, and his mood was light. He set down the origin of the sound to one of the superstitious freaks or frolicsome scrimmages between sweethearts that still survived in Hintock from old-English times.

The Woodlanders

March 4. A Village story recalled to me yesterday:

Mary L., a handsome wench, had come to Bockhampton, leaving a lover at Askerswell, her native parish. William K. fell in love with her at the new place. The old lover, who was a shoemaker, smelling a rat, came anxiously to see her, with a present of a dainty pair of shoes he had made. He met her by chance at the pathway stile, but alas, on the arm of the other lover. In the rage of love the two men fought for her till they were out of breath, she looking on and holding both their hats the while; till William, wiping his face, said: "Now, Polly, which of we two do you love best? Say it out straight!" She would not state then, but said she would consider (the hussy!). The young man to whom she had been fickle left her indignantly – throwing the shoes at her and her new lover as he went.

She never saw or heard of him again, and accepted the other. But she kept the shoes, and was married in them. I knew her well as an old woman.

The Life of Thomas Hardy

'What women do know nowadays!' observed the hollow-turner. 'You can't deceive 'em as you could in my time.'

'What they knowed then was not small,' said John Upjohn. 'Always a good deal more than the men! Why, when I went courting my wife that is now, the skilfulness that she would show in keeping me on her pretty side as she walked was beyond all belief. Perhaps you've noticed that she's got a pretty side to her face as well as a plain one?'

'I can't say I've noticed it particular much,' said the hollow-turner blandly.

'Well,' continued Upjohn, not disconcerted, 'she has. All women under the sun be prettier one side than t'other. And, as I was saying, the pains she would take to make me walk on the pretty side were unending! I warrant that whether we were going with the sun or against the sun, uphill or downhill, in wind or in lewth, that wart of hers was always towards the hedge, and that dimple towards me. There was I, too simple to see her wheelings and turnings; and she so artful, though two years younger, that she could lead me with a cotton thread, like a blind ram; for that was in the third climate of our courtship. . . . No: I don't think the women have got cleverer, for they was never otherwise.'

'How many climates may there be in courtship, Mr Upjohn?' inquired a youth.

'Five – from the coolest to the hottest – leastwise there was five in mine.'

'Can ye give us the chronicle of 'em, Mr Upjohn?'

'Yes – I could. I could certainly. But 'tis quite unnecessary. They'll come to ye by nater, young man, too soon for your good.'

The Woodlanders

'Clerk Crickett, I d' fancy you d' know everything about everybody,' said Gad.

'Well, so's,' said the clerk modestly. 'I do know a little. It comes to me.'

'And I d' know where from.'

'Ah.'

'That wife o' thine. She's an entertainen woman, not to speak disrespectful.'

'She is: and a winnen one. Look at the husbands she've had – God bless her!'

'I wonder you could stand third in that list, Clerk Crickett,' said Mr Springrove.

'Well, 't has been a power o' marvel to myself often-times. Yes, matrimony do begin wi' "Dearly beloved," and ends wi' "Amazement," as the prayer-books says. But what could I do, naibour Springrove? 'Twas ordained to be. Well do I call to mind what your poor lady said to me when I had just married. "Ah, Mr Crickett," says she, "your wife will soon settle you as she did her other two: here's a glass o' rum, for I shan't see your poor face this time next year." I swallered the rum, called again next year, and said, "Mrs Springrove, you gave me a glass o' rum last year because I was going to die – here I be alive still, you see." "Well said, clerk! Here's two glasses for you now, then," says she. "Thank you, mem," I said, and swallered the rum. Well, dang my old sides, next year I thought I'd call again and get three. And call I did. But she wouldn't give me a drop o' the commonest. "No, clerk," says she, "you be too tough for a woman's pity." . . . Ah, poor soul, 'twas true enough! Here be I, that was expected to die, alive and hard as a nail, you see, and there's she moulderen in her grave.'

'I used to think 'twas your wife's fate not to have a liven husband when I zid 'em die off so,' said Gad.

'Fate? Bless thy simplicity, so 'twas her fate; but she struggled to have one, and would, and did. Fate's nothen beside a woman's schemen!'

Desperate Remedies

'I don't speak so warm as that,' said the hollow-turner, 'but if 'tis right for couples to make a country talk about their parting for ever, and excite the neighbours, and then make fools of 'em like this, why, I haven't stood upon one leg for five-and-twenty year.'

All his listeners knew that when he alluded to his foot-lathe in these enigmatic terms, the speaker meant to be impressive.

'But this deceiving of folks is nothing unusual in matrimony,' said Farmer Cawtree. 'I know'd a man and wife – faith, I don't mind owning, as there's no strangers here, that the pair were my own relations – they'd be at it that hot one hour that you'd hear the poker, and the tongs, and the bellows, and the warming-pan, flee across the house with the movements of their vengeance; and the next hour you'd hear 'em singing "The Spotted Cow" together, as peaceable as two holy twins; yes – and very good voices they had, and would strike in like street ballet-singers to one another's support in the high notes.'

"Tis so with couples: they do make up differences in all manner of queer ways,' said the bark-ripper. 'I knowed a woman, and the husband o' her went away for four-and-twenty year. And one night he came home when she was sitting by the fire, and thereupon he sat down himself on the other side of the chimney-corner. "Well," says she, "have ye got any news?" "Don't know as I have," says he; "have you?" "No," says she, "except that my daughter by the husband that succeeded 'ee was married last month, which was a year after I was made a widow by him." "Oh! Anything else?" he says. "No," says she. And there they sat, one on each side of that chimney-corner, and were found by the neighbours sound asleep in their chairs, not having known what to talk about at all.'

The Woodlanders

'Didst ever know a man, neighbour, that no woman at all would marry?' inquired Humphrey.

'I never did,' said the turf-cutter.

'Nor I,' said another.

'Nor I,' said Grandfer Cantle.

'Well, now, I did once,' said Timothy Fairway, adding more firmness to one of his legs. 'I did know of such a man. But only once, mind.' He gave his throat a thorough rake round, as if it were the duty of every person not to be mistaken through thickness of voice. 'Yes, I knew of such a man,' he said.

'And what ghastly gallicrow might the poor fellow have been like, Master Fairway?' asked the turf-cutter.

'Well, 'a was neither a deaf man, nor a dumb man, nor a blind man. What 'a was I don't say.'

'Is he known in these parts?' said Olly Dowden.

'Hardly,' said Timothy; 'but I name no name. . . . Come, keep the fire up there, youngsters.'

'Whatever is Christian Cantle's teeth a-chattering for?' said a boy from amid the smoke and shades on the other side of the blaze. 'Be ye a-cold, Christian?'

A thin jibbering voice was heard to reply, 'No, not at all.'

'Come forward, Christian, and show yourself. I didn't know you were here,' said Fairway, with a humane look across towards that quarter.

Thus requested, a faltering man, with reedy hair, no shoulders, and a great quantity of wrist and ankle beyond his clothes, advanced a step or two by his own will, and was pushed by the will of others half a dozen steps more. He was Grandfer Cantle's youngest son.

'What be ye quaking for, Christian?' said the turf-cutter kindly.

'I'm the man.'

'What man?'

'The man no woman will marry.'

'The deuce you be!' said Timothy Fairway, enlarging his gaze to cover Christian's whole surface and a great deal more; Grandfer Cantle meanwhile staring as a hen stares at the duck she has hatched.

'Yes, I be he; and it makes me afeard,' said Christian. 'D'ye think 'twill hurt me? I shall always say I don't care, and swear to it, though I do care all the while.'

'Well, be damned if this isn't the queerest start ever I know'd,' said Mr Fairway. 'I didn't mean you at all. There's another in the country, then! Why did ye reveal yer misfortune, Christian?'

''Twas to be if 'twas, I suppose. I can't help it, can I?' He turned upon them his painfully circular eyes, surrounded by concentric lines like targets.

'No, that's true. But 'tis a melancholy thing, and my blood ran cold when you spoke, for I felt there were two poor fellows where I had thought only one. 'Tis a sad thing for ye, Christian. How'st know the women won't hae thee?'

'I've asked 'em.'

'Sure I should never have thought you had the face. Well, and what did the last one say to ye? Nothing that can't be got over, perhaps, after all?'

'"Get out of my sight, you slack-twisted, slim-looking maphrotight fool," was the woman's words to me.'

'Not encouraging, I own,' said Fairway. '"Get out of my sight, you slack-twisted, slim-looking maphrotight fool," is rather a hard way of saying No. But even that might be overcome by time and patience, so as to let a few grey hairs show themselves in the hussy's head. How old be you, Christian?'

'Thirty-one last tatie-digging, Mister Fairway.'

'Not a boy – not a boy. Still there's hope yet.'

'That's my age by baptism, because that's put down in the great book of the Judgment that they keep in church vestry; but mother told me I was born some time afore I was christened.'

'Ah!'

'But she couldn't tell when, to save her life, except that there was no moon.'

'No moon: that's bad. Hey, neighbours, that's bad for him!'

'Yes, 'tis bad,' said Grandfer Cantle, shaking his head.

'Mother know'd 'twas no moon, for she asked another woman that had an almanac, as she did whenever a boy was born to her, because of the saying, "No moon, no man" which made her afeard every man-child she had. Do ye really think it serious, Mister Fairway, that there was no moon?'

'Yes; "No moon, no man." 'Tis one of the truest sayings ever spit out. The boy never comes to anything that's born at new moon. A bad job for thee, Christian, that you should have showed your nose then of all days in the month.'

'I suppose the moon was terrible full when you were born?' said Christian, with a look of hopeless admiration at Fairway.

'Well, 'a was not new,' Mr Fairway replied, with a disinterested gaze.

The Return of the Native

'And did any of you know Miss Everdene's father and mother?' inquired the shepherd, who found some difficulty in keeping the conversation in the desired channel.

'I knew them a little,' said Jacob Smallbury; 'but they were townsfolk, and didn't live here. They've been dead for years. Father, what sort of people were mis'ess' father and mother?'

'Well,' said the maltster, 'he wasn't much to look at; but she was a lovely woman. He was fond enough of her as his sweetheart.'

'Used to kiss her scores and long-hundreds o' times, so 'twas said,' observed Coggan.

'He was very proud of her, too, when they were married, as I've been told,' said the maltster.

'Ay,' said Coggan. 'He admired her so much that he used to light the candle three times a night to look at her.'

'Boundless love; I shouldn't have supposed it in the universe!' murmured Joseph Poorgrass, who habitually spoke on a large scale in his moral reflections.

'Well, to be sure,' said Gabriel.

'Oh, 'tis true enough. I knowed the man and woman both well. Levi Everdene – that was the man's name, sure. "Man," said I in my hurry, but he were of a higher circle of life than that – 'a was a gentleman-tailor really, worth scores of pounds. And he became a very celebrated bankrupt two or three times.'

'Oh, I thought he was quite a common man!' said Joseph.

'O no, no! That man failed for heaps of money; hundreds in gold and silver.'

The maltster being rather short of breath, Mr Coggan, after absently scrutinizing a coal which had fallen among the ashes, took up the narrative, with a private twirl of his eye:

'Well, now, you'd hardly believe it, but that man – our Miss Everdene's father – was one of the ficklest husbands alive, after a while. Understand, 'a didn't want to be fickle, but he couldn't help it. The poor feller were faithful and true enough to her in his wish, but his heart would rove, do what he would. He spoke to me in real tribulation about it once. "Coggan," he said, "I could never wish for a handsomer woman than I've got, but feeling she's ticketed as my lawful wife, I can't help my wicked heart wandering, do what I will." But at last I believe he cured it by making her take off her wedding-ring and calling her by her maiden name as they sat together after the shop was shut, and so 'a would get to fancy she was only his sweetheart, and not married to him at all. And as soon as he could thoroughly fancy he was doing wrong and committing the seventh, 'a got to like her as well as ever, and they lived on a perfect picture of mutel love.'

'Well, 'twas a most ungodly remedy,' murmured Joseph Poorgrass; 'but we ought to feel deep cheerfulness that a happy Providence kept it from being any worse. You see, he might have gone the bad road and given his eyes to unlawfulness entirely – yes, gross unlawfulness, so to say it.'

'You see,' said Billy Smallbury, 'the man's will was to do right, sure enough, but his heart didn't chime in.'

'He got so much better, that he was quite godly in his later years, wasn't he, Jan?' said Joseph Poorgrass. 'He got himself confirmed over again in a more serious way, and took to saying "Amen" almost as loud as the clerk, and he liked to copy comforting verses from the tombstones. He used, too, to hold the money-plate at Let Your Light so Shine, and stand godfather to poor little come-by-chance children; and he kept a missionary box upon his table to nab folks unawares when they called; yes, and he would box the charity-boys' ears, if they laughed in church, till they could hardly stand upright, and do other deeds of piety natural to the saintly inclined.'

'Ay, at that time he thought of nothing but high things,' added Billy Smallbury. 'One day Parson Thirdly met him and said, "Good morning, Mister Everdene; 'tis a fine day!" "Amen," said Everdene, quite absent-like, thinking only of religion when he seed a parson. Yes, he was a very Christian man.'

Far from the Madding Crowd

The door was ajar; Farfrae knocked; and he who stood before them was Whittle, as they had conjectured.

His face showed marks of deep sadness, his eyes lighting on them with an unfocused gaze; and he still held in his hand the few sticks he had been out to gather. As soon as he recognized them he started.

'What, Abel Whittle; is it that ye are heere?' said Farfrae.

'Ay, yes, sir! You see he was kind-like to mother when she were here below, though 'a was rough to me.'

'Who are you talking of?'

'O sir – Mr Henchet! Didn't ye know it? He's just gone – about half-an-hour ago, by the sun; for I've got no watch to my name.'

'Not – dead?' faltered Elizabeth-Jane.

'Yes, ma'am, he's gone! He was kind-like to mother when she were here below, sending her the best ship-coal, and hardly any ashes from it at all; and taties, and such-like that were very needful to her. I seed en go down street on the night of your worshipful's wedding to the lady at yer side, and I thought he looked low and faltering. And I followed en over Grey's Bridge, and he turned and zeed me, and said, "You go back!" But I followed, and he turned again, and said, "Do you hear, sir? Go back!" But I zeed that he was low, and I followed on still. Then 'a said, "Whittle, what do ye follow me for when I've told ye to go back all these times?" And I said, "Because, sir, I see things be bad with 'ee, and ye wer kind-like to mother if ye were rough to me, and I would fain be kind-like to you." Then he walked on, and I followed; and he never complained at me no more.'

The Mayor of Casterbridge

4

THE PEOPLE'S MUSIC

'Nothing moved Henchard like an old melody', Hardy wrote in *The Mayor of Casterbridge*; and again, 'with Henchard music was of regal power'. The same is true of many other Hardy characters; music, whether sacred or profane, can stir emotional depths in them that are otherwise concealed. The reader is constantly made aware of what, in Tess's case, is described as an 'innate love of melody'. When Hardy is on his home ground the very air seems to vibrate with echoes of hymn and psalm, jig and reel and ballad.

Of his mother Hardy wrote that she was 'a woman with an extraordinary store of local memories, reaching back to the days when the ancient ballads were every-where heard at country feasts, in weaving shops, and at spinning-wheels'. Perhaps there is more than a passing resemblance to her in Tess's mother, singing 'The Spotted Cow' as she rocks the cradle: no great leap of the imagination is demanded to picture Jemima Hardy rocking her younger children, Henry and Kate, and singing a similar ditty while the boy Thomas sat and listened. From her, and also doubtless from his Hardy grandmother, he inherited a store of melodic narrative, in which crude story-telling sometimes achieved flashes of poetic felicity and additional power from its haunting tune. It is from this early, fertile soil that there sprang such a magnificent poem as 'A Trampwoman's Tragedy'; and is it too fanciful to think of *Tess of the d'Urbervilles* as the fleshing-out of an old ballad with some such title as 'The Milkmaid's Lament'? Certainly the ballad tradition touches and transmutes some of the most compelling moments in Hardy's story-telling.

Making instrumental music passed to Hardy on his father's side. The long-established Hardy tradition of performing in church came to an end when the new taste for barrel-organ and harmonium replaced the little bands of local musicians, in the way described in *Under the Greenwood Tree*; otherwise Hardy would have taken his place with his father and his uncle in Stinsford church. He was taught to play as soon as he could hold a fiddle and at an early age was competent enough to accompany his father when called upon to perform at barn dances and private 'randys'. There are surely elements of a self-portrait in the boy-fiddler at Shepherd Fennel's dance in 'The Three Strangers'.

Though they might no longer play during church services the Hardys continued to take part in performances of religious music in the form of carols and hymns, to be played and sung on suitable occasions and particularly during the Christmas perambulation of the village. The long memories of the old-timers were fortified by the individual music books in which words and tunes were carefully copied out for personal use and handed down from one generation to the next. It is here, in the cherishing of a vernacular tradition of music-making, that Hardy and his ancestors were most intimately bonded together.

The combination in the same book of religious music (starting from the front page) and secular music (starting in reverse from the back page) neatly illustrates the all-purpose character of the village musicians, though some instruments might be more versatile than others. Fiddle and bass-viol were never out of place but clarinet and serpent were subjects for much debating that Hardy must have heard. The tambourine had a special role in dance music. For dancing of the more genteel kind a combination of harp and piano was favoured, as when Christopher Julian and his sister played at Wyndway House in *The Hand of Ethelberta*. The sound of a harp occurs again in that evocative scene in the poem 'On the Esplanade' where the moonlight shimmering on Weymouth Bay reveals a pleasure-steamer

> Whereon to the strings
> Plucked sweetly and low
> Of a harp, they dance.

It was at that period in Weymouth that Hardy extended his own repertoire as a dancer by attending a dancing-class where he could practise the newest styles of ballroom dancing: not that he had much to learn, since his earlier years in London had given him opportunities to visit the dance halls whose names he celebrated as a pilgrim celebrates temples and shrines. In 'Reminiscences of a Dancing Man' he conjured up the fading Regency glories of Almack's, gay Cremorne and the Argyle Rooms.

Dancing in all its forms was for Hardy an inexhaustible subject, in his novels, short stories and poems. Reluctantly I have omitted one of the best-known examples, 'The Fiddler of the Reels', which concentrates on the spellbinding music of Mop Ollamoor, the gypsy-style fiddler whose playing can take on an evil power. Absent also here is that short story compressed into verse-form, 'The Dance at the Phoenix', though I abstract from it a single verse in which Hardy lovingly chronicles the old dances of his youth:

> The favourite Quick-step 'Speed the Plough' –
> (Cross hands, cast off, and wheel) –
> 'The Triumph', 'Sylph', 'The Row-dow-dow',
> Famed 'Major Malley's Reel',
> 'The Duke of York's', 'The Fairy Dance',
> 'The Bridge of Lodi' (brought from France),
> She beat out, toe and heel.

To seize any opportunity, in poem or story, to preserve the names of the old dance tunes was one of the little indulgences that Hardy, as a writer, allowed himself. To cherish them, to play them and to dance to them were for him as natural a part of life as eating and breathing. Gertrude Bugler has described Hardy in his later years at a rehearsal of the Hardy Players, picking up a violin and playing a traditional tune; and then demonstrating the old style of dancing to it. He himself relates a story of his last dance in the open air, as the guest of General Pitt-Rivers in 1895 at the Larmer Tree Gardens in Cranborne Chase. The bandsmen played the fashionable dances of the time – polka, schottische and the like – but Hardy led off some country dances with the General's daughter Agnes (later Lady Grove). Over thirty years afterwards, when he heard of Lady Grove's death, it was his recurring wish 'to dance with that fair woman yet once more' which inspired him to write the moving elegy 'Concerning Agnes'.

He had indeed been, in his own words, 'passionately fond of dancing from earliest childhood'. Its power to stir and quicken emotion gave it a special value in his writing. As Emily Hardcome says, in 'The History of the Hardcomes', 'People get quite crazy sometimes in a dance'. Eustacia Vye, in Wildeve's arms, drifted into a transcendental romanticism; Tess's workmates in the haze of peat dust at Chaseborough spun relentlessly to a primitive weekly orgy; the hearty, sweaty, heavily built men at the tranter's threw aside the nicer decorum of jackets and took to the floor like triumphant footballers. It is in these varieties of mode and mood that Hardy handled his dance scenes so memorably.

'Your plain music well done is as worthy as your other sort done bad, a'
b'lieve, souls; so say I.'

Mr Penny in Under the Greenwood Tree

Nothing moved Henchard like an old melody.

The Mayor of Casterbridge

If he could have summoned music to his aid, his existence might even
now have been borne; for with Henchard music was of regal power. The
merest trumpet or organ tone was enough to move him, and high
harmonies transubstantiated him.

The Mayor of Casterbridge

Joan Durbeyfield was a passionate lover of tune. No ditty floated into
Blackmoor Vale from the outer world but Tess's mother caught up its
notation in a week.

Tess of the d'Urbervilles

[Tess] liked to hear the chanting – such as it was – and the old Psalms,
and to join in the Morning Hymn. That innate love of melody, which she
had inherited from her ballad-singing mother, gave the simplest music a
power over her which could well-nigh drag her heart out of her bosom at
times.

Tess of the d'Urbervilles

'If I could afford it, be hanged if I wouldn't keep a church choir at my
own expense to play and sing to me at these low, dark times of my life.'

The Mayor of Casterbridge

'A new music greets our ears now,' said Miss Fancy, alluding, with the
sharpness that her position as village sharpener demanded, to the
contrast between the rattle of knives and forks and the late notes of the
fiddlers.

    'Ay; and I don't know but what 'tis sweeter in tone when you get
above forty,' said the tranter; 'except, in faith, as regards father there.
Never such a mortal man as he for tunes. They do move his soul; don't
'em, father?'

    The eldest Dewy smiled across from his distant chair an assent to
Reuben's remark.

'Spaking of being moved in soul,' said Mr Penny, 'I shall never forget the first time I heard the "Dead March". 'Twas at poor Corp'l Nineman's funeral at Casterbridge. It fairly made my hair creep and fidget about like a vlock of sheep – ah, it did, souls! And when they had done, and the last trump had sounded, and the guns was fired over the dead hero's grave, a' icy-cold drop o' moist sweat hung upon my forehead, and another upon my jawbone. Ah, 'tis a very solemn thing!'

'Well, as to father in the corner there,' the tranter said, pointing to old William, who was in the act of filling his mouth; 'he'd starve to death for music's sake now, as much as when he was a boy-chap of fifteen.'

'Truly, now,' said Michael Mail, clearing the corner of his throat in the manner of a man who meant to be convincing; 'there's a friendly tie of some sort between music and eating.' He lifted the cup to his mouth, and drank himself gradually backwards from a perpendicular position to a slanting one, during which time his looks performed a circuit from the wall opposite him to the ceiling overhead. Then clearing the other corner of his throat: 'Once I was a-setting in the little kitchen of the Dree Mariners at Casterbridge, having a bit of dinner, and a brass band struck up in the street. Such a beautiful band as that were! I was setting eating fried liver and lights, I well can mind – ah, I was! and to save my life, I couldn't help chawing to the tune. Band played six-eight time; six-eight chaws I, willynilly. Band plays common; common time went my teeth among the liver and lights as true as a hair. Beautiful 'twere! Ah, I shall never forget that there band!'

Under the Greenwood Tree

One is inclined to regret the displacement of these ecclesiastical bandsmen by an isolated organist (often at first a barrel-organist) or harmonium player; and despite certain advantages in point of control and accomplishment which were, no doubt, secured by installing the single artist, the change has tended to stultify the professed aims of the clergy, its direct result being to curtail and extinguish the interest of parishioners in church doings. Under the old plan, from half a dozen to ten full grown players, in addition to the numerous more or less grown-up singers, were officially occupied with the Sunday routine, and concerned in trying their best to make it an artistic outcome of the combined musical taste of the congregation. With a musical executive limited, as it mostly is limited now, to the parson's wife or daughter and the school-children, or to the school-teacher and the children, an important union of interests has disappeared.

The zest of these bygone instrumentalists must have been keen and staying, to take them, as it did, on foot every Sunday after a toilsome week through all weathers to the church, which often lay at a distance from their homes. They usually received so little in payment for their performance that their efforts were really a labour of love. In the parish I had in my mind when writing the present tale, the gratuities received yearly by the musicians at Christmas were somewhat as follows: From the manor-house ten shillings and a supper; from the vicar ten shillings; from the farmers five shillings each; from each cottage-household one shilling; amounting altogether to not more than ten shillings a head annually – just enough, as an old executant told me, to pay for their fiddle-strings, repairs, rosin, and music-paper (which they mostly ruled themselves). Their music in those days was all in their own manuscript, copied in the evenings after work, and their music-books were home-bound.

It was customary to inscribe a few jigs, reels, hornpipes, and ballads in the same book, by beginning it at the other end, the insertions being continued from front and back till sacred and secular met together in the middle, often with bizarre effect, the words of some of the songs exhibiting that ancient and broad humour which our grandfathers, and possibly grandmothers, took delight in, and is in these days unquotable.

Under the Greenwood Tree

On afternoons of drowsy calm
      We stood in the panelled pew,
Singing one-voiced a Tate-and-Brady psalm
      To the tune of 'Cambridge New'.

We watched the elms, we watched the rooks,
      The clouds upon the breeze,
Between the whiles of glancing at our books,
      And swaying like the trees.

So mindless were those outpourings! –
      Though I am not aware
That I have gained by subtle thought on things
      Since we stood psalming there.

'Afternoon Service at Mellstock'

'As 'tis Sunday, neighbours, suppose we raise the Fourth Psa'am, to Samuel Wakely's tune, as improved by me?'

'Hang Samuel Wakely's tune, as improved by thee!' said Henchard. 'Chuck across one of your psalters – old Wiltshire is the only tune worth singing – the psalm tune that would make my blood ebb and flow like the sea when I was a steady chap.'

The Mayor of Casterbridge

Shortly after ten o'clock the singing-boys arrived at the tranter's house, which was invariably the place of meeting, and preparations were made for the start. The older men and musicians wore thick coats, with stiff perpendicular collars, and coloured handkerchiefs wound round and round the neck till the end came to hand, over all which they just showed their ears and noses, like people looking over a wall. The remainder, stalwart ruddy men and boys, were dressed mainly in snow-white smock-frocks, embroidered upon the shoulders and breasts in ornamental forms of hearts, diamonds, and zigzags. The cider-mug was emptied for the ninth time, the music-books were arranged, and the pieces finally decided upon. The boys in the meantime put the old horn-lanterns in order, cut candles into short lengths to fit the lanterns; and, a thin fleece of snow having fallen since the early part of the evening, those who had no leggings went to the stable and wound wisps of hay round their ankles to keep the insidious flakes from the interior of their boots.

Mellstock was a parish of considerable acreage, the hamlets composing it lying at a much greater distance from each other than is ordinarily the case. Hence several hours were consumed in playing and singing within hearing of every family, even if but a single air were bestowed on each. There was Lower Mellstock, the main village; half a mile from this were the church and vicarage, and a few other houses, the spot being rather lonely now, though in past centuries it had been the most thickly-populated quarter of the parish. A mile north-east lay the hamlet of Upper Mellstock, where the tranter lived; and at other points knots of cottages, besides solitary farmsteads and dairies.

Old William Dewy, with the violoncello, played the bass; his grandson Dick the treble violin; and Reuben and Michael Mail the tenor and second violins respectively. The singers consisted of four men and seven boys, upon which devolved the task of carrying and attending to the lanterns, and holding the books open for the players. Directly music was the theme old William ever and instinctively came to the front.

'Now mind, neighbours,' he said, as they all went out one by one at the door, he himself holding it ajar and regarding them with a critical face as they passed, like a shepherd counting out his sheep. 'You two counter-boys, keep your ears open to Michael's fingering, and don't ye go straying into the treble part along o' Dick and his set, as ye did last year; and mind this especially when we be in "Arise, and hail". Billy Chimlen, don't you sing quite so raving mad as you fain would; and, all o' ye, whatever ye do, keep from making a great scuffle on the ground when we go in at people's gates; but go quietly, so as to strike up all of a sudden, like spirits.'

'Farmer Ledlow's first?'

'Farmer Ledlow's first; the rest as usual.'

'And, Voss,' said the tranter terminatively, 'you keep house here till about half-past two; then heat the metheglin and cider in the warmer you'll find turned up upon the copper; and bring it wi' the victuals to church-hatch, as th'st know.'

Just before the clock struck twelve they lighted the lanterns and started. The moon, in her third quarter, had risen since the snow-storm; but the dense accumulation of snow-cloud weakened her power to a faint twilight which was rather pervasive of the landscape than traceable to the sky. The breeze had gone down, and the rustle of their feet and tones of their speech echoed with an alert rebound from every post, boundary-stone, and ancient wall they passed, even where the distance of the echo's origin was less than a few yards. Beyond their own slight noises nothing was to be heard save the occasional bark of foxes in the direction of Yalbury Wood, or the brush of a rabbit among the grass now and then as it scampered out of their way.

Most of the outlying homesteads and hamlets had been visited by about two o'clock; they then passed across the outskirts of a wooded park toward the main village, nobody being at home at the Manor. Pursuing no recognized track, great care was necessary in walking lest their faces should come in contact with the low-hanging boughs of the old lime-trees, which in many spots formed dense overgrowths of interlaced branches.

'Times have changed from the times they used to be,' said Mail, regarding nobody can tell what interesting old panoramas with an inward eye, and letting his outward glance rest on the ground because it was as convenient a position as any. 'People don't care much about us now! I've been thinking we must be almost the last left in the county of the old string players? Barrel-organs, and the things next door to 'em that you blow wi' your foot, have come in terribly of late years.'

'Ay!' said Bowman shaking his head; and old William on seeing him did the same thing.

'More's the pity,' replied another. 'Time was – long and merry ago now! – when not one of the varmits was to be heard of; but it served some of the quires right. They should have stuck to strings as we did, and kept out clarinets, and done away with serpents. If you'd thrive in musical religion, stick to strings, says I.'

'Strings be safe soul-lifters, as far as that do go,' said Mr Spinks.

'Yet there's worse things than serpents,' said Mr Penny. 'Old things pass away, 'tis true; but a serpent was a good old note: a deep rich note was the serpent.'

'Clar'nets, however, be bad at all times,' said Michael Mail. 'One Christmas – years agone now, years – I went the rounds wi' the Weatherbury quire. 'Twas a hard frosty night, and the keys of all the clar'nets froze – ah, they did freeze! – so that 'twas like drawing a cork every time a key was opened; and the players o' 'em had to go into a hedger-and-ditcher's chimley-corner, and thaw their clar'nets every now and then. An icicle o' spet hung down from the end of every man's

clar'net a span long; and as to fingers — well, there, if ye'll believe me, we
had no fingers at all, to our knowing.'

'I can well bring back to my mind,' said Mr Penny, 'what I said to
poor Joseph Ryme (who took the treble part in Chalk-Newton Church for
two-and-forty year) when they thought of having clar'nets there.
"Joseph," I said says I, "depend upon't, if so be you have them tooting
clar'nets you'll spoil the whole set-out. Clar'nets were not made for the
service of the Lard; you can see it by looking at 'em," I said. And what
came o't? Why, souls, the parson set up a barrel-organ on his own
account within two years o' the time I spoke, and the old quire went to
nothing.'

'As far as look is concerned,' said the tranter, 'I don't for my part see
that a fiddle is much nearer heaven than a clar'net. 'Tis further off.
There's always a rakish, scampish twist about a fiddle's looks that seems
to say the Wicked One had a hand in making o'en; while angels be
supposed to play clar'nets in heaven, or som'at like 'em if ye may believe
picters.'

'Robert Penny, you was in the right,' broke in the eldest Dewy. 'They
should ha' stuck to strings. Your brass-man is a rafting dog – well and
good; your reed-man is a dab at stirring ye — well and good; your drum-
man is a rare bowel-shaker – good again. But I don't care who hears me
say it, nothing will spak to your heart wi' the sweetness o' the man of
strings!'

'Strings for ever!' said little Jimmy.

'Strings alone would have held their ground against all the
newcomers in creation.' ('True, true!' said Bowman.) 'But clarinets was
death.' ('Death they was!' said Mr Penny.) 'And harmonions,' William
continued in a louder voice, and getting excited by these signs of
approval, 'harmonions and barrel-organs' ('Ah!' and groans from
Spinks) 'be miserable – what shall I call 'em? – miserable –'

'Sinners,' suggested Jimmy, who made large strides like the men and
did not lag behind with the other little boys.

'Miserable dumbledores!'

'Right, William, and so they be – miserable dumbledores!' said the
choir with unanimity.

Under the Greenwood Tree

'I was one of the quire-boys at that time, and we and the players were to
appear at the manor-house as usual that Christmas week, to play and
sing in the hall to the Squire's people and visitors (among 'em being the
archdeacon, Lord and Lady Baxby, and I don't know who); afterwards
going, as we always did, to have a good supper in the servants' hall.
Andrew knew this was the custom, and meeting us when we were starting
to go, he said to us: "Lord, how I should like to join in that meal of beef,

and turkey, and plum-pudding, and ale, that you happy ones be going to just now! One more or less will make no difference to the Squire. I am too old to pass as a singing boy, and too bearded to pass as a singing girl; can ye lend me a fiddle, neighbours, that I may come with ye as a bandsman?"

'Well, we didn't like to be hard upon him, and lent him an old one, though Andrew knew no more of music than the Giant o' Cernel; and armed with the instrument he walked up to the Squire's house with the others of us at the time appointed, and went in boldly, his fiddle under his arm. He made himself as natural as he could in opening the music-books and moving the candles to the best points for throwing light upon the notes; and all went well till we had played and sung "While shepherds watch," and "Star, arise," and "Hark the glad sound." Then the Squire's mother, a tall gruff old lady, who was much interested in church-music, said quite unexpectedly to Andrew: "My man, I see you don't play your instrument with the rest. How is that?"

'Every one of the quire was ready to sink into the earth with concern at the fix Andrew was in. We could see that he had fallen into a cold sweat, and how he would get out of it we did not know.

'"I've had a misfortune, mem," he says, bowing as meek as a child. "Coming along the road I fell down and broke my bow."

'"Oh, I am sorry to hear that," says she. "Can't it be mended?"

'"Oh no, mem," says Andrew. "'Twas broke all to splinters."

'"I'll see what I can do for you," says she.

'And then it seemed all over, and we played "Rejoice, ye drowsy mortals all," in D and two sharps. But no sooner had we got through it than she says to Andrew:

'"I've sent up into the attic, where we have some old musical instruments, and found a bow for you." And she hands the bow to poor wretched Andrew, who didn't even know which end to take hold of. "Now we shall have the full accompaniment," says she.

'Andrew's face looked as if it were made of rotten apple as he stood in the circle of players in front of his book; for if there was one person in the parish that everybody was afraid of, 'twas this hook-nosed old lady. However, by keeping a little behind the next man he managed to make pretence of beginning, sawing away with his bow without letting it touch the strings, so that it looked as if he were driving into the tune with heart and soul. 'Tis a question if he wouldn't have got through all right if one of the Squire's visitors (no other than the archdeacon) hadn't noticed that he held the fiddle upside down, the nut under his chin, and the tail-piece in his hand; and they began to crowd round him, thinking 'twas some new way of performing.

'This revealed everything; the Squire's mother had Andrew turned out of the house as a vile impostor, and there was great interruption to the harmony of the proceedings, the Squire declaring he should have notice to leave his cottage that day fortnight. However, when we got to the servants' hall there sat Andrew, who had been let in at the back door by the orders of the Squire's wife, after being turned out at the front by the orders of the Squire, and nothing more was heard about his leaving his cottage. But Andrew never performed in public as a musician after that night; and now he's dead and gone, poor man, as we all shall be!'

'Old Andrey's Experience as a Musician':
'A Few Crusted Characters'

'Well,' said Timothy Fairway, feeling demands upon his praise in some form or other, ''tis a worthy thing to be married, Mr Wildeve; and the woman you've got is a dimant, so says I. Yes,' he continued, to Grandfer Cantle, raising his voice so as to be heard through the partition; 'her father (inclining his head towards the inner room) was as good a feller as ever lived. He always had his great indignation ready against anything underhand.'

'Is that very dangerous?' said Christian.

'And there were few in these parts that were upsides with him,' said Sam. 'Whenever a club walked he'd play the clarinet in the band that marched before 'em as if he'd never touched anything but a clarinet all his life. And then, when they got to church-door he'd throw down the clarinet, mount the gallery, snatch up the bass-viol and rozum away as if he'd never played anything but a bass-viol. Folk would say   folk that knowed what a true stave was – "Surely, surely that's never the same man that I saw handling the clarinet so masterly by now!"'

'I can mind it,' said the furze-cutter. ''Twas a wonderful thing that one body could hold it all and never mix the fingering.'

'There was Kingsbere church likewise,' Fairway recommenced, as one opening a new vein of the same mine of interest.

Wildeve breathed the breath of one intolerably bored, and glanced through the partition at the prisoners.

'He used to walk over there of a Sunday afternoon to visit his old acquaintance Andrew Brown, the first clarinet there; a good man enough, but rather screechy in his music, if you can mind?'

''A was.'

'And neighbour Yeobright would take Andrey's place for some part of the service, to let Andrey have a bit of a nap, as any friend would naturally do.'

'As any friend would,' said Grandfer Cantle, the other listeners expressing the same accord by the shorter way of nodding their heads.

'No sooner was Andrey asleep and the first whiff of neighbour Yeobright's wind had got inside Andrey's clarinet than every one in church felt in a moment there was a great soul among 'em. All heads

would turn, and they'd say, "Ah, I thought 'twas he!" One Sunday I can
well mind – a bass-viol day that time, and Yeobright had brought his
own. 'Twas the Hundred-and-thirty-third to "Lydia"; and when they'd
come to "Ran down his beard and o'er his robes its costly moisture
shed", neighbour Yeobright, who had just warmed to his work, drove his
bow into them strings that glorious grand that he e'en a'most sawed the
bass-viol into two pieces. Every winder in church rattled as if 'twere a
thunderstorm. Old Pa'son Williams lifted his hands in his great holy
surplice as natural as if he'd been in common clothes, and seemed to say
to hisself, "O for such a man in our parish!" But not a soul in Kingsbere
could hold a candle to Yeobright.'

The Return of the Native

'And 'a can play the peanner, so 'tis said. Can play so clever that 'a can
make a psalm tune sound as well as the merriest loose song a man can
wish for.'

Billy Smallbury in *Far from the Madding Crowd*

'I had quite forgotten the old choir, with their fiddles and bass-viols,' said
the home-comer, musingly. 'Are they still going on the same as of old?'

'Bless the man!' said Christopher Twink, the master-thatcher; 'why,
they've been done away with these twenty year. A young teetotaller plays
the organ in church now, and plays it very well; though 'tis not quite such
good music as in old times, because the organ is one of them that go with
a winch, and the young teetotaller says he can't always throw the proper
feeling into the tune without wellnigh working his arms off.'

'Why did they make the change, then?'

'Well, partly because of fashion, partly because the old musicians got
into a sort of scrape. A terrible scrape 'twas too – wasn't it, John? I shall
never forget it – never! They lost their character as officers of the church
as complete as if they'd never had any character at all.'

'That was very bad for them.'

'Yes.' The master-thatcher attentively regarded past times as if they
lay about a mile off, and went on:-

'It happened on Sunday after Christmas – the last Sunday ever they
played in Longpuddle church gallery, as it turned out, though they didn't
know it then. As you may know, sir, the players formed a very good band
– almost as good as the Mellstock parish players that were led by the
Dewys; and that's saying a great deal. There was Nicholas Puddingcome,
the leader, with the first fiddle; there was Timothy Thomas, the bass-viol
man; John Biles, the tenor fiddler; Dan'l Hornhead, with the serpent;
Robert Dowdle, with the clarionet; and Mr Nicks, with the oboe – all
sound and powerful musicians, and strong-winded men – they that

blowed. For that reason they were very much in demand Christmas week
for little reels and dancing parties; for they could turn a jig or a horn-pipe
out of hand as well as ever they could turn out a psalm, and perhaps
better, not to speak irreverent. In short, one half-hour they could be
playing a Christmas carol in the Squire's hall to the ladies and
gentlemen, and drinking tay and coffee with 'em as modest as saints; and
the next, at The Tinker's Arms, blazing away like wild horses with the
"Dashing White Sergeant" to nine couple of dancers and more, and
swallowing rum-and-cider hot as flame.

'Well, this Christmas they'd been out to one rattling randy after
another every night, and had got next to no sleep at all. Then came the
Sunday after Christmas, their fatal day. 'Twas so mortal cold that year
that they could hardly sit in the gallery; for though the congregation
down in the body of the church had a stove to keep off the frost, the
players in the gallery had nothing at all. So Nicholas said at morning
service, when 'twas freezing an inch an hour, "Please the Lord I won't
stand this numbing weather no longer: this afternoon we'll have
something in our insides to make us warm, if it cost a king's ransom."

'So he brought a gallon of hot brandy and beer, ready mixed, to
church with him in the afternoon, and by keeping the jar well wrapped up
in Timothy Thomas's bass-viol bag it kept drinkably warm till they
wanted it, which was just a thimbleful in the Absolution, and another
after the Creed, and the remainder at the beginning o' the sermon. When
they'd had the last pull they felt quite comfortable and warm, and as the
sermon went on – most unfortunately for 'em it was a long one that
afternoon – they fell asleep, every man jack of 'em; and there they slept
on as sound as rocks.

''Twas a very dark afternoon, and by the end of the sermon all you
could see of the inside of the church were the pa'son's two candles
alongside of him in the pulpit, and his spaking face behind 'em. The
sermon being ended at last, the pa'son gie'd out the Evening Hymn. But
no quire set about sounding up the tune, and the people began to turn
their heads to learn the reason why, and then Levi Limpet, a boy who sat
in the gallery, nudged Timothy and Nicholas, and said, "Begin! begin!"

'"Hey? what?" says Nicholas, starting up; and the church being so
dark and his head so muddled he thought he was at the party they had
played at all the night before, and away he went, bow and fiddle, at "The
Devil among the Tailors," the favourite jig of our neighbourhood at that
time. The rest of the band, being in the same state of mind and nothing
doubting, followed their leader with all their strength, according to
custom. They poured out that there tune till the lower bass notes of "The
Devil among the Tailors" made the cobwebs in the roof shiver like ghosts;
then Nicholas, seeing nobody moved, shouted out as he scraped (in his
usual commanding way at dances when the folk didn't know the figures),

"Top couples cross hands! And when I make the fiddle squeak at the end, every man kiss his pardner under the mistletoe!"

'The boy Levi was so frightened that he bolted down the gallery stairs and out homeward like lightning. The pa'son's hair fairly stood on end when he heard the evil tune raging through the church, and thinking the quire had gone crazy he held up his hand and said: "Stop, stop, stop! Stop, stop! What's this?" But they didn't hear'n for the noise of their own playing, and the more he called the louder they played.

'Then the folks came out of their pews, wondering down to the ground, and saying: "What do they mean by such wickedness! We shall be consumed like Sodom and Gomorrah!"

'And the Squire, too, came out of his pew lined wi' green baize, where lots of lords and ladies visiting at the house were worshipping along with him, and went and stood in front of the gallery, and shook his fist in the musicians' faces, saying, "What! In this reverent edifice! What!"

'And at last they heard'n through their playing, and stopped.

'"Never such an insulting, disgraceful thing – never!" says the Squire, who couldn't rule his passion.

'"Never!" says the pa'son, who had come down and stood beside him.

'"Not if the Angels of Heaven," says the Squire (he was a wickedish man, the Squire was, though now for once he happened to be on the Lord's side) – "not if the Angels of Heaven come down," he says, "shall one of you villainous players ever sound a note in this church again; for the insult to me, and my family, and my visitors, and the pa'son, and God Almighty, that you've a-perpetrated this afternoon!"

'Then the unfortunate church band came to their senses, and remembered where they were; and 'twas a sight to see Nicholas Puddingcome and Timothy Thomas and John Biles creep down the gallery stairs with their fiddles under their arms, and poor Dan'l Hornhead with his serpent, and Robert Dowdle with his clarionet, all looking as little as ninepins; and out they went. The pa'son might have forgi'ed 'em when he learned the truth o't, but the Squire would not. That very week he sent for a barrel-organ that would play two-and-twenty new psalm-tunes, so exact and particular that, however sinful inclined you was, you could play nothing but psalm-tunes whatsomever. He had a really respectable man to turn the winch, as I said, and the old players played no more.'

'Absent-mindedness in a parish Choir':
'A Few Crusted Characters'

'I don't care a curse what the words be,' said Henchard. 'Hymns, ballets or rantipole rubbish; the Rogue's March or the cherubin's warble – 'tis all the same to me if 'tis good harmony, and well put out'.

The Mayor of Casterbridge

The lusty notes of the East Egdon band had directed her unerringly, and she now beheld the musicians themselves, sitting in a blue waggon with red wheels scrubbed as bright as new, and arched with sticks, to which boughs and flowers were tied. In front of this was the grand central dance of fifteen or twenty couples, flanked by minor dances of inferior individuals whose gyrations were not always in strict keeping with the tune.

The young men wore blue and white rosettes, and with a flush on their faces footed it to the girls, who, with the excitement and the exercise, blushed deeper than the pink of their numerous ribbons. Fair ones with long curls, fair ones with short curls, fair ones with love-locks, fair ones with braids, flew round and round; and a beholder might well have wondered how such a prepossessing set of young women of like size, age, and disposition, could have been collected together where there were only one or two villages to choose from. In the background was one happy man dancing by himself, with closed eyes, totally oblivious of all the rest.

The Return of the Native

The fiddler was a boy of those parts, about twelve years of age, who had a wonderful dexterity in jigs and reels, though his fingers were so small and short as to necessitate a constant shifting for the high notes, from which he scrambled back to the first position with sounds not of unmixed purity of tone. At seven the shrill tweedle-dee of this youngster had begun, accompanied by a booming ground-bass from Elijah New, the parish-clerk, who had thoughtfully brought with him his favourite musical instrument, the serpent. Dancing was instantaneous, Mrs Fennel privately enjoining the players on no account to let the dance exceed the length of a quarter of an hour.

But Elijah and the boy in the excitement of their position quite forgot the injunction. Moreover, Oliver Giles, a man of seventeen, one of the dancers, who was enamoured of his partner, a fair girl of thirty-three rolling years, had recklessly handed a new crown-piece to the musicians, as a bribe to keep going as long as they had muscle and wind. Mrs Fennel, seeing the steam begin to generate on the countenances of her guests, crossed over and touched the fiddler's elbow and put her hand on the serpent's mouth. But they took no notice, and fearing she might lose her character of genial hostess if she were to interfere too markedly, she retired and sat down helpless. And so the dance whizzed on with cumulative fury, the performers moving in their planet-like courses, direct and retrograde, from apogee to perigee, till the hand of the well-kicked clock at the bottom of the room had travelled over the circumference of an hour.

'The Three Strangers'

In addition to the local musicians present a man who had a thorough
knowledge of the tambourine was invited from the village of Tantrum
Clangley, – a place long celebrated for the skill of its inhabitants as
performers on instruments of percussion. These important members of
the assembly were relegated to a height of two or three feet from the
ground, upon a temporary erection of planks supported by barrels.
Whilst the dancing progressed the older persons sat in a group under the
trunk of the tree, – the space being allotted to them somewhat grudgingly
by the young ones, who were greedy of pirouetting room, – and fortified
by a table against the heels of the dancers. Here the gaffers and gammers
whose dancing days were over told stories of great impressiveness, and at
intervals surveyed the advancing and retiring couples from the same
retreat, as people on shore might be supposed to survey a naval
engagement in the bay beyond.

Under the Greenwood Tree

This was the night which had been selected by Sergeant Troy – ruling
now in the room of his wife – for giving the harvest supper and dance. As
Oak approached the building the sound of violins and a tambourine, and
the regular jigging of many feet, grew more distinct. He came close to the
large doors, one of which stood slightly ajar, and looked in.

The central space, together with the recess at one end, was emptied of
all incumbrances, and this area, covering about two-thirds of the whole,
was appropriated for the gathering, the remaining end, which was piled
to the ceiling with oats, being screened off with sail-cloth. Tufts and
garlands of green foliage decorated the walls, beams, and extemporized
chandeliers, and immediately opposite to Oak a rostrum had been
erected, bearing a table and chairs. Here sat three fiddlers, and beside
them stood a frantic man with his hair on end, perspiration streaming
down his cheeks, and a tambourine quivering in his hand.

The dance ended, and on the black oak floor in the midst a new row of
couples formed for another.

'Now, ma'am, and no offence I hope, I ask what dance you would like
next?' said the first violin.

'Really, it makes no difference,' said the clear voice of Bathsheba, who
stood at the inner end of the building, observing the scene from behind a
table covered with cups and viands. Troy was lolling beside her.

'Then,' said the fiddler, 'I'll venture to name that the right and proper
thing is "The Soldier's Joy" – there being a gallant soldier married into
the farm – hey, my sonnies, and gentlemen all?'

'It shall be "The Soldier's Joy,"' exclaimed a chorus.

'Thanks for the compliment,' said the sergeant gaily, taking
Bathsheba by the hand and leading her to the top of the dance. 'For

though I have purchased my discharge from Her Most Gracious Majesty's regiment of cavalry the 11th Dragoon Guards, to attend to the new duties awaiting me here, I shall continue a soldier in spirit and feeling as long as I live.'

So the dance began. As to the merits of 'The Soldier's Joy', there cannot be, and never were, two opinions. It has been observed in the musical circles of Weatherbury and its vicinity that this melody, at the end of three-quarters of an hour of thunderous footing, still possesses more stimulative properties for the heel and toe than the majority of other dances at their first opening. 'The Soldier's Joy' has, too, an additional charm in being so admirably adapted to the tambourine aforesaid – no mean instrument in the hands of a performer who understands the proper convulsions, spasms, St Vitus's dances, and fearful frenzies necessary when exhibiting its tones in their highest perfection.

Far from the Madding Crowd

The dance it is a great thing,
    A great thing to me,
With candles lit and partners fit
    For night-long revelry;
And going home when day-dawning
    Peeps pale upon the lea:
O dancing is a great thing,
    A great thing to me!

'Great Things'

'Before we begin,' said the tranter, 'my proposal is, that 'twould be a right and proper plan for every mortal man in the dance to pull off his jacket, considering the heat.'

'Such low notions as you have, Reuben! Nothing but strip will go down with you when you are a-dancing. Such a hot man as he is!'

'Well, now, look here, my sonnies,' he argued to his wife, whom he often addressed in the plural masculine for economy of epithet merely; 'I don't see that. You dance and get hot as fire; therefore you lighten your clothes. Isn't that nature and reason for gentle and simple? If I strip by myself and not necessary, 'tis rather pot-housey I own; but if we stout chaps strip one and all, why, 'tis the native manners of the country, which no man can gainsay? Hey – what did you say, my sonnies?'

'Strip we will!' said the three other heavy men who were in the dance; and their coats were accordingly taken off and hung in the passage, whence the four sufferers from heat soon reappeared marching in close column, with flapping shirt-sleeves, and having as common to them all a general glance of being now a match for any man or dancer in England or Ireland.

Under the Greenwood Tree

They alighted and went in, Christopher shouldering Faith's harp, and she marching modestly behind, with curly-eared music-books under her arm. They were shown into the house-steward's room, and ushered thence along a badly-lit passage and past a door within which a hum and laughter were audible. The door next to this was then opened for them, and they entered.

Scarcely had Faith, or Christopher either, ever beheld a more shining scene than was presented by the saloon in which they now found themselves. Coming direct from the gloomy park, and led to the room by that back passage from the servants' quarter, the light from the chandelier and branches along the walls, striking on gilding at all points, quite dazzled their sight for a minute or two; it caused Faith to move forward with her eyes on the floor, and filled Christopher with an impulse to turn back again into some dusky corner where every thread of his not over-new dress suit – rather moth-eaten through lack of feasts for airing it – could be counted less easily.

He was soon seated before a grand piano, and Faith sat down under the shadow of her harp, both being arranged on a dais within an alcove at one end of the room. A screen of ivy and holly had been constructed across the front of this recess for the games of the children on Christmas Eve, and it still remained there, a small creep-hole being left for entrance and exit.

Then the merry guests tumbled through doors at the further end, and dancing began. The mingling of black-coated men and bright ladies gave a charming appearance to the groups as seen by Faith and her brother, the whole spectacle deriving an unexpected novelty from the accident of reaching their eyes through interstices in the tracery of green leaves, which added to the picture a softness that it would not otherwise have possessed.

The Hand of Ethelberta

The cold moon hangs to the sky by its horn,
    And centres its gaze on me;
The stars, like eyes in reverie,
Their westering as for a while forborne,
    Quiz downward curiously.

Old Robert draws the backbrand in,
    The green logs steam and spit;
The half-awakened sparrows flit
From the riddled thatch; and owls begin
    To whoo from the gable-slit.

Yes; far and nigh things seem to know
    Sweet scenes are impending here;
That all is prepared; that the hour is near
For welcomes, fellowships, and flow
    Of sally, song, and cheer;

That spigots are pulled and viols strung;
    That soon will arise the sound
Of measures trod to tunes renowned;
That She will return in Love's low tongue
    My vows as we wheel around.

'The Night of the Dance'

To dance with a man is to concentrate a twelvemonth's regulation fire upon him in the fragment of an hour. To pass to courtship without acquaintance, to pass to marriage without courtship, is a skipping of terms reserved for those alone who tread this royal road.

The Return of the Native

In August or September a new assistant came to Mr Crickmay's drawing-offices, who was afterwards sketched in *Desperate Remedies* as 'Edward Springrove' – and in November this young man persuaded Hardy to join a quadrille class in the town, which was a source of much amusement to them both. Dancing was still an art in those days, though Hardy remarked once that he found the young ladies of Weymouth heavier on the arm than their London sisters. By the time that winter drew on he had finished all the drawings for church-restoration that had been placed in his hands, but he remained at his Weymouth lodgings, working at the MS. of *Desperate Remedies*.

So 1869 passed, and at the beginning of February in the year following Hardy gave up his rooms at Weymouth and returned to his rural home to be able to concentrate more particularly on the MS. than he could do in a lively town and as a member of a dancing-class where a good deal of flirtation went on, the so-called 'class' being, in fact, a gay gathering for dances and love-making by adepts of both sexes.

The Life of Thomas Hardy

Wildeve gave her his arm and took her down on the outside of the ring to
the bottom of the dance, which they entered. In two minutes more they
were involved in the figure and began working their way upwards to the
top. Till they had advanced half-way thither Eustacia wished more than
once that she had not yielded to his request; from the middle to the top
she felt that, since she had come out to seek pleasure, she was only doing
a natural thing to obtain it. Fairly launched into the ceaseless glides and
whirls which their new position as top couple opened up to them,
Eustacia's pulses began to move too quickly for longer rumination of any
kind.

    Through the length of five-and-twenty couples they threaded their
giddy way, and a new vitality entered her form. The pale ray of evening
lent a fascination to the experience. There is a certain degree and tone of
light which tends to disturb the equilibrium of the senses, and to promote
dangerously the tenderer moods; added to movement, it drives the
motions to rankness, the reason becoming sleepy and unperceiving in
inverse proportion; and this light fell now upon these two from the disc of
the moon. All the dancing girls felt the symptoms, but Eustacia most of
all. The grass under their feet became trodden away, and the hard,
beaten surface of the sod, when viewed aslant towards the moonlight,
shone like a polished table. The air became quite still; the flag above the
waggon which held the musicians clung to the pole, and the players
appeared only in outline against the sky; except when the circular mouths
of the trombone, ophicleide, and French horn gleamed out like huge eyes
from the shade of their figures. The pretty dresses of the maids lost their
subtler daycolours and showed more or less of a misty white. Eustacia
floated round and round on Wildeve's arm, her face rapt and statuesque;
her soul had passed away from and forgotten her features, which were left
empty and quiescent, as they always are when feeling goes beyond their
register.

The Return of the Native

''Twas the dancing,' said she. 'People get quite crazy sometimes in a
dance.'

'The History of the Hardcomes':
'A Few Crusted Characters'

> The fiddler knows what's brewing
>   To the lilt of his lyric wiles:
> The fiddler knows what rueing
>   Will come of this night's smiles!

He sees couples join them for dancing,
    And afterwards joining for life,
He sees them pay high for their prancing
    By a welter of wedded strife.

He twangs: 'Music hails from the devil,
    Though vaunted to come from heaven,
For it makes people do at a revel
    What multiplies sins by seven.

'There's many a heart now mangled,
    And waiting its time to go,
Whose tendrils were first entangled
    By my sweet viol and bow!'

                      'The Fiddler'

The kitchen was cleared of furniture for dancing, and the old folk played at 'Put' and 'All-fours' in the parlour, though at last they gave that up to join in the dance. The top of the figure was by the large front window of the room, and there were so many couples that the lower part of the figure reached through the door at the back, and into the darkness of the out-house; in fact, you couldn't see the end of the row at all, and 'twas never known exactly how long that dance was, the lowest couples being lost among the faggots and brushwood in the out-house.

                   'The History of the Hardcomes':
                       'A Few Crusted Characters'

Here it is hanging in the sun
    By the pawn-shop door,
A dress-suit – all its revels done
    Of heretofore.
Long drilled to the waltzers' swing and sway,
    As its tokens show:
What it has seen, what it could say
    If it did but know!

The sleeve bears still a print of powder
    Rubbed from her arms
When she warmed up as the notes swelled louder
    And livened her charms –
Or rather theirs, for beauties many
    Leant there, no doubt,
Leaving these tell-tale traces when he
    Spun them about.

Its cut seems rather in bygone style
    On looking close,
So it mayn't have bent it for some while
    To the dancing pose:
Anyhow, often within its clasp
    Fair partners hung
Assenting to the wearer's grasp
    With soft sweet tongue.

Where is, alas, the gentleman
    Who wore this suit?
And where are his ladies? Tell none can:
    Gossip is mute.
Some of them may forget him quite
    Who smudged his sleeve,
Some think of a wild and whirling night
    With him, and grieve.

             'A Gentleman's Second-hand Suit'

Beside the Mead of Memories,
Where Church-way mounts to Moaning Hill
The sad man sighed his phantasies:
    He seems to sigh them still.

''Twas the Birth-tide Eve, and the hamleteers
Made merry with ancient Mellstock zest,
But the Mellstock quire of former years
    Had entered into rest.

'Old Dewy lay by the gaunt yew tree,
And Reuben and Michael a pace behind,
And Bowman with his family
    By the wall that the ivies bind.

'The singers had followed one by one,
Treble, and tenor, and thorough-bass;
And the worm that wasteth had begun
    To mine their mouldering place.

'For two-score years, ere Christ-day light,
Mellstock had throbbed to strains from these
But now there echoed on the night
    No Christmas harmonies.

'Three meadows off, at a dormered inn,
The youth had gathered in high carouse,
And, ranged on settles, some therein
     Had drunk them to a drowse.

'Loud, lively, reckless, some had grown,
Each dandling on his jigging knee
Eliza, Dolly, Nance, or Joan –
     Livers in levity.

'The taper flames and hearthfire shine
Grew smoke-hazed to a lurid light,
And songs on subjects not divine
     Were warbled forth that night.

'Yet many were sons and grandsons here
Of those who, on such eves gone by,
At that still hour had throated clear
     Their anthems to the sky.

'The clock belled midnight; and ere long
One shouted, "Now 'tis Christmas morn;
Here's to our women old and young,
     And to John Barleycorn!"

'They drink the toast and shout again:
The pewter-ware rings back the boom,
And for a breath-while follows then
     A silence in the room.

'When nigh without, as in old days,
The ancient quire of voice and string
Seemed singing words of prayer and praise
     As they had used to sing:

'While shepherds watch'd their flocks by night, –
Thus swells the long familiar sound
In many a quaint symphonic flight –
     To, Glory shone around.

'The sons defined their fathers' tones,
The widow his whom she had wed,
And others in the minor moans
     The viols of the dead.

'Something supernal has the sound
As verse by verse the strain proceeds,
And stilly staring on the ground
     Each roysterer holds and heeds.

'Towards its chorded closing bar
Plaintively, thinly, waned the hymn,
Yet lingered, like the notes afar
    Of banded seraphim.

'With brows abashed, and reverent tread,
The hearkeners sought the tavern door:
But nothing, save wan moonlight, spread
    The empty highway o'er.

'While on their hearing fixed and tense
The aerial music seemed to sink,
As it were gently moving thence
    Along the river brink.

'Then did the Quick pursue the Dead
By crystal Froom that crinkles there;
And still the viewless quire ahead
    Voiced the old holy air.

'By Bank-walk, wicket, brightly bleached,
It passed, and 'twixt the hedges twain,
Dogged by the living; till it reached
    The bottom of Church Lane.

'There, at the turning, it was heard
Drawing to where the churchyard lay:
But when they followed thitherward
    It smalled, and died away.

'Each headstone of the quire, each mound,
Confronted them beneath the moon;
But no more floated therearound
    That ancient Birth-night tune.

'There Dewy lay by the gaunt yew tree,
There Reuben and Michael, a pace behind,
And Bowman with his family
    By the wall that the ivies bind . . .

'As from a dream each sobered son
Awoke, and musing reached his door:
''Twas said that of them all, not one
    Sat in a tavern more.'

– The sad man ceased; and ceased to heed
His listener, and crossed the leaze
From Moaning Hill towards the mead –
    The Mead of Memories.   'The Dead Quire'

5

THE CEREMONIES AND
SEASONS OF THE YEAR

'We believed in highdays then', Hardy wrote, as the opening
line of a poem, and there is no doubting the importance of
the high days and holy days that added punctuation and
paragraphing to the otherwise featureless progress of the weeks and
months in the parish of Stinsford. There were the climactic occasions
of the farming year – the sheep-shearing, the corn harvest, the brewing
of ale and cider; there were the religious festivals, with Christian and
pagan elements intermixed; and there were the celebratory family
parties for a special occasion such as a wedding. Taken together they
gave shape and coherence to the annual cycle and strengthened the
ties of kindred and clan. For Hardy they provided an indelible pattern
that continued to glow in his memory.

The appropriate starting-point is Christmas, the moment of new
birth and jubilation in the dark midwinter. It is plainly a time of
feasting and jollity, of party-giving and dancing, but it has also its
visionary elements and its ancient legends. Christmas Eve brought the
phantoms of the village dead back into view, while the stalled cattle
knelt to acknowledge the Saviour's birth. From the elders of the family
came these miraculous intimations, along with precise rules of conduct
to prevent the giving of offence to the 'sky-folk' by starting to dance
before the holy day had reached midnight.

Carol-singing has already been mentioned here in 'The People's
Music'. Then there were the mummers who similarly visited the

grander residences of the gentry and the farmers, to entertain them with their play-acting and to receive food and drink in return. Theirs is a tradition that seems to have preserved, in a degenerate form, recollections of the Crusades – with England's patron saint, St George, fighting and overcoming the Turkish Knight. The tradition lingered until the 1914 war, when its continuity was finally broken. Revivals are sometimes attempted but the indigenous quality is lost, together with the social context in which it flourished. The Christmas hobby-horse similarly, described to Hardy by his father, prances no more, though its May Day cousin flourishes at Padstow and Minehead.

Associated with Christmas, and more particularly perhaps with Twelfth Night, was the custom of wassailing the cider-apple trees to make them fruitful. The last stronghold of the custom known to me was at Athelney in Somerset where, until recently, a man would climb up to put a piece of toast dipped in cider among the branches and then lead the singing of the wassail-song. To drive away evil spirits a shotgun might be fired into the upper branches. The main duty of the owner of the orchard was to provide cider to refresh the wassailers: and, as one of them recalled to me with feeling, ''twas cider in buckets in they days'. The Hardys do not seem to have wassailed their cider-apple trees in the paddock at Bockhampton though they set great store by the year's crop. Hardy's mother was certainly familiar with the custom in the Hintock countryside before her marriage and described it to young Thomas.

The imminence of Lent signalled the last of winter's welcome moments of self-indulgence at table – Shrove Tuesday or Pancake Day. Again one of Hardy's notebooks preserved the crudely chanted doggerel of the shrovers. Easter has left surprisingly little mark on his writings but its pagan equivalent – May Day – celebrating the resurrection and burgeoning of Nature is vigorously portrayed in *The Return of the Native* and *Tess of the d'Urbervilles*. In his account of the dressing of the maypole Hardy emphasized that, in the Egdon villages, 'the instincts of merry England lingered on here with exceptional vitality'. In *Tess of the d'Urbervilles* he outlined a connection between the formal club-walks and the pagan fertility rites of May Day. In his own lifetime the walks were an annual demonstration by the health benefit club and more usually took place on Whit Monday as a convenient public holiday. In recent years May Day has become International Labour Day. Whit Monday has lost its status as an official holiday, and the local benefit clubs have been replaced by the National Health Service. A characterless Spring Bank Holiday scarcely retains those 'instincts of merry England' to which Hardy was accustomed.

Weddings have no seasonal limits but springtime and midsummer seem most appropriate for the procession through the countryside.

Indeed Whitsun was the choice of Tranter Dewy and his wife for their wedding, after which they 'went a-gaying round the parish' with their guests walking in pairs. The intention was to show to the community that bride and groom were duly wedded. To have some friendly musicians in the party must have put a spring into the steps of the walkers, as in the poem 'The Country Wedding', where Hardy seems to draw on personal recollections of a family occasion at Puddletown.

Harvest Home would always have been one of the year's great occasions, promising a bountiful table to reward the workers. It marked the conclusion of the most arduous spell of labour, when corn was reaped by the scythe and stooked by hand; and fears of famine and starvation were still real enough to need the reassurance given by a good yield. It provided the mood and the setting for one of the great scenes in *Far from the Madding Crowd*, which certainly derives from Hardy's own boyhood experience. When he was about ten years old he was taken to a harvest supper where soldiers had been invited to swell the numbers of partners to dance with the farm-women. What made the deepest impression on him was the singing of the old traditional ballads which were so soon to be displaced and almost forgotten as the popular songs of the London music-halls caught the fancy of the workpeople. Richard Jefferies mourned the same loss of a tradition in neighbouring Wiltshire in 1880 when he noted, in *Hodge and his Masters*, that the song of the contemporary labourer

> tells you nothing of wheat, or hay, or flocks and herds, nothing of the old gods and heroes. It is a street ditty such as you may hear the gutter arabs yelling in London, and coming from a music hall.

One ballad in particular so possessed Hardy's imagination that he preserved his recollection of it in the poem 'The Harvest Supper'.

Between harvest and Christmas the year's remaining festival centred on the autumn bonfires and Hallow-E'en, celebrated in various forms as Punky Night, Guy Fawkes Night etc. Beneath the modern forms lay ancient rituals which retained some of their potency – for acts of divination, for supernatural appearances, for the purging and renewal by fire of Nature's spent energies. Hardy's sensitivity to such intimations is shown remarkably in the climax of the bonfire dance in *The Return of the Native*. Here the heathfolk affirm their kinship with tribal dancers performing an age-old ritual in other lands and other centuries. It is in such scenes that Hardy's deep-rooted sense of the long perspective, expressed in poetic intuitions, is so telling.

Christmas Eve, and twelve of the clock.
    'Now they are all on their knees,'
An elder said as we sat in a flock
    By the embers in hearthside ease.

We pictured the meek mild creatures where
    They dwelt in their strawy pen,
Nor did it occur to one of us there
    To doubt they were kneeling then.

So fair a fancy few would weave
    In these years! Yet, I feel,
If someone said on Christmas Eve,
    'Come; see the oxen kneel

'In the lonely barton by yonder coomb
    Our childhood used to know,'
I should go with him in the gloom,
    Hoping it might be so.

                    'The Oxen'

Here we broached the Christmas barrel,
    Pushed up the charred log-ends;
Here we sang the Christmas carol,
    And called in friends.

Time has tired me since we met here
    When the folk now dead were young,
Since the viands were outset here
    And quaint songs sung.

And the worm has bored the viol
    That used to lead the tune,
Rust eaten out the dial
    That struck night's noon.

Now no Christmas brings in neighbours,
    And the New Year comes unlit;
Where we sang the mole now labours,
    And spiders knit.

Yet at midnight if here walking,
    When the moon sheets wall and tree,
I see forms of old time talking,
    Who smile on me.

            'The House of Hospitalities'

It was dusk, and Eustacia was sitting by the fire in the dining room or hall, which they occupied at this time of the year in preference to the parlour, because of its large hearth, constructed for turf-fires, a fuel the captain was partial to in the winter season. The only visible articles in the room were those on the window-sill, which showed their shapes against the low sky: the middle article being the old hour-glass, and the other two a pair of ancient British urns which had been dug from a barrow near, and were used as flower-pots for two razor-leaved cactuses. Somebody knocked at the door. The servant was out; so was her grandfather. The person, after waiting a minute, came in and tapped at the door of the room.

'Who's there?' said Eustacia.

'Please, Cap'n Vye, will you let us –'

Eustacia arose and went to the door. 'I cannot allow you to come in so boldly. You should have waited.'

'The cap'n said I might come in without any fuss,' was answered in a lad's pleasant voice.

'Oh, did he?' said Eustacia more gently. 'What did you want, Charley?'

'Please will your grandfather lend us his fuel-house to try over our parts in, to-night at seven o'clock?'

'What, are you one of the Egdon mummers for this year?'

'Yes, miss. The cap'n used to let the old mummers practise here.'

'I know it. Yes, you may use the fuel-house if you like,' said Eustacia languidly.

The choice of Captain Vye's fuel-house as the scene of rehearsal was dictated by the fact that his dwelling was nearly in the centre of the heath. The fuel-house was as roomy as a barn, and was a most desirable place for such a purpose. The lads who formed the company of players lived at different scattered points around, and by meeting in this spot the distances to be traversed by all the comers would be about equally proportioned.

For mummers and mumming Eustacia had the greatest contempt. The mummers themselves were not afflicted with any such feeling for their art, though at the same time they were not enthusiastic. A traditional pastime is to be distinguished from a mere revival in no more striking feature than in this, that while in the revival all is excitement and fervour, the survival is carried on with a stolidity and absence of stir which sets one wondering why a thing that is done so perfunctorily should be kept up at all. Like Baalam and other unwilling prophets, the agents seem moved by an inner compulsion to say and do their allotted parts whether they will or no. This unweeting manner of performance is the true ring by which, in this refurbishing age, a fossilized survival may be known from a spurious reproduction.

The piece was the well-known play of 'Saint George', and all who were behind the scenes assisted in the preparations, including the women of each household. Without the co-operation of sisters and sweethearts the dresses were likely to be a failure; but on the other hand, this class of assistance was not without its drawbacks. The girls could never be brought to respect tradition in designing and decorating the armour; they insisted on attaching loops and bows of silk and velvet in any situation pleasing to their taste. Gorget, gusset, basinet, cuirass, gauntlet, sleeve, all alike in the view of these feminine eyes were practicable spaces whereon to sew scraps of fluttering colour.

It might be that Joe, who fought on the side of Christendom, had a sweetheart, and that Jim, who fought on the side of the Moslem, had one likewise. During the making of the costumes it would come to the knowledge of Joe's sweetheart that Jim's was putting brilliant silk scallops at the bottom of her lover's surcoat, in addition to the ribbons of the visor, the bars of which, being invariably formed of coloured strips about half an inch wide hanging before the face, were mostly of that material. Joe's sweetheart straightway placed brilliant silk on the scallops of the hem in question, and, going a little further, added ribbon tufts to the shoulder pieces. Jim's, not to be out-done, would affix bows and rosettes everywhere.

The result was that in the end the Valiant Soldier, of the Christian army, was distinguished by no peculiarity of accoutrement from the Turkish Knight; and what was worse, on a casual view Saint George himself might be mistaken for his deadly enemy, the Saracen. The guisers themselves, though inwardly regretting this confusion of persons, could not afford to offend those by whose assistance they so largely profited, and the innovations were allowed to stand.

There was, it is true, a limit to this tendency to uniformity. The Leech or Doctor preserved his character intact: his darker habiliments, peculiar hat, and the bottle of physic slung under his arm, could never be mistaken. And the same might be said of the conventional figure of Father Christmas, with his gigantic club, an older man, who accompanied the band as general protector in long night journeys from parish to parish, and was bearer of the purse.

Seven o'clock, the hour of the rehearsal, came round, and in a short time Eustacia could hear voices in the fuel-house. To dissipate in some trifling measure her abiding sense of the murkiness of human life she went to the 'linhay' or lean-to shed, which formed the root-store of their dwelling and abutted on the fuel-house. Here was a small rough hole in the mud wall, originally made for pigeons, through which the interior of the next shed could be viewed. A light came from it now; and Eustacia stepped upon a stool to look in upon the scene.

On a ledge in the fuel-house stood three tall rushlights, and by the light of them seven or eight lads were marching about, haranguing, and confusing each other, in endeavours to perfect themselves in the play. Humphrey and Sam, the furze and turf cutters, were there looking on, so also was Timothy Fairway, who leant against the wall and prompted the boys from memory, interspersing among the set words remarks and anecdotes of the superior days when he and others were the Egdon mummers-elect that these lads were now.

'Well, ye be as well up to it as ever ye will be,' he said. 'Not that such mumming would have passed in our time. Harry as the Saracen should strut a bit more, and John needn't holler his inside out. Beyond that perhaps you'll do. Have you got all your clothes ready?'

'We shall by Monday.'

'Your first outing will be Monday night, I suppose?'

'Yes. At Mrs Yeobright's.'

'Oh, Mrs Yeobright's. What makes her want to see ye? I should think a middle-aged woman was tired of mumming.'

'She's got up a bit of a party, because 'tis the first Christmas that her son Clym has been home for a long time.'

'To be sure, to be sure – her party! I am going myself. I almost forgot it, upon my life.'

Eustacia's face flagged. There was to be a party at the Yeobrights'; she, naturally, had nothing to do with it. She was a stranger to all such local gatherings, and had always held them as scarcely appertaining to her sphere. But had she been going, what an opportunity would have been afforded her of seeing the man whose influence was penetrating her like summer sun! To increase that influence was coveted excitement; to cast it off might be to regain serenity; to leave it as it stood was tantalizing.

The lads and men prepared to leave the premises, and Eustacia returned to her fireside. She was immersed in thought, but not for long. In a few minutes the lad Charley, who had come to ask permission to use the place, returned with the key to the kitchen. Eustacia heard him, and opening the door into the passage said, 'Charley, come here.'

The lad was surprised. He entered the front room not without blushing; for he, like many, had felt the power of this girl's face and form.

She pointed to a seat by the fire, and entered the other side of the chimney-corner herself. It could be seen in her face that whatever motive she might have had in asking the youth indoors would soon appear.

'Which part do you play, Charley – the Turkish Knight, do you now?' inquired the beauty, looking across the smoke of the fire to him on the other side.

'Yes, miss, the Turkish Knight,' he replied diffidently.

'Is yours a long part?'

'Nine speeches, about.'

'Can you repeat them to me? If so I should like to hear them.'
The lad smiled into the glowing turf and began –

> 'Here come I, a Turkish Knight,
> Who learnt in Turkish land to fight'

continuing the discourse throughout the scenes to the concluding
catastrophe of his fall by the hand of Saint George.

Eustacia had occasionally heard the part recited before. When the lad
ended she began, precisely in the same words, and ranted on without
hitch or divergence till she too reached the end. It was the same thing, yet
how different. Like in form, it had the added softness and finish of a
Raffaelle after Perugino, which, while faithfully reproducing the original
subject, entirely distances the original art.

Charley's eyes rounded with surprise. 'Well, you be a clever lady!' he
said, in admiration. 'I've been three weeks learning mine.'

'I have heard it before,' she quietly observed. 'Now, would you do
anything to please me, Charley?'

'I'd do a good deal, miss.'

'Would you let me play your part for one night?'

'O, miss! But your woman's gown – you couldn't.'

'I can get boy's clothes – at least all that would be wanted besides the
mumming dress. What should I have to give you to lend me your things,
to let me take your place for an hour or two on Monday night, and on no
account to say a word about who or what I am? You would, of course,
have to excuse yourself from playing that night, and to say that somebody
– a cousin of Miss Vye's – would act for you. The other mummers have
never spoken to me in their lives, so that it would be safe enough; and if it
were not, I should not mind. Now, what must I give you to agree to this?
Half a crown?' ...

[Later, at Bloom's End]

... 'Why does Mrs Yeobright give parties of this sort?' Eustacia asked, a
little surprised to hear merriment so pronounced.

'It is not one of her bettermost parlour-parties. She's asked the plain
neighbours and workpeople without drawing any lines, just to give 'em a
good supper and such like. Her son and she wait upon the folks.'

'I see,' said Eustacia.

''Tis the last strain, I think,' said Saint George, with his ear to the
panel. 'A young man and woman have just swung into this corner, and
he's saying to her, "Ah, the pity; 'tis over for us this time, my own".'

'Thank God,' said the Turkish Knight, stamping, and taking from the
wall the conventional lance that each of the mummers carried. Her boots
being thinner than those of the young men, the hoar had damped her feet
and made them cold.

'Upon my song 'tis another ten minutes for us,' said the Valiant

Soldier, looking through the keyhole as the tune modulated into another without stopping. 'Grandfer Cantle is standing in this corner, waiting his turn.'

''Twon't be long; 'tis a six-handed reel,' said the Doctor.

'Why not go in, dancing or no? They sent for us,' said the Saracen.

'Certainly not,' said Eustacia authoritatively, as she paced smartly up and down from door to gate to warm herself. 'We should burst into the middle of them and stop the dance, and that would be unmannerly.'

'He thinks himself somebody because he has had a bit more schooling than we,' said the Doctor.

'You may go to the deuce!' said Eustacia.

There was a whispered conversation between three or four of them, and one turned to her.

'Will you tell us one thing?' he said, not without gentleness. 'Be you Miss Vye? We think you must be.'

'You may think what you like,' said Eustacia slowly. 'But honourable lads will not tell tales upon a lady.'

'We'll say nothing, miss. That's upon our honour.'

'Thank you,' she replied

At this moment the fiddles finished off with a screech, and the serpent emitted a last note that nearly lifted the roof. When, from the comparative quiet within, the mummers judged that the dancers had taken their seats, Father Christmas advanced, lifted the latch, and put his head inside the door.

'Ah, the mummers, the mummers!' cried several guests at once. 'Clear a space for the mummers.'

Hump-backed Father Christmas then made a complete entry, swinging his huge club, and in a general way clearing the stage for the actors proper, while he informed the company in smart verse that he was come, welcome or welcome not; concluding his speech with

> Make room, make room, my gallant boys,
>   And give us space to rhyme;
> We've come to show Saint George's play,
>   Upon this Christmas time.'

The guests were now arranging themselves at one end of the room, the fiddler was mending a string, the serpent-player was emptying his mouthpiece, and the play began. First of those outside the Valiant Soldier entered, in the interest of Saint George –

> Here come I, the Valiant Soldier;
>   Slasher is my name;

and so on. This speech concluded with a challenge to the infidel, at the end of which it was Eustacia's duty to enter as the Turkish Knight. She, with the rest who were not yet on, had hitherto remained in the moonlight which streamed under the porch. With no apparent effort or backwardness she came in, beginning –

> Here come I, a Turkish Knight,
> Who learnt in Turkish land to fight;
> I'll fight this man with courage bold:
> If his blood's hot I'll make it cold!

During her declamation Eustacia held her head erect, and spoke as roughly as she could, feeling pretty secure from observation. But the concentration upon her part necessary to prevent discovery, the newness of the scene, the shine of the candles, and the confusing effect upon her vision of the ribboned visor which hid her features, left her absolutely unable to perceive who were present as spectators. On the further side of a table bearing candles she could faintly discern faces, and that was all.

Meanwhile Jim Starks as the Valiant Soldier had come forward, and, with a glare upon the Turk, replied –

> If then, thou art that Turkish Knight,
> Draw out thy sword, and let us fight!

And fight they did; the issue of the combat being that the Valiant Soldier was slain by a preternaturally inadequate thrust from Eustacia, Jim, in his ardour for genuine histrionic art, coming down like a log upon the stone floor with force enough to dislocate his shoulder. Then, after more words from the Turkish Knight, rather too faintly delivered, and statements that he'd fight Saint George and all his crew, Saint George himself magnificently entered with the well-known flourish –

> Here come I, Saint George, the valiant man,
> With naked sword and spear in hand,
> Who fought the dragon and brought him to the slaughter,
> And by this won fair Sabra, the King of Egypt's daughter;
> What mortal man would dare to stand
> Before me with my sword in hand?

This was the lad who had first recognised Eustacia; and when she now, as the Turk, replied with suitable defiance, and at once began the combat, the young fellow took especial care to use his sword as gently as possible. Being wounded, the Knight fell upon one knee, according to the direction. The Doctor now entered, restored the Knight by giving him a draught from the bottle which he carried, and the fight was again resumed, the Turk sinking by degrees until quite overcome – dying as hard in this venerable drama as he is said to do at the present day.

This gradual sinking to the earth was, in fact, one reason why Eustacia had thought that the part of the Turkish Knight, though not the shortest, would suit her best. A direct fall from upright to horizontal, which was the end of the other fighting characters, was not an elegant or decorous part for a girl. But it was easy to die like a Turk, by a dogged decline.

Eustacia was now among the number of the slain, though not on the floor, for she had managed to sink into a sloping position against the clock-case, so that her head was well elevated. The play proceeded between Saint George, the Saracen, the Doctor, and Father Christmas; and Eustacia, having no more to do, for the first time found leisure to observe the scene around, and to search for the form that had drawn her hither.

The Return of the Native

There used to be dancing parties at Christmas, and some weeks after. This kind of party was called a Jacob's Join, in which every guest contributed a certain sum to pay the expenses of the entertainment – it was mostly half a crown in this village [Stinsford].

The Life of Thomas Hardy

The guests had all assembled, and the tranter's party had reached the degree of development which accords with ten o'clock p.m. in rural assemblies. At that hour the sound of a fiddle in process of tuning was heard from the inner pantry.

'That's Dick,' said the tranter. 'That lad's crazy for a jig.'

'Dick! Now I cannot – really, I cannot have any dancing at all till Christmas-day is out,' said old William emphatically. 'When the clock ha' done striking twelve, dance as much as ye like.'

'Well, I must say there's reason in that, William,' said Mrs Penny. 'If you do have a party on Christmas-night, 'tis only fair and honourable to the sky-folk to have it a sit-still party. Jigging parties be all very well on the Devil's holidays; but a jigging party looks suspicious now. O yes; stop till the clock strikes, young folk – so say I.'

It happened that some warm mead accidentally got into Mr Spinks's head about this time.

'Dancing,' he said, 'is a most strengthening, livening, and courting movement, 'specially with a little beverage added! And dancing is good. But why disturb what is ordained, Richard and Reuben, and the company zhinerally? Why, I ask, as far as that do go?'

'Then nothing till after twelve,' said William.

Though Reuben and his wife ruled on social points, religious questions were mostly disposed of by the old man, whose firmness on this head quite counterbalanced a certain weakness in his handling of

domestic matters. The hopes of the younger members of the household
were therefore relegated to a distance of one hour and three-quarters – a
result that took visible shape in them by a remote and listless look about
the eyes – the singing of songs being permitted in the interim.

At five minutes to twelve the soft tuning was again heard in the back
quarters; and when at length the clock had whizzed forth the last stroke,
Dick appeared ready primed, and the instruments were boldly handled;
old William very readily taking the bass-viol from its accustomed nail,
and touching the strings as irreligiously as could be desired.

Under the Greenwood Tree

> We believed in highdays then,
>   And could glimpse at night
>   On Christmas Eve
> Imminent oncomings of radiant revel –
>   Doings of delight: –
>   Now we have no such sight.
>
> We had eyes for phantoms then,
>   And at bridge or stile
>   On Christmas Eve
> Clear beheld those countless ones who had crossed it
>   Cross again in file: –
>   Such has ceased longwhile!
>
> We liked divination then,
>   And, as they homeward wound
>   On Christmas Eve,
> We could read men's dreams within them spinning
>   Even as wheels spin round: –
>   Now we are blinker-bound.
>
> We heard still small voices then,
>   And, in the dim serene
>   Of Christmas Eve,
> Caught the fartime tones of fire-filled prophets
>   Long on earth unseen . . .
>   – Can such ever have been?

'Yuletide in a Younger World'

At Melbury, on a certain day of the year, a family used to go round to the
houses saying –

Wassail, wassail,
All round the town
The cup is white
And the ale is brown:
The cup is made of an ashen tree
And the ale is made of good bar-ley.
We'll set the cup upon the bron' [brand]
And hope we shall have good luck anon,
Hope all the apple-trees 'ill bud, bear & bloo',
This year, next year, the year after too,
For this our 'sail, our jolly wassail,
O joy go with our jolly wassail!

Personal Notebooks of Thomas Hardy

Shroving in Dorset

When going shroving they used to carry a bag for flour, & a basin for fat.
Their words were:

'Ma'am, ma'am, ma'am
I be come a shroving
For a piece of pancake
Or a piece of bacon
Or a round ruggle-cheese
Of your own making
Ma'am, ma'am, ma'am.

Subjoined
at
Puddlehinton
& other
villages.

Hot, hot, the pan's hot,
Buttery doors open,
Pray mis'ess, good mis'ess
Is your heart open?
I be come 'ithout my bag,
Afeard I shall have nothing.'

Personal Notebooks of Thomas Hardy

''Tis Maypole-day to-morrow, and the Shadwater folk have clubbed with a few of your neighbours here to have a pole just outside your palings in the heath, as it is a nice green place.' Venn waved his elbow towards the patch in front of the house. 'I have been talking to Fairway about it,' he continued, 'and I said to him that before we put up the pole it would be as well to ask Mrs Wildeve.'

'I can say nothing against it,' she answered. 'Our property does not reach an inch further than the white palings.'

'But you might not like to see a lot of folk going crazy round a stick, under your very nose?'

'I shall have no objection at all.'   .

Venn soon after went away, and in the evening Yeobright strolled as far as Fairway's cottage. It was a lovely May sunset, and the birch trees which grew on this margin of the vast Egdon wilderness had put on their new leaves, delicate as butterflies' wings, and diaphanous as amber. Beside Fairway's dwelling was an open space recessed from the road, and here were now collected all the young people from within a radius of a couple of miles. The pole lay with one end supported on a trestle, and women were engaged in wreathing it from the top downwards with wild-flowers. The instincts of merry England lingered on here with exceptional vitality, and the symbolic customs which tradition had attached to each season of the year were yet a reality on Egdon. Indeed, the impulses of all such outlandish hamlets are pagan still: in these spots homage to nature, self-adoration, frantic gaieties, fragments of Teutonic rites to divinities whose names are forgotten, seem in some way or other to have survived mediaeval doctrine.

Yeobright did not interrupt the preparations, and went home again. The next morning, when Thomasin withdrew the curtains of her bedroom window, there stood the Maypole in the middle of the green, its top cutting into the sky. It had sprung up in the night, or rather early morning, like Jack's bean-stalk. She opened the casement to get a better view of the garlands and posies that adorned it. The sweet perfume of the flowers had already spread into the surrounding air, which, being free from every taint, conducted to her lips a full measure of the fragrance received from the spire of blossom in its midst. At the top of the pole were crossed hoops decked with small flowers; beneath these came a milk-white zone of Maybloom; then a zone of bluebells, then of cowslips, then of lilacs, then of ragged-robins, daffodils, and so on, till the lowest stage was reached. Thomasin noticed all these, and was delighted that the May-revel was to be so near.

The Return of the Native

The forests have departed, but some old customs of their shades remain. Many, however, linger only in a metamorphosed or disguised form. The May-Day dance, for instance, was to be discerned on the afternoon under notice, in the guise of the club revel, or 'club-walking,' as it was there called.

It was an interesting event to the younger inhabitants of Marlott, though its real interest was not observed by the participators in the ceremony. Its singularity lay less in the retention of a custom of walking in procession and dancing on each anniversary than in the members being solely women. In men's clubs such celebrations were, though expiring, less uncommon; but either the natural shyness of the softer sex, or a sarcastic attitude on the part of male relatives, had denuded such women's clubs as remained (if any other did) of this their glory and consummation. The club of Marlott alone lived to uphold the local Cerealia. It had walked for hundreds of years, if not as benefit-club, as votive sisterhood of some sort; and it walked still.

The banded ones were all dressed in white gowns – a gay survival from Old Style days, when cheerfulness and May-time were synonyms – days before the habit of taking long views had reduced emotions to a monotonous average. Their first exhibition of themselves was in a processional march of two and two round the parish. Ideal and real clashed slightly as the sun lit up their figures against the green hedges and creeper-laced house-fronts; for, though the whole troop wore white garments, no two whites were alike among them. Some approached pure blanching; some had a bluish pallor; some worn by the older characters (which had possibly lain by folded for many a year) inclined to a cadaverous tint, and to a Georgian style.

In addition to the distinction of a white frock, every woman and girl carried in her right hand a peeled willow wand, and in her left a bunch of white flowers. The peeling of the former, and the selection of the latter, had been an operation of personal care.

Tess of the d'Urbervilles

'And then, of course, when 'tis all over,' continued the tranter, 'we shall march two and two round the parish.'

'Yes, sure,' said Mr Penny: 'two and two: every man hitched up to his woman, 'a b'lieve'.

'I never can make a show of myself in that way!' said Fancy, looking at Dick to ascertain if he could.

'I'm agreed to anything you and the company like, my dear!' said Mr Richard Dewy heartily.

'Why, we did when we were married, didn't we, Ann?' said the tranter; 'and so do everybody, my sonnies.'

'And so did we,' said Fancy's father.

'And so did Penny and I,' said Mrs Penny: 'I wore my best Bath clogs, I remember, and Penny was cross because it made me look so tall.'

'And so did father and mother,' said Miss Mercy Onmey.

'And I mean to, come next Christmas!' said Nat the groomsman vigorously, and looking towards the person of Miss Vashti Sniff.

'Respectable people don't nowadays,' said Fancy. 'Still, since poor mother did, I will.'

'Ay,' resumed the tranter, ''twas on a White Tuesday when I

committed it. Mellstock Club walked the same day, and we new-married folk went a-gaying round the parish behind 'em. Everybody used to wear something white at Whitsuntide in them days. My sonnies, I've got the very white trousers that I wore, at home in box now. Ha'nt I, Ann?'

'You had till I cut 'em up for Jimmy,' said Mrs Dewy.

'And we ought, by rights, after doing this parish, to go round Higher and Lower Mellstock, and call at Viney's, and so work our way hither again across He'th,' said Mr Penny, recovering scent of the matter in hand. 'Dairyman Viney is a very respectable man, and so is Farmer Kex, and we ought to show ourselves to them.'

'True,' said the tranter, 'we ought to go round Mellstock to do the thing well. We shall form a very striking object walking along in rotation, good-now, neighbours?'

'That we shall: a proper pretty sight for the nation,' said Mrs Penny.

Under the Greenwood Tree

Approaching the hill Fitzpiers discerned a gay procession of people coming down the way, and was not long in perceiving it to be a wedding-party. Though the wind was keen, the women were in light attire, and the flowered waistcoats of the men had a pleasing vividness of pattern. Each of the gentler ones clung to the arm of her partner so tightly as to have with him one step, rise, swing, gait, almost one centre of gravity. In the buxom bride Fitzpiers recognized no other than Suke Damson, who in her light gown looked a giantess; the small husband beside her he saw to be Tim Tangs.

Fitzpiers could not escape, for they had seen him; though of all the beauties of the world whom he did not wish to meet Suke was the chief. But he put the best face on the matter that he could, and came on, the approaching company evidently discussing him and his separation from Mrs Fitzpiers. As the couples closed upon him he expressed his congratulations.

'We be just walking round the parishes to show ourselves a bit,' said Tim. 'First we het across to Great Hintock, then back to here, and from here we go to Revellers Inn and Marshwood, and then round by the cross roads home.'

The Woodlanders

> Little fogs were gathered in every hollow,
> But the purple hillocks enjoyed fine weather
> As we marched with our fiddles over the heather
> – How it comes back! – to their wedding that day.

Our getting there brought our neighbours and all, O!
Till, two and two, the couples stood ready.
And her father said: 'Souls, for God's sake, be steady!'
And we strung up our fiddles, and sounded out 'A'.

The groomsman he stared, and said, 'You must follow!'
But we'd gone to fiddle in front of the party,
(Our feelings as friends being true and hearty)
And fiddle in front we did – all the way.

Yes, from their door by Mill-tail-Shallow,
And up Styles-Lane, and by Front-Street houses,
Where stood maids, bachelors, and spouses,
Who cheered the songs that we knew how to play.

I bowed the treble before her father,
Michael the tenor in front of the lady,
The bass-viol Reub – and right well played he! –
The serpent Jim; ay, to church and back.

I thought the bridegroom was flurried rather,
As we kept up the tune outside the chancel,
While they were swearing things none can cancel
Inside the walls to our drumstick's whack.

'Too gay!' she pleaded. 'Clouds may gather,
And sorrow come.' But she gave in, laughing,
And by supper-time when we'd got to the quaffing
Her fears were forgot, and her smiles weren't slack.

A grand wedding, 'twas! And what would follow
We never thought. Or that we should have buried her
On the same day with the man that married her,
A day like the first, half hazy, half clear.

Yes: little fogs were in every hollow,
Though the purple hillocks enjoyed fine weather,
When we went to play 'em to church together,
And carried 'em there in an after year.

'The Country Wedding'

It may be worthy of note that this harvest-home [*c.* 1850] was among the last at which the old traditional ballads were sung, the railway having been extended to Dorchester just then, and the orally transmitted ditties of centuries being slain at a stroke by the London comic songs that were introduced. The particular ballad which he remembered hearing that night from the lips of the farm-women was that one variously called 'The Outlandish Knight', 'May Colvine', 'The Western Tragedy', etc. He could recall to old age the scene of the young women in their light gowns sitting on a bench against the wall in the barn, and leaning against each other as they warbled the Dorset version of the ballad, which differed a little from the northern:

> Lie there, lie there, thou false-hearted man,
>   Lie there instead o' me;
> For six pretty maidens thou hast a-drown'd here,
>   But the seventh hath drown-ed thee!
>
> O tell no more, my pretty par-rot,
>   Lay not the blame on me;
> And your cage shall be made o' the glittering gold,
>   Wi' a door o' the white ivo-rie!

> *The Life of Thomas Hardy*

> Nell and the other maids danced their best
>   With the Scotch-Greys in the barn;
> These had been asked to the harvest-feast;
>   Red shapes amid the corn.
>
> Nell and the other maids sat in a row
>   Within the benched barn-nook;
> Nell led the songs of long ago
>   She'd learnt from never a book.
>
> She sang of the false Sir John of old,
>   The lover who witched to win,
> And the parrot, and cage of glittering gold;
>   And the other maids joined in.
>
> Then whispered to her a gallant Grey,
>   'Dear, sing that ballet again!
> For a bonnier mouth in a bonnier way
>   Has sung not anywhen!'
>
> As she loosed her lips anew there sighed
>   To Nell through the dark barn-door
> The voice of her Love from the night outside,
>   Who was buried the month before:
>
> 'O Nell, can you sing ballets there,
>   And I out here in the clay,
> Of lovers false of yore, nor care
>   What you vowed to me one day!

'O can you dance with soldiers bold,
    Who kiss when dancing's done,
Your little waist within their hold,
    As ancient troth were none!'

She cried: 'My heart is pierced with a wound!
    There's something outside the wall
That calls me forth to a greening mound:
    I can sing no more at all!

'My old Love rises from the worms,
    Just as he used to be,
And I must let gay gallants' arms
    No more encircle me!'

They bore her home from the merry-making;
    Bad dreams disturbed her bed:
'Nevermore will I dance and sing,'
    Mourned Nell; 'and never wed!'

               'The Harvest Supper' – circa 1850

'We workfolk shall have some lordly junketing to-night,' said Cainy Ball, casting forth his thoughts in a new direction. 'This morning I see 'em making the great puddens in the milking-pails – lumps of fat as big as yer thumb, Mister Oak! I've never seed such splendid large knobs of fat before in the days of my life – they never used to be bigger than a horse-bean. And there was a great black crock upon the brandise with his legs a-sticking out, but I don't know what was in within.'

'And there's two bushels of biffins for apple-pies,' said Maryann.

'Well, I hope to do my duty by it all,' said Joseph Poorgrass, in a pleasant, masticating manner of anticipation. 'Yes; victuals and drink is a cheerful thing, and gives nerves to the nerveless, if the form of words may be used. 'Tis the gospel of the body, without which we perish, so to speak it.'

               Far from the Madding Crowd

'How dark 'tis now the fire's gone down! said Christian Cantle, looking behind him with his hare eyes. 'Don't ye think we'd better get home-along, neighbours? The heth isn't haunted, I know; but we'd better get home ... Ah, what was that?'

'Only the wind,' said the turf-cutter.

'I don't think Fifth-of-Novembers ought to be kept up by night except in towns. It should be by day in outstep, ill-accounted places like this.'

'Nonsense, Christian. Lift up your spirits like a man! Susy, dear, you and I will have a jig – hey, my honey? – before 'tis quite too dark to see how well-favoured you be still, though so many summers have passed since your husband, a son of a witch, snapped you up from me.'

This was addressed to Susan Nunsuch; and the next circumstance of which the beholders were conscious was a vision of the matron's broad form whisking off towards the space whereon the fire had been kindled. She was lifted bodily by Mr Fairway's arm, which had been flung round her waist before she had become aware of his intention. The site of the fire was now merely a circle of ashes flecked with red embers and sparks, the furze having burnt completely away. Once within the circle he whirled her round and round in a dance. She was a woman noisily constructed; in addition to her enclosing framework of whalebone and lath, she wore pattens summer and winter, in wet weather and in dry, to preserve her boots from wear; and when Fairway began to jump about with her, the clicking of the pattens, the creaking of the stays, and her screams of surprise, formed a very audible concert.

'I'll crack thy numskull for thee, you mandy chap!' said Mrs Nunsuch, as she helplessly danced round with him, her feet playing like drumsticks among the sparks. 'My ankles were all in a fever before, from walking through that prickly furze, and now you must make 'em worse with these vlankers!'

The vagary of Timothy Fairway was infectious. The turf-cutter seized old Olly Dowden, and, somewhat more gently, poussetted with her likewise. The young men were not slow to imitate the example of their elders, and seized the maids; Grandfer Cantle and his stick jigged in the form of a three-legged object among the rest; and in half a minute all that could be seen on Rainbarrow was a whirling of dark shapes amid a boiling confusion of sparks, which leapt around the dancers as high as their waists.

The Return of the Native

6

CIDER, MEAD AND ALE

In the matter of what Mr Spinks called 'stimmilents' Hardy's first loyalty was undoubtedly to cider. He rated it among the 'great things' of life, on a par with dancing and love-making. It was the native drink of his earliest years, made from the apples that he saw from his bedroom window and helped to pick each autumn on the family plot at Bockhampton for his father's annual cider-making. In later life it was the scenes and odours of the year's apple-pressing that were to be one of Hardy's fondest recollections of his youth and young manhood; and when wartime conditions brought about a shortage of imported wines it was cider that Hardy recommended for the table.

It is not difficult to imagine a young Thomas among the children participating in the cider-making at The Three Tranters in *Desperate Remedies*. The falling of the apples is surely drawn from first-hand experience. His tribute to the fame of the Hintock villages is a reminder that his mother also embodied a cider-making tradition, coming from one of those villages where the dunghills smelt of pomace. There is a kinship here, or at least a fellow feeling, with Japheth Johns in 'Interlopers at the Knap' proclaiming 'I am a cider-drinker on my mother's side'.

It is in his portrayal of the Hintock villages in *The Woodlanders* that Hardy gave his fullest attention to cider and more particularly to the itinerant cider-maker 'and apple-tree shaker', Giles Winterborne. Coming before us 'like Autumn's very brother', Winterborne reveals the mysteries of his craft in a wealth of detail that Hardy evidently took pleasure in describing. It is in *The Woodlanders* also that we see the everyday drinking of cider – by the workfolk as they labour and pause to quench their thirst, and at home when Mr Melbury fills his drinking-horn from the pitcher of cider standing on the hearth.

A homely, commonplace drink it might be, but cider also aroused a connoisseurship among those with more judicious palates. The varieties of apple suitable for cider-making and the art of blending them propitiously were conversational topics of endless possibility in Victorian Dorset; and few could rival Reuben Dewy and Miller Loveday in that respect. When they broached a cask on some hospitable occasion the liquor they poured was no common tipple.

Cider was not the only strong drink that a cottager with a modest plot of land could create from his own resources. Among his cider-apple trees there might be seen a few beehives, indicating that the owner could also keep himself supplied with mead if he had the wish and the skill to do so. That was certainly the case with Shepherd Fennel in 'The Three Strangers'. I have known Wessex countrymen like the Shepherd who made mead in the traditional way from the honey of their own bees: at its best the cloudy excessive sweetness should be refined to a pure spirit that does not cloy. The medicated form of mead spiced with herbs and known as metheglin has never come my way and must be a rarity nowadays. Its name is Welsh, which tends therefore to set it apart from Dorset's pristine customs.

In his *Cottage Economy* William Cobbett claimed that, until the latter part of the eighteenth century, a labourer would normally brew his own beer at home. The dawning nineteenth century saw the rise of the commercial breweries and of public houses tied to the breweries, causing – to Cobbett's regret – a consequent decline in home-brew. Hardy's references to ale or beer are fewer than might be expected and confirm Cobbett's forebodings. The provenance of Farmer Everdene's ale, so gratefully enjoyed by Jan Coggan, is not plainly stated and may therefore have been brewed by the farmer himself; but he lived near Casterbridge and it is at least as likely that he bought it from that celebrated brewery which supplied Miller Loveday with the barrel laid in for Captain Bob's wedding. The potency of Casterbridge's 'strong' was legendary; but, when the immediate aim was to summon up Dutch courage, Tranter Dewy preferred the older combination of cider and mead together. In 'The Romantic Adventures of a Milkmaid' Richard Vine liked to have a mug of perry to accompany the smoking of his clay pipe but I can think of no other Hardy character who shared his preference. Perhaps Hardy thought the pear suggested a more Devonian style than the apple of his native Dorset.

Sweet cyder is a great thing,
    A great thing to me,
Spinning down to Weymouth town
    By Ridgway thirstily,
And maid and mistress summoning
    Who tend the hostelry:
O cyder is a great thing,
    A great thing to me.

'Great Things'

This autumn [1873] Hardy assisted at his father's cider-making – a proceeding he had always enjoyed from childhood – the apples being from huge old trees that have now long perished. It was the last time he ever took part in a work whose sweet smells and oozings in the crisp autumn air can never be forgotten by those who have had a hand in it.

The Life of Thomas Hardy

'Though I inherit the malt-liquor principle from my father, I am a cider-drinker on my mother's side. She came from these parts, you know. And there's this to be said for't – 'tis a more peaceful liquor, and don't lie about a man like your hotter drinks. With care, one may live on it a twelve-month without knocking down a neighbour, or getting a black eye from an old acquaintance'.

'Interlopers at the Knap'

By the way we drink cider – in wine glassses to make it seem precious – and find it just as good for us as wine and better than spirits. If you want to get up with a clear head in the morning, try cider for dinner.

Letter to Clement Shorter, 15 March 1916

. . . an old-fashioned village – one of the Hintocks (several villages of that name, with a distinctive prefix or affix, lying thereabouts) – where the people make the best cider and cider-wine in all Wessex, and where the dunghills smell of pomace instead of stable refuse as elsewhere.

'Interlopers at the Knap'

Smells of pomace, and the hiss of fermenting cider, which reached him from the back quarters of other tenements, revealed the recent occupation of some of the inhabitants, and joined with the scent of decay from the perishing leaves underfoot.

The Woodlanders

The cottages along Carriford village street were not so close but that on one side or other of the road was always a hedge of hawthorn or privet, over or through which could be seen gardens or orchards rich with produce. It was about the middle of the early apple-harvest, and the laden trees were shaken at intervals by the gatherers; the soft pattering of the falling crop upon the grassy ground being diversified by the loud rattle of vagrant ones upon a rail, hencoop, basket, or lean-to roof, or upon the rounded and stooping backs of the collectors – mostly children, who would have cried bitterly at receiving such a smart blow from any other quarter, but smilingly assumed it to be but fun in apples.

The Three Tranters Inn, a many-gabled, mediaeval building, constructed almost entirely of timber, plaster, and thatch, stood close to the line of the roadside, almost opposite the churchyard, and was connected with a row of cottages on the left by thatched outbuildings.

On a green plot at the other end of the building grew two or three large, wide-spreading elm-trees, from which the sign was suspended – representing the three men called tranters (irregular carriers), standing side by side, and exactly alike to a hair's-breadth, the grain of the wood and joints of the boards being visible through the thin paint depicting their forms, which were still further disfigured by red stains running downwards from the rusty nails above.

Under the trees now stood a cider-mill and press, and upon the spot sheltered by the boughs were gathered Mr Springrove himself, his men, the parish clerk, two or three other men, grinders and supernumeraries, a woman with an infant in her arms, a flock of pigeons, and some little boys with straws in their mouths, endeavouring, whenever the men's backs were turned, to get a sip of the sweet juice issuing from the vat.

Edward Springrove the elder, the landlord, now more particularly a farmer, and for two months in the year a cider-maker, was an employer of labour of the old school, who worked himself among his men. He was now engaged in packing the pomace into horsehair bags with a rammer, and Gad Weedy, his man, was occupied in shovelling up more from a tub at his side.

Desperate Remedies

Their way homeward ran along the western flank of the Vale, whence afar they beheld a wide district, differing somewhat in feature and atmosphere from the Hintock precincts. It was the cider country more especially, which met the woodland district some way off. There the air was blue as sapphire – such a blue as outside that apple-region was never seen. Under the blue the orchards were in a blaze of pink bloom, some of the richly flowered trees running almost up to where they drove along. At a gate, which opened down an incline, a man leant on his arms, regarding this fair promise so intently that he did not observe their passing.

'That was Giles,' said Melbury, when they had gone by 'All that apple-blooth means heavy autumn work for him and his hands. If no blight happens before the setting, the cider yield will be such as we have not had for years.'

The Woodlanders

Who is this coming with pondering pace,
Black and ruddy, with white embossed,
His eyes being black, and ruddy his face,
And the marge of his hair like morning frost?
 It's the cider-maker,
 And appletree-shaker,
And behind him on wheels, in readiness,
His mill, and tubs, and vat and press.

'Shortening Days at the Homestead'

He looked and smelt like Autumn's very brother, his face being sunburnt to wheat-colour, his eyes blue as corn-flowers, his sleeves and leggings dyed with fruit-stains, his hands clammy with the sweet juice of apples, his hat sprinkled with pips, and everywhere about him that atmosphere of cider which at its first return each season has such an indescribable fascination for those who have been born and bred among the orchards.

The Woodlanders

In the yard between Grace and the orchards there progressed a scene natural to the locality at this time of the year. An apple-mill and press had been erected on the spot, to which some men were bringing fruit from divers points in mawn-baskets, while others were grinding them, and others wringing down the pomace, whose sweet juice gushed forth into tubs and pails. The superintendent of these proceedings, to whom the others spoke as master, was a young yeoman of prepossessing manner and aspect, whose form she recognized in a moment. He had hung his coat to a nail of the outhouse wall, and wore his shirt-sleeves rolled up beyond his elbows, to keep them unstained while he rammed the pomace into the bags of horsehair. Fragments of apple-rind had alighted upon the brim of his hat – probably from the bursting of a bag – while brown pips of the same fruit were sticking among the down upon his fine round arms, and in his beard.

She realized in a moment how he had come there. Down in the heart of the apple-country nearly every farmer kept a cider-making apparatus and wring-house for his own use, building up the pomace in great straw 'cheeses' as they were called; but here, on the margin of Pomona's plain, was a debatable land neither orchard nor sylvan exclusively, where the apple-produce was hardly sufficient to warrant each proprietor in keeping a mill of his own. This was the field of the travelling cider-maker. His press and mill were fixed to wheels instead of being set up in a cider-house; and with a couple of horses, buckets, tubs, strainers, and an assistant or two, he wandered from place to place, deriving very satisfactory returns for his trouble in such a prolific season as the present.

The outskirts of the town were just now abounding with apple-gatherings. They stood in the yards in carts, baskets, and loose heaps; and the blue stagnant air of autumn which hung over everything was heavy with a sweet cidery smell. Cakes of pomace lay against the walls in the yellow sun, where they were drying to be used as fuel. Yet it was not the great make of the year as yet; before the standard crop came in there accumulated, in abundant times like this, a large superfluity of early apples, and windfalls from the trees of later harvest, which would not keep long. Thus in the baskets, and quivering in the hopper of the mill, she saw specimens of mixed dates, including the mellow countenances of streaked-jacks, codlins, costards, stubbards, ratheripes and other well-known friends of her ravenous youth.

The Woodlanders

'Hullo, my sonnies, here you be, then!' said Reuben Dewy at length, standing up and blowing forth a vehement gust of breath. 'How the blood do puff up in anybody's head, to be sure, a-stooping like that! I was just going out to gate to hark for ye.' He then carefully began to wind a strip of brown paper round a brass tap he held in his hand. 'This in the cask here is a drop o' the right sort' (tapping the cask); ''tis a real drop o' cordial from the best picked apples – Sansoms, Stubbards, Five-corners, and such-like – you d'mind the sort, Michael?' (Michael nodded.) 'And there's a sprinkling of they that grow down by the orchard-rails – streaked ones – rail apples we d'call 'em, as 'tis by the rails they grow, and not knowing the right name. The water-cider from 'em is as good as most people's best cider is.'

'Ay, and of the same make too,' said Bowman. '"It rained when we wrung it out, and the water got into it," folk will say. But 'tis on'y an excuse. Watered cider is too common among us.'

'Yes, yes; too common it is!' said Spinks with an inward sigh, whilst his eyes seemed to be looking at the case in an abstract form rather than at the scene before him. 'Such poor liquor do make a man's throat feel very melancholy – and is a disgrace to the name of stimmilent.'

Under the Greenwood Tree

In addition, Mr Loveday also tapped a hogshead of fine cider that he had had mellowing in the house for several months, having bought it of an honest down-country man, who did not colour, for any special occasion like the present. It had been pressed from fruit judiciously chosen by an old hand – Horner and Cleeves apple for the body, a few Tom-Putts for colour, and just a dash of Old Five-corners for sparkle – a selection originally made to please the palate of a well-known temperate earl who was a regular cider-drinker, and lived to be eighty-eight.

The Trumpet-Major

'Now let's see what we can do,' was heard spoken about this time by the tranter in a private voice to the barrel, beside which he had again established himself, and was stooping to cut away the cork.

'Reuben, don't make such a mess o' tapping that barrel as is mostly made in this house,' Mrs Dewy cried from the fireplace. 'I'd tap a hundred without wasting more than you do in one. Such a squizzling and squirting job as 'tis in your hands! There, he always was such a clumsy man indoors.'

'Ay, ay; I know you'd tap a hundred beautiful, Ann – I know you would; two hundred, perhaps. But I can't promise. This is a' old cask, and the wood's rotted away about the tap-hole. The husbird of a feller Sam Lawson – that ever I should call 'n such, now he's dead and gone, poor heart! – took me in completely upon the feat of buying this cask. "Reub," says he – 'a always used to call me plain Reub, poor old heart! – "Reub," he said says he, "that there cask, Reub, is as good as new; yes, good as new. 'Tis a wine-hogshead; the best port-wine in the commonwealth have been in that there cask; and you shall have en for ten shillens, Reub," – 'a said says he – "he's worth twenty, ay, five-and-twenty, if he's worth one; and an iron hoop or two put round en among the wood ones will make en worth thirty shillens of any man's money, if – "'

'I think I should have used the eyes that Providence gave me to use afore I paid any ten shillens for a jimcrack wine-barrel; a saint is sinner enough not to be cheated. But 'tis like all your family was, so easy to be deceived.'

'That's as true as gospel of this member,' said Reuben.

Mrs Dewy began a smile at the answer, then altering her lips and refolding them so that it was not a smile, commenced smoothing little Bessy's hair; the tranter having meanwhile suddenly become oblivious to conversation, occupying himself in a deliberate cutting and arrangement of some more brown paper for the broaching operation.

'Ah, who can believe sellers!' said old Michael Mail in a carefully-cautious voice, by way of tiding-over this critical point of affairs.

'No one at all,' said Joseph Bowman, in the tone of a man fully agreeing with everybody.

'Ay,' said Mail, in the tone of a man who did not agree with everybody as a rule, though he did now; 'I knowed a' auctioneering feller once – a very friendly feller 'a was too. And so one hot day as I was walking down the front street o' Casterbridge, jist below the King's Arms, I passed a' open winder and see him inside, stuck upon his perch, a-selling off. I jist nodded to en in a friendly way as I passed, and went on my way, and thought no more about it. Well, next day, as I was oilen my boots by fuel-house door, if a letter didn't come wi' a bill charging me with a feather-bed, bolster, and pillers, that I had bid for at Mr Taylor's sale. The slim-faced martel had knocked 'em down to me because I nodded to en in my friendly way; and I had to pay for 'em too. Now, I hold that that was coming it very close, Reuben?'

''Twas close, there's no denying,' said the general voice.

'Too close, 'twas,' said Reuben, in the rear of the rest. 'And as to Sam Lawson – poor heart! now he's dead and gone too! – I'll warrant, that if so be I've spent one hour in making hoops for that barrel, I've spent fifty, first and last. That's one of my hoops' – touching it with his elbow – 'that's one of mine, and that, and that, and all these.'

'Ah, Sam was a man,' said Mr Penny, contemplatively.

'Sam was!' said Bowman.

'Especially for a drap o' drink,' said the tranter.

'Good, but not religious-good,' suggested Mr Penny.

The tranter nodded. Having at last made the tap and hole quite ready, 'Now then, Suze, bring a mug,' he said. 'Here's luck to us, my sonnies!'

The tap went in, and the cider immediately squirted out in a horizontal shower over Reuben's hands, knees, and leggings, and into the eyes and neck of Charley, who, having temporarily put off his grief under pressure of more interesting proceedings, was squatting down and blinking near his father.

'There 'tis again!' said Mrs Dewy.

'Devil take the hole, the cask, and Sam Lawson too, that good cider should be wasted like this!' exclaimed the tranter. 'Your thumb! Lend me your thumb, Michael! Ram it in here, Michael! I must get a bigger tap, my sonnies.'

Under the Greenwood Tree

Wildeve made no reply; and probably feeling that the sooner he treated them the sooner they would go, he produced a stone jar, which threw a warm halo over matters at once.

'That's a drop of the right sort, I can see,' said Grandfer Cantle, with the air of a man too well-mannered to show any hurry to taste it.

'Yes,' said Wildeve, ''tis some old mead. I hope you will like it.'

'O ay!' replied the guests, in the hearty tones natural when the words demanded by politeness coincide with those of deepest feeling. 'There isn't a prettier drink under the sun.'

'I'll take my oath there isn't,' added Grandfer Cantle. 'All that can be said against mead is that 'tis rather heady, and apt to lie about a man a good while. But to-morrow's Sunday, thank God.'

'I feel'd for all the world like some bold soldier after I had had some once,' said Christian.

'You shall feel so again,' said Wildeve, with condescension. 'Cups or glasses, gentlemen?'

'Well, if you don't mind, we'll have the beaker, and pass 'en round; 'tis better than heling it out in dribbles.'

'Jown the slippery glasses,' said Grandfer Cantle. 'What's the good of a thing that you can't put down in the ashes to warm, hey, neighbours; that's what I ask?'

'Right, Grandfer,' said Sam; and the mead then circulated.

The Return of the Native

The table had been pushed so closely into the chimney-corner, to give all available room to the dancers, that its inner edge grazed the elbow of the man who had ensconced himself by the fire; and thus the two strangers were brought into close companionship. They nodded to each other by way of breaking the ice of unacquaintance, and the first stranger handed his neighbour the family mug – a huge vessel of brown ware, having its upper edge worn away like a threshold by the rub of whole generations of thirsty lips that had gone the way of all flesh, and bearing the following inscription burnt upon its rotund side in yellow letters: –

THERE IS NO FUN
UNTILL i CUM

The other man, nothing loth, raised the mug to his lips, and drank on, and on, and on – till a curious blueness overspread the countenance of the shepherd's wife, who had regarded with no little surprise the first stranger's free offer to the second of what did not belong to him to dispense.

'I knew it,' said the toper to the shepherd with much satisfaction. 'When I walked up your garden before coming in, and saw the hives all of a row, I said to myself, "Where there's bees there's honey, and where there's honey there's mead." But mead of such a truly comfortable sort as this I really didn't expect to meet in my older days.' He took yet another pull at the mug, till it assumed an ominous elevation.

'Glad you enjoy it!' said the shepherd warmly.

'It is goodish mead,' assented Mrs Fennel, with an absence of enthusiasm which seemed to say that it was possible to buy praise for one's cellar at too heavy a price. 'It is trouble enough to make – and really I hardly think we shall make any more. For honey sells well, and we ourselves can make shift with a drop o' small mead and metheglin for common use from the comb-washings.'

'O, but you'll never have the heart!' reproachfully cried the stranger in cinder-gray, after taking up the mug a third time and setting it down empty. 'I love mead, when 'tis old like this, as I love to go to church o' Sundays or to relieve the needy any day of the week.'

'Ha, ha, ha!' said the man in the chimney-corner, who, in spite of the taciturnity induced by the pipe of tobacco, could not or would not refrain from this slight testimony to his comrade's humour.

Now the old mead of those days, brewed of the purest first-year or maiden honey, four pounds to the gallon – with its due complement of white of eggs, cinnamon, ginger, cloves, mace, rosemary, yeast, and processes of working, bottling, and cellaring – tasted remarkably strong; but it did not taste so strong as it actually was. Hence, presently, the stranger in cinder-gray at the table, moved by its creeping influence, unbuttoned his waistcoat, threw himself back in his chair, spread his legs, and made his presence felt in various ways.

'The Three Strangers'

'I used to go to his house a-courting my first wife, Charlotte, who was his dairymaid. Well, a very good-hearted man were Farmer Everdene, and I being a respectable young fellow was allowed to call and see her and drink as much ale as I liked, but not to carry away any – outside my skin I mane, of course.'

'Ay, ay, Jan Coggan; we know yer maning.'

'And so you see 'twas beautiful ale, and I wished to value his kindness as much as I could, and not to be so ill-mannered as to drink only a thimbleful, which would have been insulting the man's generosity – '

'True, Master Coggan, 'twould so,' corroborated Mark Clark.

' – And so I used to eat a lot of salt fish afore going, and then by the time I got there I were as dry as a lime-basket – so thoroughly dry that that ale would slip down – ah, 'twould slip down sweet! Happy times! heavenly times! Such lovely drunks as I used to have at that house! You can mind, Jacob? You used to go wi' me sometimes.'

'I can – I can,' said Jacob. 'That one, too, that we had at Buck's Head on a White Monday was a pretty tipple.'

''Twas. But for a wet of the better class, that brought you no nearer to the horned man than you were afore you begun, there was none like those in Farmer Everdene's kitchen. Not a single damn allowed; no, not a bare poor one, even at the most cheerful moment when all were blindest, though the good old word of sin thrown in here and there at such times is a great relief to a merry soul.'

'True,' said the maltster. 'Nater requires her swearing at the regular times, or she's not herself; and unholy exclamations is a necessity of life.'

'But Charlotte,' continued Coggan – 'not a word of the sort would Charlotte allow, nor the smallest item of taking in vain ... Ay, poor Charlotte, I wonder if she had the good fortune to get into Heaven when 'a died! But 'a was never much in luck's way and perhaps 'a went downwards after all, poor soul.'

Far from the Madding Crowd

In the liquor line Loveday laid in an ample barrel of Casterbridge 'strong beer'. This renowned drink – now almost as much a thing of the past as Falstaff's favourite beverage – was not only well calculated to win the hearts of soldiers blown dry and dusty by residence in tents on a hill-top, but of any wayfarer whatever in that land. It was of the most beautiful colour that the eye of an artist in beer could desire; full in body, yet brisk as a volcano; piquant, yet without a twang; luminous as an autumn sunset; free from streakiness of taste; but, finally, rather heady. The masses worshipped it, the minor gentry loved it more than wine, and by the most illustrious county families it was not despised. Anybody brought up for being drunk and disorderly in the streets of its natal borough, had only to prove that he was a stranger to the place and its liquor to be honourably dismissed by the magistrates, as one overtaken in a fault that no man could guard against who entered the town unawares.

The Trumpet-Major

'Now,' continued the tranter, dispersing by a new tone of voice these digressions about Leaf; 'as to going to see the pa'son, one of us might call and ask en his meaning, and 'twould be just as well done; but it will add a bit of a flourish to the cause if the quire waits on him as a body. Then the great thing to mind is, not for any of our fellers to be nervous; so before starting we'll one and all come to my house and have a rasher of bacon; then every man-jack het a pint of cider into his inside; then we'll warm up an extra drop wi' some mead and a bit of ginger; every one take a thimbleful – just a glimmer of a drop, mind ye, no more, to finish off his inner man – and march off to Pa'son Mayble. Why, sonnies, a man's not himself till he is fortified wi' a bit and a drop! We shall be able to look any gentleman in the face then without shrink or shame.'

Under the Greenwood Tree

7

THE WORLD OF NATURE:
Landscape and Wildlife

In his response to the Wessex landscape Hardy was very much a child of the Romantic Movement. His boyhood was spent almost entirely in the midst of rural scenes and his mind was indelibly impressed with the features of heath and downland and water-meadow in all the variety of their seasonal moods. His emotional participation in these surroundings was Wordsworthian in its intensity and its spiritual overtones. Hill and river, tree and field composed a cryptic statement in which some measure of religious or philosophical truth was implicit. What Hardy sought was, in his words, 'the deeper reality underlying the scenic'. The supreme example of this treatment of landscape – Egdon Heath – has an earlier chapter to itself (pp. 13–20). My choice here is the scene in *Far from the Madding Crowd* on Norcombe Hill where at midnight, in Hardy's majestic phrase, 'the roll of the world eastward is almost a palpable movement'.

To reinforce the bold strokes of his pen Hardy drew on a repertoire of minute, close details. He was peculiarly sensitive to sound, distinguishing fine differences of tone in his elaborate acoustic pictures of heath or woodland. He admired the subtle knowledge of field-workers whose day-long intimacy with a single scene gave them special insights into the ways of plants and animals. This knowledge was not gained by them casually but in their working roles as an integral part of the process. In his contemplation of Giles and Marty at work in the Hintock woodlands Hardy remarks: 'The artifices of the seasons were seen by them from the conjuror's own point of view, and not from that of the spectator'.

In that respect Hardy himself was often a spectator and not always a reliable one. Though he might choose to present himself as a 'country boy' imbued with 'the life of the fields', his family circumstances placed him on the brink of the mainstream of country life rather than up to his neck in it as was his Wiltshire contemporary, Richard Jefferies. To make the point with a crude but instantly comprehensible example, I doubt if Hardy ever wrung the neck of a fowl or paunched a rabbit: to Jefferies these were the normal incidents of farm life. In their attitudes to field sports the two men again differed strongly. Hardy's developing sympathies allied him with the urban middle class against the traditional practices of Jefferies. The fact that animals tend to die sudden, violent deaths – axiomatic in farming communities – was always a source of distress for Hardy. His one obvious personal experience was his father's killing of the pig he fattened for the family's needs from time to time. Not until he came to write his final novel, *Jude the Obscure*, did Hardy draw on that grim youthful memory of what Jude called 'a hateful business'. In his description of Jude's reluctant and clumsy killing of the pig Hardy's own revulsion is clearly expressed in his contemplation of the pig's blood falling on the snow-covered ground: 'The white snow, stained with the blood of his fellow-mortal, wore an illogical look to him as a lover of justice, not to say a Christian'.

The expression *fellow-mortal* is perhaps the key to Hardy's approach to the natural world. He wished to acknowledge a kinship with all forms of life. The interplay of people, plants, trees and animals in pastoral and sylvan complexes is a source of strength in his lighter sketches of rural scenes. I have chosen three which show him celebrating the things he knew best. Here are the spontaneous unforced observations of a country-bred boy – of an owl, a nightjar and a stoat, of the wintry creaking of branches, of the sudden unfurling of leaves, of the first springtime singing of nightingales. Here Hardy is at one with Jefferies, and indeed superior to him in poetic range and literary skill.

Where Hardy moves apart and pursues a highly individual course of his own is in the philosophical implications that he perceives in the procedures of Nature. In some instances he is simply staying true to his early attitudes but deepening them with more mature emotion. In others he is grafting on to them the intellectual apparatus of his manhood – most notably in the form of the Darwinian concept of the survival of the fittest. The competitive character of the evolutionary process, and the necessary role of the predator, aroused in Hardy an increasing repugnance. He cherished the hope – and usually conceded it to be a vain hope – that the quality of altruism would spread gradually through mankind and thence downwards to the lower forms of creation, until the lion might lie down with the lamb. In the accepted manner of his time he cultivated an anthropomorphic view of animals, superimposing human thoughts and emotions on them. In the poem 'The Darkling Thrush' the bird's singing is made to bear the speculation that it is expressing 'some blessed Hope, whereof he knew/ And I was unaware'. When Marty South watches the roosting pheasants in *The Woodlanders* she first makes a sharp practical observation and then looks whimsically for some human correlation. More strikingly, in the poem 'The Last Chrysanthemum' Hardy first endows the flower with human powers of reasoned decision, but then checks himself –

> I talk as if the thing were born
>   With sense to work its mind;
> Yet it is but one mask of many worn
>   By the Great Face behind.

In that concluding moment Hardy looked ahead to modern ethology, to the observation of behaviour which is innate, instinctive; and of that which is learned. After discounting his occasional sentimentalities, his anthropomorphism and his overworking of the pathetic fallacy, what remains most impressive in Hardy is his determined search for that Great Face behind the many masks of Nature. It was this which led him to write:

> The 'simply natural' is interesting no longer. The much-decried, mad, late-Turner rendering is now necessary to create my interest. The exact truth as to material fact ceases to be of importance in art.

If Wordsworth was unmistakably one of Hardy's models, Turner was certainly another. Of his watercolours Hardy wrote: 'each is a landscape *plus* a man's soul'. It was in that spirit, and with an indifference to 'exact truth as to material fact', that Hardy created the bitter landscape of Flintcomb-Ash where Tess worked miserably in severe wintry conditions. To crown the effect of desolation Hardy introduced some birds of curious aspect – 'gaunt spectral creatures with tragical eyes'. They are not identified as any particular species, which is just as well in view of their origins. In an earlier novel, *The Return of the Native*, Diggory Venn noticed a wild mallard 'just arrived from the home of the north wind'. Developing this thought Hardy speculated on the remote arctic scenes that were familiar to the duck but scarcely imaginable to Venn. When he came to write his description of Flintcomb-Ash and wanted to stress the almost tundra-like severity of the scene he decided to refurbish Diggory Venn's duck with added melodramatic detail. The one obvious drawback was the unsuitability of the mallard to promote an imagery of horror and weirdness. 'Ducks', as the poet F. W. Harvey wrote, 'are soothy things'. It was with understandable discretion that Hardy preserved his spectral birds' anonymity. They would not be found in any field-guide of European birds. They have their honourable place, however, in that nature reserve of the poets which contains the basilisk, the unicorn and the mermaid – and without which our literature would be the poorer.

There could be no better example of Hardy's insistence on the unimportance of 'exact truth as to material fact', which supported his claim that 'Art is the secret of how to produce by a false thing the effect of a true'. This is not of course to deny that birds were a weak point in Hardy's general knowledge. He grew up, as most people do, with no comprehensively analytical curiosity about the familiar everyday world that he took for granted. Like most village boys he had an easy acquaintance with the common birds of garden, field and hedgerow, was not altogether secure in distinguishing house martins, swifts and swallows, and admitted in a letter to Mrs Henniker that his second wife, Florence, could identify the varieties of tits in the garden more accurately than he could. In his formative years ornithology was a minority interest that he did not share. His account of the birds of Egdon Heath – notably the cream-coloured courser – is not so much a diversion as a loss of bearings; and readers familiar with the hunting methods of the marsh harrier will be startled by the highly circumstantial episode at the beginning of *The Hand of Ethelberta*.

Here again it is important to recognize where Hardy's real talents lay. His account of the holly-roost beside his birthplace is vivid and charming, drawn at first hand. The description of a blackbird's bill as 'crocus-yellow' is beautifully exact. The bird sound that haunts him is the sustained churring of the nightjar. It is the dominantly characteristic summer sound of his native countryside and he draws on its atmospheric effect accordingly; and what a lovely alternative name he coined for it – 'the dewfall-hawk', with its soft unheard flight 'like an eyelid's soundless blink'.

It is the eye of the poet, not the field naturalist or the landscape photographer, that is Hardy's strength. With this he was able to evoke that deeper reality 'underlying the scenic' which adds an unforgettable quality to his Wessex landscapes. And his sense of kinship with his 'fellow-mortals' of the animal kingdom found expression in a humility and a sense of wonder that created fresh perceptions. Knowledge of the long-haul migrations of some species of waterfowl and pelagic birds drew from him a homage to their wider experience, in certain respects, of Earth's mysteries. With the same humility and insight he contemplated a solitary deer passing a house or the assortment of 'God's humblest' clustering round the light in his study at midnight: 'they know Earth-secrets that know not I'.

It is in such moments that Hardy's genius comes unequivocally off the page.

As Nature was hardly invented at this early point of the [nineteenth] century, Bob's Matilda could not say much about the glamour of the hills, or the shimmering of the foliage, or the wealth of glory in the distant sea, as she would doubtless have done had she lived later on.

The Trumpet-Major

Norcombe Hill – not far from lonely Toller-Down – was one of the spots which suggest to a passer-by that he is in the presence of a shape approaching the indestructible as nearly as any to be found on earth. It was a featureless convexity of chalk and soil – an ordinary specimen of those smoothly-outlined protuberances of the globe which may remain undisturbed on some great day of confusion, when far grander heights and dizzy granite precipices topple down.

The hill was covered on its northern side by an ancient and decaying plantation of beeches, whose upper verge formed a line over the crest, fringing its arched curve against the sky, like a mane. To-night these trees sheltered the southern slope from the keenest blasts, which smote the wood and floundered through it with a sound as of grumbling, or gushed over its crowning boughs in a weakened moan. The dry leaves in the ditch simmered and boiled in the same breezes, a tongue of air occasionally ferreting out a few, and sending them spinning across the grass. A group or two of the latest in date amongst the dead multitude had remained till this very mid-winter time on the twigs which bore them, and in falling rattled against the trunks with smart taps.

Between this half-wooded half-naked hill, and the vague still horizon that its summit indistinctly commanded, was a mysterious sheet of fathomless shade – the sounds from which suggested that what it concealed bore some reduced resemblance to features here. The thin grasses, more or less coating the hill, were touched by the wind in breezes of differing powers, and almost of differing natures – one rubbing the blades heavily, another raking them piercingly, another brushing them like a soft broom. The instinctive act of humankind was to stand and listen, and learn how the trees on the right and the trees on the left wailed or chaunted to each other in the regular antiphonies of a cathedral choir; how hedges and other shapes to leeward then caught the note, lowering it to the tenderest sob; and how the hurrying gust then plunged into the south, to be heard no more.

The sky was clear – remarkably clear – and the twinkling of all the stars seemed to be but throbs of one body, timed by a common pulse. The North Star was directly in the wind's eye, and since evening the Bear had swung round it outwardly to the east, till he was now at a right angle with the meridian. A difference of colour in the stars – oftener read of than seen in England – was really perceptible here. The sovereign brilliancy of Sirius pierced the eye with a steely glitter, the star called Capella was yellow, Aldebaran and Betelgueux shone with a fiery red.

To persons standing alone on a hill during a clear midnight such as this, the roll of the world eastward is almost a palpable movement. The sensation may be caused by the panoramic glide of the stars past earthly objects, which is perceptible in a few minutes of stillness, or by the better outlook upon space that a hill affords, or by the wind, or by the solitude; but whatever be its origin the impression of riding along is vivid and abiding. The poetry of motion is a phrase much in use, and to enjoy the epic form of that gratification it is necessary to stand on a hill at a small hour of the night, and, having first expanded with a sense of difference from the mass of civilized mankind, who are dreamwrapt and disregardful of all such proceedings at this time, long and quietly watch your stately progress through the stars. After such a nocturnal reconnoitre it is hard to get back to earth, and to believe that the consciousness of such majestic speeding is derived from a tiny human frame.

Far from the Madding Crowd

Her reason for standing so dead still as the pivot of this circle of heath-country was just as obscure. Her extraordinary fixity, her conspicuous loneliness, her heedlessness of night, betokened among other things an utter absence of fear. A tract of country unaltered from that sinister condition which made Caesar anxious every year to get clear of its glooms before the autumnal equinox, a kind of landscape and weather which leads travellers from the South to describe our island as Homer's Cimmerian land, was not, on the face it it, friendly to women.

It might reasonably have been supposed that she was listening to the wind, which rose somewhat as the night advanced, and laid hold of the attention. The wind, indeed, seemed made for the scene, as the scene seemed made for the hour. Part of its tone was quite special; what was heard there could be heard nowhere else. Gusts in innumerable series followed each other from the north-west, and when each one of them raced past the sound of its progress resolved into three. Treble, tenor, and bass notes were to be found therein. The general ricochet of the whole over pits and prominences had the gravest pitch of the chime. Next there could be heard the baritone buzz of a holly tree. Below these in force, above them in pitch, a dwindled voice strove hard at a husky tune, which was the peculiar local sound alluded to. Thinner and less immediately traceable than the other two, it was far more impressive than either. In it lay what may be called the linguistic peculiarity of the heath; and being audible nowhere on earth off a heath, if afforded a shadow of reason for the woman's tenseness, which continued as unbroken as ever.

Throughout the blowing of these plaintive November winds that note bore a great resemblance to the ruins of human song which remain to the throat of fourscore and ten. It was a worn whisper, dry and papery, and it brushed so distinctly across the ear that, by the accustomed, the material minutiae in which it originated could be realized as by touch. It was the united products of infinitesimal vegetable causes, and these were neither stems, leaves, fruit, blades, prickles, lichen, nor moss.

They were the mummied heath-bells of the past summer, originally tender and purple, now washed colourless by Michaelmas rains, and dried to dead skins by October suns. So low was an individual sound from these that a combination of hundreds only just emerged from silence, and the myriads of the whole declivity reached the woman's ear but as a shrivelled and intermittent recitative. Yet scarcely a single accent among the many afloat to-night could have such power to impress a listener with thoughts of its origin. One inwardly saw the infinity of those combined multitudes; and perceived that each of the tiny trumpets was seized on, entered, scoured and emerged from by the wind as thoroughly as if it were as vast as a crater.

The Return of the Native

The casual glimpses which the ordinary population bestowed upon that wondrous world of sap and leaves called the Hintock woods had been with these two, Giles and Marty, a clear gaze. They had been possessed of its finer mysteries as of commonplace knowledge; had been able to read its hieroglyphs as ordinary writing; to them the sights and sounds of night, winter, wind, storm, amid those dense boughs, which had to Grace a touch of the uncanny, and even of the supernatural, were simple occurrences, whose origin, continuance, and laws they foreknew. They had planted together, and together they had felled; together they had, with the run of the years, mentally collected those remoter signs and symbols which seen in few were of runic obscurity, but all together made an alphabet. From the light lashing of the twigs upon their faces when brushing through them in the dark, either could pronounce upon the species of the tree whence they stretched; from the quality of the wind's murmur through a bough, either could in like manner name its sort afar off. They knew by a glance at a trunk if its heart were sound, or tainted with incipient decay; and by the state of its upper twigs the stratum that had been reached by its roots. The artifices of the seasons were seen by them from the conjuror's own point of view, and not from that of the spectator.

The Woodlanders

Acoustic pictures were returned from the darkened scenery; they could hear where the tracts of heather began and ended; where the furze was growing stalky and tall; where it had been recently cut; in what direction the fir-clump lay, and how near was the pit in which the hollies grew; for these differing features had their voices no less than their shapes and colours.

The Return of the Native

The town-bred boy will often appreciate nature more than the country boy, but he does not know it in the same sense. He will rush to pick a flower which the country boy does not seem to notice. But it is part of the country boy's life. It grows in his soul – he does not want it in his button-hole.

Hardy in *Real Conversations*: William Archer

'What are picturesque ravines and mists to us who see nothing else?'

Wildeve in *The Return of the Native*

There was now a distinct manifestation of morning in the air, and presently the bleared white visage of a sunless winter day emerged like a dead-born child. The woodlanders everywhere had already bestirred themselves, rising this month of the year at the far less dreary time of absolute darkness. It had been above an hour earlier, before a single bird had untucked his head, that twenty lights were struck in as many bedrooms, twenty pairs of shutters opened, and twenty pairs of eyes stretched to the sky to forecast the weather for the day.

Owls that had been catching mice in the outhouses, rabbits that had been eating the winter-greens in the gardens, and stoats that had been sucking the blood of the rabbits, discerning that their human neighbours were on the move, discreetly withdrew from publicity, and were seen and heard no more till nightfall.

The Woodlanders

Spring weather came on rather suddenly, the unsealing of buds that had long been swollen accomplishing itself in the space of one warm night. The rush of sap in the veins of the trees could almost be heard. The flowers of late April took up a position unseen, and looked as if they had been blooming a long while, though there had been no trace of them the day before yesterday; birds began not to mind getting wet. In-door people said they had heard the nightingale, to which out-door people replied contemptuously that they had heard him a fortnight before.

The Woodlanders

The leaves over Hintock unrolled their creased tissues, and the woodland seemed to change from an open filigree to a solid opaque body of infinitely larger shape and importance. The boughs cast green shades, which disagreed with the complexion of the girls who walked there; and a fringe of the same boughs which overhung Mr Melbury's garden dripped on his seed-plots when it rained, pitting their surface all over as with pock-marks, till Melbury declared that gardens in such a place were no good at all. The two trees that had creaked all the winter left off creaking, the whirr of the night-hawk, however, forming a very satisfactory continuation of uncanny music from that quarter. Except at midday the sun was not seen complete by the Hintock people, but rather in the form of numerous little stars staring through the leaves.

The Woodlanders

In spite of myself I cannot help noticing countenances and tempers in objects of scenery, e.g. trees, hills, houses.

The Life of Thomas Hardy

They went noiselessly over mats of starry moss, rustled through interspersed tracts of leaves, skirted trunks with spreading roots whose mossed rinds made them like hands wearing green gloves; elbowed old elms and ashes with great forks, in which stood pools of water that overflowed on rainy days, and ran down their stems in green cascades. On older trees still than these huge lobes of fungi grew like lungs. Here, as everywhere, the Unfulfilled Intention, which makes life what it is, was as obvious as it could be among the depraved crowds of a city slum. The leaf was deformed, the curve was crippled, the taper was interrupted; the lichen ate the vigour of the stalk, and the ivy slowly strangled to death the promising sapling.

The Woodlanders

I sometimes look upon all things in inanimate Nature as pensive mutes.

The Life of Thomas Hardy

In regard of sport for instance, will ever the great body of human beings, of whom the commonplace & degenerate breed most, ever see its immorality? Worse than that, supposing they do, when will the still more numerous terrestrial animals – our kin, having the same ancestry – learn to be merciful? The fact is that when you get to the bottom of things you find no bed-rock of righteousness to rest on – nature is *unmoral* . . .

Letter to Frederic Harrison, 17 October 1906

She looked towards the western sky, which was now aglow like some vast foundry wherein new worlds were being cast. Across it the bare bough of a tree stretched horizontally, revealing every twig against the evening fire, and showing in dark profile every beck and movement of three pheasants that were settling themselves down on it in a row to roost.

'It will be fine to-morrow,' said Marty, observing them with the vermilion light of the sun in the pupils of her eyes, 'for they are a croupied down nearly at the end of the bough. If it were going to be stormy they'd squeeze close to the trunk. The weather is almost all they have to think of, isn't it, Mr Winterborne? And so they must be lighter-hearted than we.'

'I dare say they are,' said Winterborne.

The Woodlanders

Here in front of him was a wild mallard – just arrived from the home of the north wind. The creature brought within him an amplitude of Northern knowledge. Glacial catastrophies, snowstorm episodes, glittering auroral effects, Polaris in the zenith, Franklin underfoot – the category of his commonplaces was wonderful.

The Return of the Native

After this season of congealed dampness came a spell of dry frost, when strange birds from behind the North Pole began to arrive silently on the upland of Flintcomb-Ash; gaunt spectral creatures with tragical eyes – eyes which had witnessed scenes of cataclysmal horror in inaccessible polar regions of a magnitude such as no human being had ever conceived, in curdling temperatures that no man could endure; which had beheld the crash of icebergs and the slide of snow-hills by the shooting light of the Aurora; been half blinded by the whirl of colossal storms and terraqueous distortions; and retained the expression of feature that such scenes had engendered. These nameless birds came quite near to Tess and Marian, but of all they had seen which humanity would never see, they brought no account.

Tess of the d'Urbervilles

The lady whose appearance had asserted a difference between herself and the Anglebury people, without too clearly showing what that difference was, passed out of the town in a few moments and, following the highway across meadows fed by the Froom, she crossed the railway and soon got into a lonely heath. She had been watching the base of a cloud as it closed down upon the line of a distant ridge, like an upper upon a lower eyelid, shutting in the gaze of the evening sun. She was about to return before dusk came on, when she heard a commotion in the air immediately behind and above her head. The saunterer looked up and saw a wild-duck flying along with the greatest violence, just in its rear being another large bird, which a countryman would have pronounced to be one of the biggest duck-hawks that he had ever beheld. The hawk neared its intended victim, and the duck screamed and redoubled its efforts.

Ethelberta impulsively started off in a rapid run that would have made a little dog bark with delight and run after, her object being, if possible, to see the end of this desperate struggle for a life so small and unheard-of. Her stateliness went away, and it could be forgiven for not remaining; for her feet suddenly became as quick as fingers, and she raced along over the uneven ground with such force of tread that, being a woman slightly heavier than gossamer, her patent heels punched little D's in the soil with unerring accuracy wherever it was bare, crippled the heather-twigs where it was not, and sucked the swampy places with a sound of quick kisses.

Her rate of advance was not to be compared with that of the two birds, though she went swiftly enough to keep them well in sight in such an open place as that around her, having at one point in the journey been so near that she could hear the whisk of the duck's feathers against the wind as it lifted and lowered its wings. When the bird seemed to be but a few yards from its enemy she saw it strike downwards, and after a level flight of a quarter of a minute, vanish. The hawk swooped after, and Ethelberta now perceived a whitely shining oval of still water, looking amid the swarthy level of the heath like a hole through to a nether sky.

Into this large pond, which the duck had been making towards from the beginning of its precipitate flight, it had dived out of sight. The excited and breathless runner was in a few moments close enough to see the disappointed hawk hovering and floating in the air as if waiting for the reappearance of its prey, upon which grim pastime it was so intent that by creeping along softly she was enabled to get very near the edge of the pool and witness the conclusion of the episode. Whenever the duck was under the necessity of showing its head to breathe, the other bird would dart towards it, invariably too late, however; for the diver was far too experienced in the rough humour of the buzzard family at this game to come up twice near the same spot, unaccountably emerging from opposite sides of the pool in succession, and bobbing again by the time its adversary reached each place, so that at length the hawk gave up the contest and flew away, a satanic moodiness being almost perceptible in the motion of its wings.

The Hand of Ethelberta

. . . though I admit such & such places were in my mind when describing the fictitious ones, the latter are by no means photographs of such places, & exist precisely as pictured nowhere but in the imaginary region I have called Wessex.

Letter to W. T. Horton, 12 February 1909

There are some heights in Wessex, shaped as if by a kindly hand
For thinking, dreaming, dying on, and at crises when I stand,
Say, on Ingpen Beacon eastward, or on Wylls-Neck westwardly,
I seem where I was before my birth, and after death may be.

'Wessex Heights'

There is what we used to call 'The Birds' Bedroom' in the plantation at Bockhampton. Some large hollies grow among leafless ash, oak, birch, etc. At this time of year the birds select the hollies for roosting in, and at dusk noises not unlike the creaking of withy-chairs arise, with a busy rustling as of people going to bed in a lodging-house; accompanied by sundry shakings, adjustings, and pattings, as if they were making their beds vigorously before turning in.

The Life of Thomas Hardy

May 30. Walking to Marnhull. The prime of bird-singing. The thrushes and blackbirds are the most prominent, – pleading earnestly rather than singing, and with such modulation that you seem to see their little tongues curl inside their bills in their emphasis. A bullfinch sings from a tree with a metallic sweetness piercing as a fife.

The Life of Thomas Hardy

One without looks in to-night
  Through the curtain-chink
From the sheet of glistening white;
One without looks in to-night
  As we sit and think
  By the fender-brink.

We do not discern those eyes
  Watching in the snow;
Lit by lamps of rosy dyes
We do not discern those eyes
  Wondering, aglow,
  Fourfooted, tiptoe.

  'The Fallow Deer at the Lonely House'

A shaded lamp and a waving blind,
And the beat of a clock from a distant floor:
On this scene enter – winged, horned, and spined –
A longlegs, a moth, and a dumbledore;
While 'mid my page there idly stands
A sleepy fly, that rubs its hands . . .

Thus meet we five, in this still place,
At this point of time, at this point in space
– My guests besmear my new-penned line,
Or bang at the lamp and fall supine.
'God's humblest, they!' I muse. Yet why?
They know Earth-secrets that know not I.

    'An August Midnight'

8

THE FARMING WORLD

At Bockhampton in 1840 there was little working activity that was not connected, in one way or another, with farming. Although the Hardys were not directly involved their livelihood depended largely on estate work, on constructing or repairing farm buildings. In any conversation the state of agriculture would be a prominent and absorbing topic, with the prospects of the harvest a subject of deep concern to everyone. In particular, the merits or demerits of the Corn Laws aroused vehement arguments. When they were finally repealed Hardy was six years old. It was an event which inaugurated a long process of radical change in farming. Hardy grew up to realize that his native countryside was undergoing nothing less than a transformation of its traditional practices. Like Richard Jefferies, Hardy found much to celebrate in the old ways but realized that many changes were inevitable and indeed desirable.

His immediate vicinity was dairying country principally. The poor soil of the heath yielded little more than furze cut for fuel and bracken for stock-bedding; as grazing land it was given over mainly to wild ponies – 'heath-croppers'. The visits of Diggory Venn with his supplies of reddle indicate the presence of some sheep, and the ewe-leaze was a feature of Hardy's local geography, but downland was the real sheep country. It was on Toller Down that Gabriel Oak grazed his sheep, not on Egdon Heath or in the Froom valley.

That valley was to be named by Hardy as the 'Valley of the Great Dairies,' where Tess admired the rich quality of the milking herds, 'their large-veined udders ponderous as sandbags, the teats sticking

out like the legs of a gipsy's crock'. Of all the farming scenes he
described it is this one which seems to spring most copiously from
first-hand knowledge. As a youth he was on friendly terms with some of
the dairymaids. He knew the valley in all its seasonal moods and
portrayed them unforgettably. He understood the complex technique
of the water-meadows, which lingered in the area until about 1950,
when I last saw it in operation. Surely Hardy was never more freely and
contentedly at home than where

> The flowery river-ooze
> Upheaves and falls; the milk purrs in the pail.

In arable country and among the sheep folds he has an experienced eye
but not quite the same masterful intimacy. The working practices of
shepherd Gabriel Oak in *Far from the Madding Crowd* can leave questions
unanswered. The time taken by him to shear a sheep, which so
impressed Bathsheba – and Hardy – has not impressed other shearers.
And his complaint that the lambing season was bringing too many
twins is difficult to reconcile with the fact, mentioned by Hardy in his
essay 'The Dorsetshire Labourer', that it was customary for a shepherd
to be paid an additional shilling for each twin reared. Could there be
too many?

   The farming scenes of Hardy's boyhood were little changed from
Chaucer's time. Scythe, pitchfork, flail and milking-pail were the
familiar hand tools. Oxen were still used as draught animals. Plough,
harrow and hoe were horse-drawn. Seed was scattered by hand. The
daily life of the farm-workers consisted largely of heavy, unremitting
labour: it is no wonder that Hezekiah Biles in *Two on a Tower* thought
that labouring men should have a second backbone. And not men only
– the physical demands on women field-workers were sometimes
grievous.

   The most obvious features of the farming revolution that Hardy
chronicled were the mechanical implements that increasingly replaced
hand labour. None could have been more welcome than the reaping-
machine, which took over the main burden from the scythe. Its
appearance in *Tess* provides one of those miniature paintings at which
Hardy excelled. The seed-drill, like the reaper, was drawn by horses.
The threshing-machine took matters a stage further, bringing steam
power to the farm. The *sheen* ('chine) as it was named, in my
experience, usually made its mysterious entry into the parish at night,
so as to be in position and with its furnace ablaze at the start of the
working day. Its operator, the engineer, was a man of an alien breed, as
Hardy shrewdly observed.

   The farm-folk themselves were changing also. In the hungry forties

Hardy knew a shepherd-boy who died of starvation, and the general lot of the farm-worker then was to be ill-paid and regarded almost as a figure of fun. 'Hodge' was the stock caricature of the countryman in his old-fashioned smock – a disparagement that Hardy resented. The workfolk as he knew them had as much individuality, and as varied a potential for tragedy and humour, as any other social group. Not easily forgotten are the ageing shepherd's difficult search for new employment at the hiring-fair and the spirit of Andrew Randle, in *Far from the Madding Crowd*, who was sacked for saying to the squire that his soul was his own 'and other iniquities'.

During the second half of the nineteenth century some of the harsher circumstances were ameliorated. Wages improved and many of the old customs and practices – the good and the bad alike – were swept away. In his correspondence with Sir Henry Rider Haggard, and elsewhere, Hardy drew a balanced picture of the interaction between old and new as he had personally witnessed it.

The time was in the years immediately before foreign competition had revolutionized the trade in grain, when still, as from the earliest ages, the wheat quotations from month to month depended entirely upon the home harvest. A bad harvest, or the prospect of one, would double the price of corn in a few weeks; and the promise of a good yield would lower it as rapidly. Prices were like the roads of the period, steep in gradient, reflecting in their phases the local conditions, without engineering, levellings, or averages.

The farmer's income was ruled by the wheat-crop within his own horizon, and the wheat-crop by the weather. Thus, in person, he became a sort of flesh-barometer, with feelers always directed to the sky and wind around him. The local atmosphere was everything to him; the atmospheres of other countries a matter of indifference. The people, too, who were not farmers, the rural multitude, saw in the god of the weather a more important personage than they do now. Indeed, the feeling of the peasantry in this matter was so intense as to be almost unrealizable in these equable days. Their impulse was well-nigh to prostrate themselves in lamentation before untimely rains and tempests, which came as the Alastor of those households whose crime it was to be poor.

After midsummer they watched the weather-cocks as men waiting in antechambers watch the lackey. Sun elated them; quiet rain sobered them; weeks of watery tempest stupefied them. That aspect of the sky which they now regard as disagreeable they then beheld as maleficent.

The Mayor of Casterbridge

It was an eighty-cow dairy, and the troop of milkers, regular and
supernumerary, were all at work; for, though the time of year was as yet
but early April, the feed lay entirely in water-meadows, and the cows
were 'in full pail.' The hour was about six in the evening, and three-
fourths of the large, red, rectangular animals having been finished off,
there was opportunity for a little conversation.

'He do bring home his bride to-morrow, I hear. They've come as far
as Anglebury to-day.'

The voice seemed to proceed from the belly of the cow called Cherry,
but the speaker was a milking-woman, whose face was buried in the flank
of that motionless beast.

'Hav' anybody seen her?' said another.

There was a negative response from the first. 'Though they say she's a
rosy-cheeked, tisty-tosty little body enough,' she added; and as the
milkmaid spoke she turned her face so that she could glance past her
cow's tail to the other side of the barton, where a thin, fading woman of
thirty milked somewhat apart from the rest.

'Years younger than he, they say,' continued the second, with also a
glance of reflectiveness in the same direction.

'How old do you call him, then?'

'Thirty or so.'

'More like forty,' broke in an old milkman near, in a long white
pinafore or 'wropper,' and with the brim of his hat tied down, so that he
looked like a woman. ''A was born before our Great Weir was builded,
and I hadn't man's wages when I laved water there.'

The discussion waxed so warm that the purr of the milk-streams
became jerky, till a voice from another cow's belly cried with authority,
'Now then, what the Turk do it matter to us about Farmer Lodge's age,
or Farmer Lodge's new mis'ess? I shall have to pay him nine pound a
year for the rent of every one of these milchers, whatever his age or hers.
Get on with your work, or 'twill be dark afore we have done. The evening
is pinking in a'ready.' This speaker was the dairyman himself, by whom
the milkmaids and men were employed.

'The Withered Arm'

About this time they would hear Dairyman Crick's voice, lecturing the
non-resident milkers for arriving late, and speaking sharply to old
Deborah Fyander for not washing her hands.

'For Heaven's sake, pop thy hands under the pump, Deb! Upon my
soul, if the London folk only knowed of thee and thy slovenly ways, they'd
swaller their milk and butter more mincing than they do a'ready; and
that's saying a good deal.'

Tess of the d'Urbervilles

'To my thinking,' said the dairyman, rising suddenly from a cow he had just finished off, snatching up his three-legged stool in one hand and the pail in the other, and moving on to the next hard-yielder in his vicinity; 'to my thinking, the cows don't gie down their milk to-day as usual. Upon my life, if Winker do begin keeping back like this, she'll not be worth going under by midsummer.'

'"Tis because there's a new hand come among us,' said Jonathan Kail. 'I've noticed such things afore.'

'To be sure. It may be so. I didn't think o't.'

'I've been told that it goes up into their horns at such times,' said a dairymaid.

'Well, as to going up into their horns,' replied Dairyman Crick dubiously, as though even witchcraft might be limited by anatomical possibilities, 'I couldn't say; I certainly could not. But as nott cows will keep it back as well as the horned ones, I don't quite agree to it. Do ye know that riddle about the nott cows, Jonathan? Why do nott cows give less milk in a year than horned?'

'I don't!' interposed the milkmaid. 'Why do they?'

'Because there bain't so many of 'em,' said the dairyman. 'Howsomever, these gam'sters do certainly keep back their milk to-day. Folks, we must lift up a stave or two – that's the only cure for't.'

Songs were often resorted to in dairies hereabout as an enticement to the cows when they showed signs of withholding their usual yield; and the band of milkers at this request burst into melody – in purely business-like tones, it is true, and with no great spontaneity; the result, according to their own belief, being a decided improvement during the song's continuance.

Tess of the d'Urbervilles

They sheared in the great barn, called for the nonce the Shearing-barn, which on ground-plan resembled a church with transepts. It not only emulated the form of the neighbouring church of the parish, but vied with it in antiquity. Whether the barn had ever formed one of a group of conventual buildings nobody seemed to be aware; no trace of such surroundings remained. The vast porches at the sides, lofty enough to admit a waggon laden to its highest with corn in the sheaf, were spanned by heavy-pointed arches of stone, broadly and boldly cut, whose very simplicity was the origin of a grandeur not apparent in erections where more ornament has been attemped. The dusky, filmed, chestnut roof, braced and tied in by huge collars, curves, and diagonals, was far nobler in design, because more wealthy in material, than nine-tenths of those in our modern churches. Along each side wall was a range of striding buttresses, throwing deep shadows on the spaces between them, which were perforated by lancet openings, combining in their proportions the precise requirements both of beauty and ventilation.

One could say about this barn, what could hardly be said of either the church or the castle, akin to it in age and style, that the purpose which had dictated its original erection was the same with that to which it was still applied. Unlike and superior to either of those two typical remnants of medievalism, the old barn embodied practices which had suffered no mutilation at the hands of time. Here at least the spirit of the ancient builders was at one with the spirit of the modern beholder. Standing before this abraded pile, the eye regarded its present usage, the mind dwelt upon its past history, with a satisfied sense of functional continuity throughout – a feeling almost of gratitude, and quite of pride, at the permanence of the idea which had heaped it up. The fact that four centuries had neither proved it to be founded on a mistake, inspired any hatred of its purpose, nor given rise to any reaction that had battered it down, invested this simple grey effort of old minds with a repose, if not a grandeur, which a too curious reflection was apt to disturb in its ecclesiastical and military compeers. For once medievalism and modernism had a common stand-point. The lanceolate windows, the time-eaten arch-stones and chamfers, the orientation of the axis, the misty chestnut work of the rafters, referred to no exploded fortifying art or worn-out religious creed. The defence and salvation of the body by daily bread is still a study, a religion, and a desire.

Today the large side doors were thrown open towards the sun to admit a bountiful light to the immediate spot of the shearers' operations, which was the wood threshing-floor in the centre, formed of thick oak, black with age and polished by the beating of flails for many generations, till it had grown as slippery and as rich in hue as the state-room floors of an Elizabethan mansion. Here the shearers knelt, the sun slanting in upon their bleached shirts, tanned arms, and the polished shears they flourished, causing these to bristle with a thousand rays strong enough to blind a weak-eyed man. Beneath them a captive sheep lay panting, quickening its pants as misgiving merged in terror, till it quivered like the hot landscape outside.

Far from the Madding Crowd

There is a loquacity that tells nothing, which was Bathsheba's; and there is a silence which says much: that was Gabriel's. Full of this dim and temperate bliss, he went on to fling the ewe over upon her other side, covering her head with his knee, gradually running the shears line after line round her dewlap, thence about her flank and back, and finishing over the tail.

'Well done, and done quickly!' said Bathsheba, looking at her watch as the last snip resounded.

'How long, miss?' said Gabriel, wiping his brow.

'Three-and-twenty minutes and a half since you took the first lock from its forehead. It is the first time that I have ever seen one done in less than half an hour.'

The clean, sleek creature arose from its fleece – how perfectly like Aphrodite rising from the foam should have been seen to be realised – looking startled and shy at the loss of its garment, which lay on the floor in one soft cloud, united throughout, the portion visible being the inner surface only, which, never before exposed, was white as snow, and without flaw or blemish of the minutest kind.

'Cain Ball!'

'Yes, Mister Oak; here I be!'

Cainy now runs forward with the tar-pot. 'B.E.' is newly stamped upon the shorn skin, and away the simple dam leaps, panting, over the board into the shirtless flock outside. Then up comes Maryann; throws the loose locks into the middle of the fleece, rolls it up, and carries it into the background as three-and-a-half pounds of unadulterated warmth for the winter enjoyment of persons unknown and far away.

Far from the Madding Crowd

A firm loud tread was now heard stamping outside; the door was opened about six inches, and somebody on the other side exclaimed –

'Neighbours, have ye got room for a few new-born lambs?'

'Ay, sure, shepherd,' said the conclave.

The door was flung back till it kicked the wall and trembled from top to bottom with the blow. Mr Oak appeared in the entry with a steaming face, hay-bands wound about his ankles to keep out the snow, a leather strap round his waist outside the smock-frock, and looking altogether an epitome of the world's health and vigour. Four lambs hung in various embarrassing attitudes over his shoulders, and the dog George, whom Gabriel had contrived to fetch from Norcombe, stalked solemnly behind.

'Well, Shepherd Oak, and how's lambing this year, if I mid say it?' inquired Joseph Poorgrass.

'Terrible trying,' said Oak. 'I've been wet through twice a-day, either in snow or rain, this last fortnight. Cainy and I haven't tined our eyes tonight.'

'A good few twins, too, I hear?'

'Too many by half. Yes; 'tis a very queer lambing this year. We shan't have done by Lady Day.'

'And last year 'twer all over by Sexajessamine Sunday,' Joseph remarked.

'Bring on the rest, Cain,' said Gabriel, 'and then run back to the ewes. I'll follow you soon.'

Cainy Ball – a cheery-faced young lad, with a small circular orifice by way of mouth, advanced and deposited two others, and retired as he was bidden. Oak lowered the lambs from their unnatural elevation, wrapped them in hay, and placed them round the fire.

'We've no lambing-hut here, as I used to have at Norcombe,' said Gabriel, 'and 'tis such a plague to bring the weakly ones to a house. If 'twasn't for your place here, malter, I don't know what I should do, this keen weather. And how is it with you today, malter?'

'Oh, neither sick nor sorry, shepherd; but no younger.'

'Ay – I understand.'

Far from the Madding Crowd

Another week passed. The oat-harvest began, and all the men were a-field under a monochromatic Lammas sky, amid the trembling air and short shadows of noon. Indoors nothing was to be heard save the droning of blue-bottle flies; out-of-doors the whetting of scythes and the hiss of tressy oat-ears rubbing together as their perpendicular stalks of amber-yellow fell heavily to each swath. Every drop of moisture not in the men's bottles and flagons in the form of cider was raining as perspiration from their foreheads and cheeks. Drought was everywhere else.

Far from the Madding Crowd

The old men on the rising straw-rick talked of the past days when they had been accustomed to thresh with flails on the oaken barn-floor; when everything, even the winnowing, was effected by hand-labour, which, to their thinking, though slow, produced better results.

Tess of the d'Urbervilles

> Only a man harrowing clods
>   In a slow silent walk
> With an old horse that stumbles and nods
>   Half asleep as they stalk.
>
> Only thin smoke without flame
>   From the heaps of couch-grass;
> Yet this will go onward the same
>   Though Dynasties pass.

'In Time of "The Breaking of Nations"'

There was a noise of horse's hoofs without, a stumbling against the door-scraper, a tethering to the window-shutter, a creaking of the door on its hinges, and a voice which Swithin recognized as Mr Torkingham's. He

greeted each of the previous arrivals by name, and stated that he was glad
to see them all so punctually assembled.

'Ay, sir,' said Haymoss Fry. ''Tis only my jints that have kept me
from assembling myself long ago. I'd assemble upon the top of Welland
Steeple, if 'tweren't for my jints. I assure ye, Pa'son Tarkenham, that in
the clitch o' my knees, where the rain used to come through when I was
cutting clots for the new lawn, in old my lady's time, 'tis as if rats wez
gnawing, every now and then. When a feller's young he's too small in the
brain to see how soon a constitution can be squandered, worse luck!'

'True,' said Biles, to fill the time while the parson was engaged in
finding the Psalms. 'A man's a fool till he's forty. Often have I thought,
when hay-pitching, and the small of my back seeming no stouter than a
harnet's, "The devil send that I had but the making of labouring men for
a twelvemonth!" I'd gie every man jack two good backbones, even if the
alteration was as wrong as forgery.'

Two on a Tower

Several days had passed, and Tess was afield. The dry winter wind still
blew, but a screen of thatched hurdles erected in the eye of the blast kept
its force away from her. On the sheltered side was a turnip-slicing
machine, whose bright blue hue of new paint seemed almost vocal in the
otherwise subdued scene. Opposite its front was a long mound or 'grave,'
in which the roots had been preserved since early winter. Tess was
standing at the uncovered end, chopping off with a bill-hook the fibres
and earth from each root, and throwing it after the operation into the
slicer. A man was turning the handle of the machine, and from its trough
came the newly-cut swedes, the fresh smell of whose yellow chips was
accompanied by the sounds of the snuffling wind, the smart swish of the
slicing-blades, and the choppings of the hook in Tess's leather-gloved
hand.

The wide acreage of blank agricultural brownness, apparent where
the swedes had been pulled, was beginning to be striped in wales of
darker brown, gradually broadening to ribands. Along the edge of each of
these something crept upon ten legs, moving without haste and without
rest up and down the whole length of the field; it was two horses and a
man, the plough going between them, turning up the cleared ground for a
spring sowing.

Tess of the d'Urbervilles

It was the new-fashioned agricultural implement called a horse-drill, till
then unknown, in its modern shape, in this part of the country, where the
venerable seed-lip was still used for sowing as in the days of the

Heptarchy. Its arrival created about as much sensation in the corn-market as a flying machine would create at Charing Cross. The farmers crowded round it, women drew near it, children crept under and into it. The machine was painted in bright hues of green, yellow, and red, and it resembled as a whole a compound of hornet, grasshopper, and shrimp, magnified enormously. Or it might have been likened to an upright musical instrument with the front gone. That was how it struck Lucetta. 'Why, it is a sort of agricultural piano,' she said.

'It has something to do with corn,' said Elizabeth.

The Mayor of Casterbridge

The sunlight, a little later, broke through chinks of cottage shutters, throwing stripes like red-hot pokers upon cupboards, chests of drawers, and other furniture within; and awakening harvesters who were not already astir.

But of all ruddy things that morning the brightest were two broad arms of painted wood, which rose from the margin of a yellow cornfield hard by Marlott village. They, with two others below, formed the revolving Maltese cross of the reaping-machine, which had been brought to the field on the previous evening to be ready for operations this day. The paint with which they were smeared, intensified in hue by the sunlight, imparted to them a look of having been dipped in liquid fire.

The field had already been 'opened'; that is to say, a lane a few feet wide had been hand-cut through the wheat along the whole circumference of the field, for the first passage of the horses and machine.

Two groups, one of men and lads, the other of women, had come down the lane just at the hour when the shadows of the eastern hedge-top struck the west hedge midway, so that the heads of the groups were enjoying sunrise while their feet were still in the dawn. They disappeared from the lane between the two stone posts which flanked the nearest field-gate.

Presently there arose from within a ticking like the love-making of the grasshopper. The machine had begun, and a moving concatenation of three horses and the aforesaid long rickety machine was visible over the gate, a driver sitting upon one of the hauling horses, and an attendant on the seat of the implement. Along one side of the field the whole wain went, the arms of the mechanical reaper revolving slowly, till it passed down the hill quite out of sight. In a minute it came up on the other side of the field at the same equable pace; the glistening brass star in the forehead of the fore horse first catching the eye as it rose into view over the stubble, then the bright arms, and then the whole machine.

Tess of the d'Urbervilles

I

If seasons all were summers,
  And leaves would never fall,
And hopping casement-comers
  Were foodless not at all,
And fragile folk might be here
  That white winds bid depart;
Then one I used to see here
  Would warm my wasted heart!

II

One frail, who, bravely tilling
  Long hours in gripping gusts,
Was mastered by their chilling,
  And now his ploughshare rusts.
So savage winter catches
  The breath of limber things,
And what I love he snatches,
  And what I love not, brings.

'The Farm-Woman's Winter'

Close under the eaves of the stack, and as yet barely visible, was the red tyrant that the women had come to serve – a timber-framed construction, with straps and wheels appertaining – the threshing-machine which, whilst it was going, kept up a despotic demand upon the endurance of their muscles and nerves.

A little way off there was another indistinct figure; this one black, with a sustained hiss that spoke of strength very much in reserve. The long chimney running up beside an ash-tree, and the warmth which radiated from the spot, explained without the necessity of much daylight that here was the engine which was to act as the *primum mobile* of this little world. By the engine stood a dark motionless being, a sooty and grimy embodiment of tallness, in a sort of trance, with a heap of coals by his side: it was the engineman. The isolation of his manner and colour lent him the appearance of a creature from Tophet, who had strayed into the pellucid smokelessness of this region of yellow grain and pale soil, with which he had nothing in common, to amaze and to discompose its aborigines.

What he looked he felt. He was in the agricultural world, but not of it. He served fire and smoke; these denizens of the fields served vegetation, weather, frost, and sun. He travelled with his engine from farm to farm, from county to county, for as yet the steam threshing-machine was itinerant in this part of Wessex. He spoke in a strange northern accent;

his thoughts being turned inwards upon himself, his eye on his iron charge, hardly perceiving the scenes around him, and caring for them not at all: holding only strictly necessary intercourse with the natives, as if some ancient doom compelled him to wander here against his will in the service of his Plutonic master. The long strap which ran from the driving-wheel of his engine to the red thresher under the rick was the sole tie-line between agriculture and him.

Tess of the d'Urbervilles

Two months passed away. We are brought on to a day in February, on which was held the yearly statute or hiring fair in the county-town of Casterbridge.

At one end of the street stood from two to three hundred blithe and hearty labourers waiting upon Chance – all men of the stamp to whom labour suggests nothing worse than a wrestle with gravitation, and pleasure nothing better than a renunciation of the same. Among these, carters and waggoners were distinguished by having a piece of whip-cord twisted round their hats; thatchers wore a fragment of woven straw; shepherds held their sheep-crooks in their hands; and thus the situation required was known to the hirers at a glance.

Far from the Madding Crowd

The conventional farm-folk of his imagination – personified in the newspaper-press by the pitiable dummy known as Hodge – were obliterated after a few days' residence. At close quarters no Hodge was to be seen.

Tess of the d'Urbervilles

The fair without the windows was now raging thick and loud. It was the chief hiring fair of the year, and differed quite from the market of a few days earlier. In substance it was a whitey-brown crowd flecked with white – this being the body of labourers waiting for places. The long bonnets of the women, like waggon-tilts, their cotton gowns and checked shawls, mixed with the carters' smockfrocks; for they, too, entered into the hiring. Among the rest, at the corner of the pavement, stood an old shepherd, who attracted the eyes of Lucetta and Farfrae by his stillness. He was evidently a chastened man. The battle of life had been a sharp one with him, for, to begin with, he was a man of small frame. He was now so bowed by hard work and years that, approaching from behind, a person could hardly see his head. He had planted the stem of his crook in the gutter, and was resting upon the bow, which was polished to silver brightness by the long friction of his hands. He had quite forgotten where he was, and what he had come for, his eyes being bent on the ground. A little way off negotiations were proceeding which had reference to him; but he did not hear them, and there seemed to be passing through his mind pleasant visions of the hiring successes of his prime, when his skill laid open to him any farm for the asking.

The negotiations were between a farmer from a distant county and the old man's son. In these there was a difficulty. The farmer would not take the crust without the crumb of the bargain, in other words, the old man without the younger; and the son had a sweetheart on his present farm, who stood by, waiting the issue with pale lips.

'I'm sorry to leave ye, Nelly,' said the young man with emotion. 'But, you see, I can't starve father, and he's out o' work at Lady-day. 'Tis only thirty-five mile.'

The girl's lips quivered. 'Thirty-five mile!' she murmured. 'Ah! 'tis enough! I shall never see 'ee again!' It was, indeed, a hopeless length of traction for Dan Cupid's magnet; for young men were young men at Casterbridge as elsewhere.

'O! no, no – I never shall,' she insisted, when he pressed her hand; and she turned her face to Lucetta's wall to hide her weeping. The farmer said he would give the young man half-an-hour for his answer, and went away, leaving the group sorrowing.

The Mayor of Casterbridge

To Mr (afterwards Sir) Rider Haggard, who was investigating the conditions of agriculture and agricultural labourers, he gave the following information:

March: 1902

My dear Haggard:

As to your question, my opinion on the past of the agricultural labourers in this county: I think, indeed know, that down to 1850 or 1855 their condition was in general one of great hardship. I say in general, for there have always been fancy-farms, resembling St Clair's in 'Uncle Tom's Cabin', whereon they lived as smiling exceptions to those of their class all around them. I recall one such, the estate-owner being his own farmer, and ultimately ruining himself by his hobby. To go to the other extreme; as a child I knew a sheep-keeping boy who to my horror shortly afterwards died of want – the contents of his stomach at the autopsy being raw turnip only. His father's wages were six shillings a week, with about two pounds at harvest, a cottage rent free, and an allowance of thorn faggots from the hedges as fuel. Between these examples came the great bulk of farms – wages whereon ranged from seven to nine shillings a week, and perquisites being better in proportion.

Secondly: as to the present. Things are of course widely different now. I am told that at the annual hiring-fair just past, the old positions were absolutely reversed, the farmers walking about and importuning the labourers to come and be hired, instead of, as formerly, the labourers anxiously entreating the stolid farmers to take them on at any pittance. Their present life is almost without exception one of comfort, if the most ordinary thrift be observed. I could take you to the cottage of a shepherd not many miles from here that has a carpet and brass-rods to the staircase, and from the open door of which you hear a piano strumming within. Of course bicycles stand by the doorway, while at night a large paraffin lamp throws out a perfect blaze of light upon the passer by.

The son of another labourer I know takes dancing lessons at a quadrille-class in the neighbouring town. Well, why not!

But changes at which we must all rejoice have brought other changes which are not so attractive. The labourers have become more and more migratory – the younger families in especial, who enjoy nothing so much as fresh scenery and new acquaintance. The consequences are curious and unexpected. For one thing, village tradition – a vast mass of unwritten folk-lore, local chronicle, local topography and nomenclature – is absolutely sinking, has nearly sunk, into eternal oblivion. I cannot recall a single instance of a labourer who still lives on the farm where he was born, and I can only recall a few who have been five years on their present farms. Thus you see, there being no continuity of environment in their lives, there is no continuity of information, the names, stories, and relics of one place being speedily forgotten under the incoming facts of the next. For example, if you ask one of the workfolk (they always used to be called 'workfolk' hereabout – 'labourers' is an imported word) the names of surrounding hills, streams; the character and circumstances of people buried in particular graves; at what spots parish personages lie interred; questions on local fairies, ghosts, herbs, &c, they can give no answer: yet I can recollect the time when the places of burial even of the poor and tombless were all remembered, and the history of the parish and squire's family for 150 years back known. Such and such ballads appertained to such and such a locality, ghost tales were attached to particular sites, and nooks wherein wild herbs grew for the cure of divers maladies were pointed out readily.

The Life of Thomas Hardy

Half-an-hour later Bathsheba, in finished dress, and followed by Liddy, entered the upper end of the old hall to find that her men had all deposited themselves on a long form and a settle at the lower extremity. She sat down at a table and opened the time-book, pen in her hand, with a canvas money-bag beside her. From this she poured a small heap of coin. Liddy chose a position at her elbow and began to sew, sometimes pausing and looking round, or, with the air of a privileged person, taking up one of the half-sovereigns lying before her, and surveying it merely as a work of art, while strictly preventing her countenance from expressing any wish to possess it as money.

'Now, before I begin, men,' said Bathsheba, 'I have two matters to speak of. The first is that the bailiff is dismissed for thieving, and that I have formed a resolution to have no bailiff at all, but to manage everything with my own head and hands.'

The men breathed an audible breath of amazement.

'The next matter is, have you heard anything of Fanny?'

'Nothing, ma'am.'

'Have you done anything?'

'I met Farmer Boldwood,' said Jacob Smallbury, 'and I went with him and two of his men, and dragged Newmill Pond, but we found nothing.'

'And the new shepherd have been to Buck's Head, by Yalbury, thinking she had gone there, but nobody had seed her,' said Laban Tall.

'Hasn't William Smallbury been to Casterbridge?'

'Yes, ma'am, but he's not yet come home. He promised to be back by six.'

'It wants a quarter to six at present,' said Bathsheba, looking at her watch. 'I daresay he'll be in directly. Well, now then' – she looked into the book – 'Joseph Poorgrass, are you there?'

'Yes, sir – ma'am I mane,' said the person addressed. 'I be the personal name of Poorgrass.'

'And what are you?'

'Nothing in my own eye. In the eye of other people – well, I don't say it; though public thought will out.'

'What do you do on the farm?'

'I do do carting things all the year, and in seed time I shoots the rooks and sparrows, and helps at pig-killing, sir.'

'How much to you?'

'Please nine and ninepence and a good halfpenny where 'twas a bad one, sir – ma'am I mane.'

'Quite correct. Now here are ten shillings in addition as a small present, as I am a new comer.'

Bathsheba blushed slightly at the sense of being generous in public, and Henery Fray, who had drawn up towards her chair, lifted his eyebrows and fingers to express amazement on a small scale.

'How much do I owe you – that man in the corner – what's your name?' continued Bathsheba.

'Matthew Moon, ma'am,' said a singular framework of clothes with

nothing of any consequence inside them, which advanced with the toes in
no definite direction forwards, but turned in or out as they chanced to
swing.

'Matthew Mark, did you say? – speak out – I shall not hurt you,'
inquired the young farmer kindly.

'Matthew Moon, mem,' said Henery Fray, correctingly, from behind
her chair, to which point he had edged himself.

'Matthew Moon,' murmured Bathsheba, turning her bright eyes to
the book. 'Ten and twopence halfpenny is the sum put down to you, I
see?'

'Yes, mis'ess,' said Matthew, as the rustle of wind among dead leaves.

'Here it is, and ten shillings. Now the next – Andrew Randle, you are
a new man, I hear. How came you to leave your last farm?'

'P–p–p–p–p–pl–pl–pl–pl–l–l–l–l–l-ease ma'am, p–p–p–p–pl–pl–pl–
pl–please, ma'am–please'm–please'm –'

''A's a stammering man, mem,' said Henery Fray in an undertone,
'and they turned him away because the only time he ever did speak plain
he said his soul was his own, and other iniquities, to the squire. 'A can
cuss, mem, as well as you or I, but 'a can't speak a common speech to
save his life.'

'Andrew Randle, here's your – finish thanking me in a day or two.
Temperance Miller – oh, here's another, Soberness – both women, I
suppose?'

'Yes'm. Here we be, 'a b'lieve,' was echoed in shrill unison.

'What have you been doing?'

'Tending thrashing-machine, and wimbling haybonds, and saying
"Hoosh!" to the cocks and hens when they go upon your seeds, and
planting Early Flourballs and Thompson's Wonderfuls with a dibble.'

'Yes – I see. Are they satisfactory women?' she inquired softly of
Henery Fray.

'O mem – don't ask me! Yielding women – as scarlet a pair as ever
was!' groaned Henery under his breath.

Far from the Madding Crowd

Having 'agreed for a place', as it is called, either at the fair, or
(occasionally) by private intelligence, or (with growing frequency) by
advertisement in the penny local papers, the terms are usually reduced to
writing: though formerly a written agreement was unknown, and is now,
as a rule, avoided by the farmer if the labourer does not insist upon one.
It is signed by both, and a shilling is passed to bind the bargain. The
business is then settled, and the man returns to his place of work, to do no
more in the matter till Lady Day, Old Style – April 6.

Of all the days in the year, people who love the rural poor of the south-west should pray for a fine day then. Dwellers near the highways of the country are reminded of the anniversary surely enough. They are conscious of a disturbance of their night's rest by noises beginning in the small hours of darkness, and intermittently continuing till daylight – noises as certain to recur on that particular night of the month as the voice of the cuckoo on the third or fourth week of the same. The day of fulfilment has come, and the labourers are on the point of being fetched from the old farm by the carters of the new. For it is always by the waggon and horses of the farmer who requires his services that the hired man is conveyed to his destination; and that this may be accomplished within the day is the reason that the noises begin so soon after midnight. . . . The aim is usually to be at the door of the removing household by six o'clock, when the loading of goods at once begins; and at nine or ten the start to the new home is made.

The goods are built up on the waggon to a well-nigh unvarying pattern, which is probably as peculiar to the country labourer as the hexagon to the bee. The dresser, with its finger-marks and domestic evidences thick upon it, stands importantly in front, over the backs of the shaft horses, in its erect and natural position, like some Ark of the Covenant, which must not be handled slightingly or overturned. The hive of bees is slung up to the axle of the waggon, and alongside it the cooking pot or crock, within which are stowed the roots of garden flowers. Barrels are largely used for crockery, and budding gooseberry bushes are suspended by the roots; while on the top of the furniture a circular nest is made of the bed and bedding for the matron and children, who sit there through the journey. If there is no infant in arms, the woman holds the head of the clock, which at any exceptional lurch of the waggon strikes one, in thin tones. The other object of solicitude is the looking-glass, usually held in the lap of the eldest girl. It is emphatically spoken of as *the* looking-glass, there being but one in the house, except possibly a small shaving-glass for the husband.

The day of removal, if fine, wears an aspect of jollity, and the whole proceeding is a blithe one. A bundle of provisions for the journey is usually hung up at the side of the vehicle, together with a three-pint stone jar of extra strong ale; for it is as impossible to move house without beer as without horses. Roadside inns, too, are patronized, where, during the halt, a mug is seen ascending and descending through the air to and from the feminine portion of the household at the top of the waggon. The drinking at these times is, however, moderate, the beer supplied to travelling labourers being of a preternaturally small brew; as was illustrated by a dialogue which took place on such an occasion quite recently. The liquor was not quite to the taste of the male travellers and they complained. But the landlady upheld its merits. ''Tis our own brewing, and there is nothing in it but malt and hops,' she said, with rectitude. 'Yes, there is,' said the traveller. 'There's water.' 'Oh! I forgot the water,' the landlady replied. 'I'm d–d if you did, mis'ess,' replied the man; 'for there's hardly anything else in the cup.'

Ten or a dozen of these families, with their goods, may be seen halting simultaneously at an out-of-the-way inn, and it is not possible to walk a mile on any of the high roads this day without meeting several. This annual migration from farm to farm is much in excess of what it was formerly. For example, on a particular farm where, a generation ago, not more than one cottage on an average changed occupants yearly, and where the majority remained all their lifetime, the whole number of tenants were changed at Lady Day just past, and this though nearly all of them had been new arrivals on the previous Lady Day. Dorset labourers now look upon an annual removal as the most natural thing in the world, and it becomes with the younger families a pleasant excitement. Change is also a certain sort of education. Many advantages accrue to the labourers from the varied experience it brings, apart from the discovery of the best market for their abilities. They have become shrewder and sharper men of the world, and have learnt how to hold their own with firmness and judgment. Whenever the habitually-removing man comes into contact with one of the old-fashioned stationary sort, who are still to be found, it is impossible not to perceive that the former is much more wide awake than his fellow-worker, astonishing him with stories of the wide world comprised in a twenty-mile radius from their homes.

They are also losing their peculiarities as a class; hence the humorous simplicity which formerly characterized the men and the unsophisticated modesty of the women are rapidly disappearing or lessening, under the constant attrition of lives mildly approximating to those of workers in a manufacturing town. . . . Their brains are less frequently than they once were 'as dry as the remainder biscuit after a voyage', and they vent less often the result of their own observations than what they have heard to be the current ideas of smart chaps in towns. The women have, in many districts, acquired the rollicking air of factory hands. That seclusion and immutability, which was so bad for their pockets, was an unrivalled fosterer of their personal charm in the eyes of those whose experiences had been less limited. But the artistic merit of their old condition is scarcely a reason why they should have continued in it when other communities were marching on so vigorously towards uniformity and mental equality. It is only the old story that progress and picturesqueness do not harmonize. They are losing their individuality, but they are widening the range of their ideas, and gaining in freedom. It is too much to expect them to remain stagnant and old-fashioned for the pleasure of romantic spectators.

'The Dorsetshire Labourer'

9

CRAFTS AND TRADES

A first glance at Hardy's native scene might suggest that the working population was almost exclusively engaged in agriculture – as shepherds, carters, dairymaids or stockmen; or in domestic service – as butlers, footmen, maids, cooks, grooms or coachmen. Certainly they formed the overwhelming majority. A youngster looking for employment in the vicinity of Bockhampton or Puddletown had few other options.

The Hardys themselves stood apart from both these dominant occupations, though with some experience of domestic service in their womenfolk. The Hardy men, as masons, belonged to the smaller and more select group of relatively independent craftsmen, of whom some served the whole community in general terms, like the bootmaker, the barber and indeed the mason; while others were ancillary to agriculture, like the hurdle-maker and the forester.

Though they are drawn on a minor scale Hardy provides an interesting range of sketches of such craftsmen, who were not given much attention in Victorian literature generally. Some of the obvious ones I have omitted, notably the various masons with implications of family biography – Old James Dewy in *Under the Greenwood Tree*, John Smith in *A Pair of Blue Eyes* and Jude 'the obscure'. I have selected those who are shown to us with an insight into the practice of their craft, particularly the more unusual ones.

One or two of these minor figures are tantalizingly slight, even anonymous, like the hollow-turner in *The Woodlanders*. Others, like the maker of boots and shoes, Mr Penny, come to us with the lively eloquence of direct observation. There are the difficult cases of occupations which scarcely qualify as the pursuit of a craft – that of the reddleman, for instance. The subject of reddle must be unique to Hardy and is characteristic of Wessex: I have watched it being quarried in the Mendip Hills. But the transporting and selling of it is not a craftsman's work.

Nor, perhaps, are two somewhat ambiguous occupations that I could not bring myself to exclude – the apple-inventor and the quack doctor. In their defence I must urge that they show those qualities of ingenuity and thoughtful application that distinguish the best of their more orthodox fellows.

The young doctor's practice being scarcely so large as a London surgeon's he frequently walked in the wood. Indeed, such practice as he had he did not follow up with the assiduity that would have been necessary for developing it to exceptional proportions.

One day, book in hand, he went to a part of the wood where the trees were mainly oaks. It was a calm afternoon, and there was everywhere around that sign of great undertakings on the part of vegetable nature which is apt to fill reflective human beings who are not undertaking much themselves with a sudden uneasiness at the contrast. He heard in the distance a curious sound, something like the quack of ducks, which, though it was common enough here about this time, was not common to him.

Looking through the trees Fitzpiers soon perceived the origin of the noise. The barking season had just commenced, and what he had heard was the tear of the ripping-tool as it ploughed its way along the sticky parting between the trunk and the rind. When he got nearer he recognized among the workmen John Upjohn, the two Timothys, and Robert Creedle, who probably had been 'lent' by Winterborne; Marty South also assisted. A milking-pail of cider stood near, a half-pint cup floating on it, with which they dipped and drank whenever they passed the pail.

Each tree doomed to the flaying process was first attacked by Upjohn. With a small bill-hook he carefully freed the collar of the tree from twigs and patches of moss which encrusted it to a height of a foot or two above the ground, an operation comparable to the 'little toilette' of the executioner's victim. After this it was barked in its erect position to a point as high as a man could reach. If a fine product of vegetable nature could ever be said to look ridiculous it was the case now, when the oak stood naked-legged, and as if ashamed, till the axe-man came and cut a ring round it, and the two Timothys finished the work with the cross-cut saw.

As soon as it had fallen the barkers attacked it like locusts, and in a short time not a particle of rind was left on the trunk and larger limbs. Marty South was an adept at peeling the upper parts; and there she stood encaged amid the mass of twigs and buds like a great bird, running her ripping-tool into the smallest branches, beyond the furthest points to which the skill and patience of the men enabled them to proceed – branches which, in their lifetime, had swayed high above the bulk of the wood, and caught the earliest rays of the sun and moon while the lower part of the forest was still in darkness.

'You seem to have a better instrument than they, Marty,' said Fitzpiers.

'No, sir,' she said, holding up the tool, a horse's leg-bone fitted into a handle and filed to an edge; ''tis only that they've less patience with the twigs, because their time is worth more than mine.'

The Woodlanders

Barber Percomb was the chief of his trade in Sherton Abbas. He had the patronage of such county off-shoots as had been obliged to seek the shelter of small houses in that venerable town, of the local clergy, and so on; for some of whom he had made wigs, while others among them had compensated for neglecting him in their lifetime by patronizing him when they were dead, and letting him shave their corpses. On the strength of all this he had taken down his pole and called himself 'Perruquier to the aristocracy.'

Nevertheless, this sort of support did not quite fill his children's mouths, and they had to be filled. So behind his house there was a little yard, reached by a passage from the back street, and in that yard was a pole, and under the pole a shop of quite another description than the ornamental one in the front street. Here on Saturday nights from seven till ten he took an almost innumerable succession of twopences from the farm-labourers who flocked thither in crowds from the country. And thus he lived.

The Woodlanders

''Od rabbit it all!' said Mr Penny, interrupting with a flash of his spectacles, and at the same time clawing at something in the depths of a large side-pocket. 'If so be I hadn't been as scatter-brained and thirtingill as a chiel I should have called at the schoolhouse wi' a boot as I cam up along. Whatever is coming to me I really can't estimate at all!'

'The brain has its weaknesses,' murmured Mr Spinks, waving his head ominously. Mr Spinks was considered to be a scholar, having once kept a night-school, and always spoke up to that level.

'Well, I must call with en the first thing tomorrow. And I'll empt my pocket o' this last too, if you don't mind, Mrs Dewy.' He drew forth a last, and placed it on a table at his elbow. The eyes of three or four followed it.

'Well,' said the shoemaker, seeming to perceive that the interest the object had excited was greater than he had anticipated, and warranted the last's being taken up again and exhibited; 'now, whose foot do ye suppose this last was made for? It was made for Geoffrey Day's father, over at Yalbury Wood. Ah, many's the pair o' boots he've had off the last! Well, when 'a died, I used the last for Geoffrey, and have ever since, though a little doctoring was wanted to make it do. Yes, a very queer natured last it is now, 'a b'lieve,' he continued, turning it over caressingly. 'Now, you notice that there' (pointing to a lump of leather bradded to the toe), 'that's a very bad bunion that he've had ever since 'a was a boy. Now, this remarkable large piece' (pointing to a patch nailed to the side), 'shows a' accident he received by the tread of a horse, that squashed his foot a'most to a pomace. The horse-shoe came full-butt on this point, you see. And so I've just been over to Geoffrey's, to know if he wanted his bunion altered or made bigger in the new pair I'm making.'

During the latter part of this speech Mr Penny's left hand wandered towards the cider-cup as if the hand had no connection with the person speaking; and bringing his sentence to an abrupt close all but the extreme margin of the boot-maker's face was eclipsed by the circular brim of the vessel.

'However, I was going to say,' continued Penny, putting down the cup, 'I ought to have called at the school' – here he went groping again in the depths of his pocket – 'to leave this without fail, though I suppose the first thing to-morrow will do.'

He now drew forth and placed upon the table a boot – small, light, and prettily shaped – upon the heel of which he had been operating.

'The new schoolmistress's!'

'Ay, no less, Miss Fancy Day; as neat a little figure of fun as ever I see and just husband-high.'

'Never Geoffrey's daughter Fancy?' said Bowman, as all glances present converged like wheel-spokes upon the boot in the centre of them.

'Yes, sure,' resumed Mr Penny, regarding the boot as if that alone were his auditor; ''tis she that's come here schoolmistress. You knowed his daughter was in training?'

'Strange, isn't it, for her to be here Christmas-night, Master Penny?'

'Yes; but here she is, 'a b'lieve.'

'I know how she comes here – so I do!' chirruped one of the children.

'Why?' Dick inquired with subtle interest.

'Pa'son Maybold was afraid he couldn't manage us all to-morrow at the dinner, and he talked o' getting her jist to come over and help him hand about the plates, and see we didn't make pigs of ourselves; and that's what she's come for!'

'And that's the boot, then,' continued its mender imaginatively, 'that she'll walk to church in to-morrow morning. I don't care to mend boots I don't make; but there's no knowing what it may lead to, and her father always comes to me.'

There, between the cider-mug and the candle, stood this interesting receptacle of the little unknown's foot; and a very pretty boot it was. A character, in fact – the flexible bend at the instep, the rounded localities of the small nestling toes, scratches from careless scampers now forgotten – all, as repeated in the tell-tale leather, evidencing a nature and a bias. Dick surveyed it with a delicate feeling that he had no right to do so without having first asked the owner of the foot's permission.

'Now, neighbours, though no common eye can see it,' the shoemaker went on, 'a man in the trade can see the likeness between this boot and that last, although that is so deformed as hardly to recall one of God's creatures, and this is one of as pretty a pair as you'd get for ten-and-sixpence in Casterbridge. To you, nothing; but 'tis father's voot and daughter's voot to me, as plain as houses.'

'I don't doubt there's a likeness, Master Penny – a mild likeness – a fantastical likeness,' said Spinks. 'But I han't got imagination enough to see it, perhaps.'

Mr Penny adjusted his spectacles.

'Now, I'll tell ye what happened to me once on this very point. You used to know Johnson the dairyman, William?'

'Ay, sure; I did.'

'Well, 'twasn't opposite his house, but a little lower down – by his paddock, in front o' Parkmaze Pool. I was a-bearing across towards Bloom's End, and lo and behold, there was a man just brought out o' the Pool, dead; he had un'rayed for a dip, but not being able to pitch it just there had gone in flop over his head. Men looked at en; women looked at en; children looked at en; nobody knowed en. He was covered wi' a sheet; but I catched sight of his voot, just showing out as they carried en along. "I don't care what name that man went by," I said, in my way, "but he's John Woodward's brother; I can swear to the family voot." At that very moment up comes John Woodward, weeping and teaving, "I've lost my brother! I've lost my brother!"'

'Only to think of that!' said Mrs Dewy.

Under the Greenwood Tree

In the room from which this cheerful blaze proceeded he beheld a girl seated on a willow chair, and busily working by the light of the fire, which was ample and of wood. With a bill-hook in one hand and a leather glove, much too large for her, on the other, she was making spars, such as are used by thatchers, with great rapidity. She wore a leather apron for this purpose, which was also much too large for her figure. On her left hand lay a bundle of the straight, smooth hazel rods called spar-gads – the raw material of her manufacture; on her right, a heap of chips and ends – the refuse – with which the fire was maintained; in front, a pile of the finished articles. To produce them she took up each gad, looked critically at it from end to end, cut it to length, split it into four, and sharpened each of the quarters with dexterous blows, which brought it to a triangular point precisely resembling that of a bayonet.

The Woodlanders

Between six and seven o'clock in the evening of the same day a young man descended the hills into the valley of the Exe, at a point about midway between Silverthorn and the residence of Margery's grand-mother, four miles to the east.

He was a thoroughbred son of the country, as far removed from what is known as the provincial, as the latter is from the out-and-out gentleman of culture. His trousers and waistcoat were of fustian, almost white, but he wore a jacket of old-fashioned blue West-of-England cloth, so well preserved that evidently the article was relegated to a box whenever its owner engaged in such active occupations as he usually pursued. His complexion was fair, almost florid, and he had scarcely any beard.

A novel attraction about this young man, which a glancing stranger would know nothing of, was a rare and curious freshness of atmosphere that appertained to him, to his clothes, to all his belongings, even to the room in which he had been sitting. It might almost have been said that by adding him and his implements to an over-crowded apartment you made it healthful. This resulted from his trade. He was a lime-burner; he handled lime daily; and in return the lime rendered him an incarnation of salubrity. His hair was dry, fair, and frizzled, the latter possibly by the operation of the same caustic agent. He carried as a walking-stick a green sapling, whose growth had been contorted to a corkscrew pattern by a twining honeysuckle.

'The Romantic Adventures of a Milkmaid'

Though few knew of it, Giles had had a serious illness during the winter; but it just now happened that after being for a long time apathetic and unemployed on that account, he had become one of the busiest men in the neighbourhood. It is often thus; fallen friends, lost sight of, we expect to find starving; we discover them going on fairly well. Without any

solicitation or desire to profit on his part, he had been asked to execute a
very large order for hurdles and other copseware, for which purpose he
had been obliged to buy several acres of hazel brushwood standing. He
was now engaged in the cutting and manufacture of the same, proceeding
with the work daily like an automaton.

The hazel-tree did not belie its name to-day. The whole of the
copsewood where the mist had cleared returned purest tints of that hue,
amid which Winterborne himself was in the act of making a hurdle, the
stakes being driven firmly into the ground in a row, over which he bent
and wove the twigs. Beside him was a square, compact pile like the altar
of Cain, formed of hurdles already finished, which bristled on all sides
with the sharp points of their stakes. At a little distance the men in his
employ were assisting him to carry out his contract. Rows of brushwood
lay on the ground as it had fallen under the axe; and a shelter had been
constructed near at hand, in front of which burnt the fire whose smoke
had attracted Melbury. The air was so dank that the smoke hung heavily,
and crept away amid the bushes without rising from the ground.

The Woodlanders

'Cainy's grandfather was a very clever man,' said Matthew Moon.
'Invented a' apple-tree out of his own head, which is called by his name
to this day – the Early Ball. You know 'em, Jan? A Quarrenden grafted
on a Tom Putt, and a Rathe-ripe upon top o' that again. 'Tis trew 'a used
to bide about in a public-house wi' a 'ooman in a way he had no business
to by rights, but there – 'a were a clever man in the sense of the term.'

Far from the Madding Crowd

Vilbert was an itinerant quack-doctor, well known to the rustic
population, and absolutely unknown to anybody else, as he, indeed, took
care to be, to avoid inconvenient investigations. Cottagers formed his
only patients, and his Wessex-wide repute was among them alone. His
position was humbler and his field more obscure than those of the quacks
with capital and an organized system of advertising. He was, in fact, a
survival. The distances he traversed on foot were enormous, and
extended nearly the whole length and breadth of Wessex. Jude had one
day seen him selling a pot of coloured lard to an old woman as a certain
cure for a bad leg, the woman arranging to pay a guinea, in instalments of
a shilling a fortnight, for the precious salve, which, according to the
physician, could only be obtained from a particular animal which grazed
on Mount Sinai, and was to be captured only at great risk to life and
limb.

Jude the Obscure

10

INN AND MALTHOUSE

In its traditional image the English inn tends to express itself in terms of coaches and horses; and the rural malthouse, tavern or beerhouse – the village pub as we now know it – provides a scene of sage elderly peasants dispensing folk-wisdom in rich dialect. As a Victorian novelist using rustic settings and characters Hardy might be expected to nourish and augment these prevailing stereotypes, and in some respects he does so. In *Far from the Madding Crowd*, particularly, the scenes in Warren's Malthouse and the Buck's Head are masterpieces of their kind.

There are, however, important distinctions to be made since the source of Hardy's descriptions was first-hand experience. He was essentially a child of the railway age. The long-distance horse-drawn stage coach was already in decline in his boyhood and the roadside coaching inns were facing ruin. He collected reminiscences of that dying world, and in later years he prophesied a revival as the roads began to stir with the new figures of cyclists and motorists. In his own formative years it was the short local journeys of the tranter and the tradesman's waggon that still found a public use for the horse. Where the historical background of a novel required a character to travel by coach – as Newson did in *The Mayor of Casterbridge* and Matilda Johnson might have done in *The Trumpet-Major* – Hardy confined himself to the essentials, having no personal experience to add a richer lustre.

Drinking in convivial company was similarly passing through a period of transition during Hardy's early years. The workfolk and the small traders would be likely to brew their own ale and cider, and perhaps also some mead and the familiar country wines of elderberry, dandelion and parsnip. Whatever was brewed at home would be drunk at home or in the fields during the working day. More memorable tipples would take place at barn dances or special festivals. The rise of the public house as the poor man's club was in progress but still as a rather innovative competitor with the older practices. The commercial breweries had by no means replaced the home-brewing so vividly described in *Under the Greenwood Tree* or the unofficial sale of home-brewed ale at Rolliver's in *Tess of the d'Urbervilles*.

Rolliver's is particularly interesting as a survival of what young Henry VIII's tutor, John Skelton, described in his poem 'The Tunning of Elinor Rumming'. In nineteenth-century terms Rolliver's held an off-licence only and was therefore breaking the law in allowing its customers to drink on the premises. It was in quite a different category from the Pure Drop tavern, in another part of Marlott, which was fully licensed but offered a less attractive ale – the more standardized product perhaps of one of the commercial breweries. This blend of contrasting social patterns would have been typical of Hardy's native setting during his young manhood.

Those hostelries that came most readily under his observation were those in Dorchester – notably The King's Arms, The Three Mariners and The Phoenix – and the two closest to his home, The Buck's Head and The Traveller's Rest. The Buck's Head was at Troy Town on the London road west of Puddletown. The Traveller's Rest is shown on the first Ordnance Survey map near Ilsington farm on the Tincleton road: it subsequently became the Duck Dairy House. Hardy made it the location of the inn known as 'The Quiet Woman' in *The Return of the Native*. Stinsford seems not to have had a licensed house and perhaps found consolation in an equivalent of Rolliver's. Puddletown was the location of Warren's Malthouse.

In Hardy's first published novel, *Desperate Remedies*, one of the important locations in the development of the plot is an inn, The Three Tranters, which seems to have a composite derivation from The Three Mariners in Dorchester and The Buck's Head at Troy Town. The description of its signboard is very similar to that of The Three Mariners, and the unusual situation of the board – suspended from an elm tree – links it closely with The Buck's Head, which displayed its sign in the same manner.

In many instances the inns and pubs in Hardy's stories occur incidentally as a normal feature in town or village, second only to the church as landmark and meeting-place. The Earl of Wessex inn at Sherton Abbas in *The Woodlanders*, for example, provides accommodation and refreshment for Fitzpiers and Grace and an exterior setting for Winterborne's cider-making, but the inner life of the bar parlour passes unnoticed. For scenes of that sort we must return to Hardy's home territory, to the little groups of regulars who gathered to gossip together at The Mariners, The Buck's Head, The Quiet Woman and Warren's Malthouse. It is here that Hardy conjures up the authentic Dorset voices of his native community, in such lofty flights as Jan Coggan's assessment of church and chapel or in the more earthy welcome given to the new shepherd, Gabriel Oak. Some of these conversations pursue themes which locate them more appropriately in other chapters of this book but I have included here a representative scene at Warren's Malthouse.

The Three Tranters Inn ... was an uncommonly characteristic and handsome specimen of the genuine roadside inn of bygone times; and standing on one of the great highways in this part of England, had in its time been the scene of as much of what is now looked upon as the romantic and genial experience of stage-coach travelling as any halting-place in the country. The railway had absorbed the whole stream of traffic which formerly flowed through the village and along by the ancient door of the inn.

Desperate Remedies

The Buck's Head was a somewhat unusual place for a man of this sort to choose as a house of sojourn in preference to some Casterbridge inn four miles further on. Before he left home it had been a lively old tavern at which High-flyers, and Heralds, and Tally-hoes had changed horses on their stages up and down the country; but now the house was rather cavernous and chilly, the stable-roofs were hollow-backed, the landlord was asthmatic, and the traffic gone.

'The Waiting Supper'

At the roadside hamlet called Roy-Town, just beyond this wood, was the old inn Buck's Head. It was about a mile and a half from Weatherbury, and in the meridian times of stage-coach travelling had been the place where many coaches changed and kept their relays of horses. All the old stabling was now pulled down, and little remained besides the habitable inn itself, which, standing a little way back from the road, signified its existence to people far up and down the highway by a sign hanging from the horizontal bough of an elm on the opposite side of the way.

Travellers – for the variety tourist had hardly developed into a

distinct species at this date – sometimes said in passing, when they cast
their eyes up to the sign-bearing tree, that artists were fond of
representing the signboard hanging thus, but that they themselves had
never before noticed so perfect an instance in actual working order. It was
near this tree that the waggon was standing into which Gabriel Oak crept
on his first journey to Weatherbury; but, owing to the darkness, the sign
and the inn had been unobserved.

The manners of the inn were of the old-established type. Indeed, in
the minds of its frequenters they existed as unalterable formulae: e.g. –

Rap with the bottom of your pint for more liquor.
For tobacco, shout.
In calling for the girl in waiting, say, 'Maid!'
Ditto for the landlady, 'Old Soul!' etc., etc.

Far from the Madding Crowd

Rolliver's inn, the single alehouse at this end of the long and broken
village, could only boast of an off-licence; hence, as nobody could legally
drink on the premises, the amount of overt accommodation for consumers
was strictly limited to a little board about six inches wide and two yards
long, fixed to the garden palings by pieces of wire, so as to form a ledge.
On this board thirsty strangers deposited their cups as they stood in the
road and drank, and threw the dregs on the dusty ground to the pattern
of Polynesia, and wished they could have a restful seat inside.

Thus the strangers. But there were also local customers who felt the
same wish; and where there's a will there's a way.

In a large bedroom upstairs, the window of which was thickly
curtained with a great woollen shawl lately discarded by the landlady
Mrs Rolliver, were gathered on this evening nearly a dozen persons, all
seeking beatitude; all old inhabitants of the nearer end of Marlott, and
frequenters of this retreat. Not only did the distance to The Pure Drop,
the fully-licensed tavern at the further part of the dispersed village,
render its accommodation practically unavailable for dwellers at this end;
but the far more serious question, the quality of the liquor, confirmed the
prevalent opinion that it was better to drink with Rolliver in a corner of
the housetop than with the other landlord in a wide house.

A gaunt four-post bedstead which stood in the room afforded sitting-
space for several persons gathered round three of its sides; a couple more
men had elevated themselves on a chest of drawers; another rested on the
oak-carved 'cwoffer'; two on the wash-stand; another on the stool; and
thus all were, somehow, seated at their ease. The stage of mental comfort
to which they had arrived at this hour was one wherein their souls
expanded beyond their skins, and spread their personalities warmly

through the room. In this process the chamber and its furniture grew more and more dignified and luxurious; the shawl hanging at the window took upon itself the richness of tapestry; the brass handles of the chest of drawers were as golden knockers; and the carved bedposts seemed to have some kinship with the magnificent pillars of Solomon's temple.

Mrs Durbeyfield, having quickly walked hitherward after parting from Tess, opened the front door, crossed the downstairs room, which was in deep gloom, and then unfastened the stair-door like one whose fingers knew the tricks of the latches well. Her ascent of the crooked staircase was a slower process, and her face, as it rose into the light above the last stair, encountered the gaze of all the party assembled in the bedroom.

' – Being a few private friends I've asked in to keep up club-walking at my own expense,' the landlady exclaimed at the sound of footsteps, as glibly as a child repeating the Catechism, while she peered over the stairs. 'Oh, 'tis you, Mrs Durbeyfield - Lard – how you frightened me! – I thought it might be some gaffer sent by Gover'ment.'

Tess of the d'Urbervilles

This going to hunt up her shiftless husband at the inn was one of Mrs Durbeyfield's still extant enjoyments in the muck and muddle of rearing children. To discover him at Rolliver's, to sit there for an hour or two by his side and dismiss all thought and care of the children during the interval, made her happy. A sort of halo, an occidental glow, came over life then. Troubles and other realities took on themselves a metaphysical impalpability, sinking to mere mental phenomena for serene contemplation, and no longer stood as pressing concretions which chafed body and soul. The youngsters, not immediately within sight, seemed rather bright and desirable appurtenances than otherwise; the incidents of daily life were not without humorousness and jollity in their aspect there. She felt a little as she had used to feel when she sat by her now wedded husband in the same spot during his wooing, shutting her eyes to his defects of character, and regarding him only in his ideal presentation as lover.

Tess of the d'Urbervilles

This ancient house [The Three Mariners] of accommodation for man and beast, now, unfortunately, pulled down, was built of mellow sandstone, with mullioned windows of the same material, markedly out of perpendicular from the settlement of foundations. The bay window projecting into the street, whose interior was so popular among the frequenters of the inn, was closed with shutters, in each of which appeared a heart-shaped aperture, somewhat more attenuated in the right and left ventricles than is seen in Nature. Inside these illuminated holes at a distance of about three inches, were ranged at this hour, as every passer knew, the ruddy polls of Billy Wills the glazier, Smart the shoemaker, Buzzford the general dealer, and others of a secondary set of worthies, of a grade somewhat below that of the diners at the King's Arms, each with his yard of clay.

A four-centred Tudor arch was over the entrance, and over the arch the signboard, now visible in the rays of an opposite lamp. Hereon the Mariners, who had been represented by the artist as persons of two dimensions only – in other words, flat as a shadow – were standing in a row in paralyzed attitudes. Being on the sunny side of the street, the three comrades had suffered largely from warping, splitting, fading, and shrinkage, so that they were but a half-invisible film upon the reality of the grain, and knots, and nails, which composed the signboard. As a matter of fact, this state of things was not so much owing to Stannidge the landlord's neglect, as from the lack of a painter in Casterbridge who would undertake to reproduce the features of men so traditional.

A long, narrow, dimly-lit passage gave access to the inn, within which passage the horses going to their stalls at the back, and the coming and departing human guests, rubbed shoulders indiscriminately, the latter running no slight risk of having their toes trodden upon by the animals. The good stabling and the good ale of the Mariners, though somewhat difficult to reach on account of there being but this narrow way to both, were nevertheless perseveringly sought out by the sagacious old heads who knew what was what in Casterbridge.

The Mayor of Casterbridge

Men drank, smoked, and spat in the inns with only a little more adulteration in their refreshments and a trifle less dialect in their speech than of yore.

The Well-Beloved

Warren's Malthouse was enclosed by an old wall inwrapped with ivy, and though not much of the exterior was visible at this hour, the character and purposes of the building were clearly enough shown by its outline upon the sky. From the walls an overhanging thatched roof sloped up to a point in the centre, upon which rose a small wooden lantern, fitted with louvre-boards on all the four sides, and from these openings a mist was dimly perceived to be escaping into the night air. There was no window in front; but a square hole in the door was glazed with a single pane, through which red, comfortable rays now stretched out upon the ivied wall in front. Voices were to be heard inside.

Oak's hand skimmed the surface of the door with fingers extended to
an Elymas-the-Sorcerer pattern, till he found a leathern strap, which he
pulled. This lifted a wooden latch, and the door swung open.

The room inside was lighted only by the ruddy glow from the kiln
mouth, which shone over the floor with the streaming horizontality of the
setting sun, and threw upwards the shadows of all facial irregularities in
those assembled around. The stone-flag floor was worn into a path from
the doorway to the kiln, and into undulations everywhere. A curved settle
of unplaned oak stretched along one side, and in a remote corner was a
small bed and bedstead, the owner and frequent occupier of which was
the maltster.

This aged man was now sitting opposite the fire, his frosty white hair
and beard overgrowing his gnarled figure like the grey moss and lichen
upon a leafless apple-tree. He wore breeches and the laced-up shoes
called ankle-jacks; he kept his eyes fixed upon the fire.

Gabriel's nose was greeted by an atmosphere laden with the sweet
smell of new malt. The conversation (which seemed to have been
concerning the origin of the fire) immediately ceased, and every one
ocularly criticized him to the degree expressed by contracting the flesh of
their foreheads and looking at him with narrowed eyelids, as if he had
been a light too strong for their sight. Several exclaimed meditatively
after this operation had been completed: –

'Oh, 'tis the new shepherd, 'a b'lieve.'

'We thought we heard a hand pawing about the door for the bobbin,
but weren't sure 'twere not a dead leaf blowed across,' said another.
'Come in, shepherd; sure ye be welcome, though we don't know yer
name.'

'Gabriel Oak, that's my name, neighbours.'

The ancient maltster sitting in the midst turned at this – his turning
being as the turning of a rusty crane.

'That's never Gable Oak's grandson over at Norcombe – never!' he
said, as a formula expressive of surprise, which nobody was supposed to
take literally.

'My father and my grandfather were old men of the name of Gabriel,'
said the shepherd placidly.

'Thought I knowed the man's face as I seed him on the rick! – thought
I did! And where be ye trading o't to now, shepherd?'

'I'm thinking of biding here,' said Mr Oak.

'Knowed yer grandfather for years and years!' continued the maltster,
the words coming forth of their own accord as if the momentum
previously imparted had been sufficient.

'Ah – and did you!'

'Knowed yer grandmother.'

'And her too!'

'Likewise knowed yer father when he was a child. Why, my boy Jacob there and your father were sworn brothers – that they were sure – weren't ye, Jacob?'

'Ay, sure,' said his son, a young man about sixty-five, with a semi-bald head and one tooth in the left centre of his upper jaw, which made much of itself by standing prominent, like a milestone in a bank. 'But 'twas Joe had most to do with him. However, my son William must have knowed the very man afore us – didn't ye, Billy, afore ye left Norcombe?'

'No, 'twas Andrew,' said Jacob's son Billy, a child of forty, or thereabouts, who manifested the peculiarity of possessing a cheerful soul in a gloomy body, and whose whiskers were assuming a chinchilla shade here and there.

'I can mind Andrew,' said Oak, 'as being a man in the place when I was quite a child.'

'Ay – the other day I and my youngest daughter, Liddy, were over at my grandson's christening,' continued Billy. 'We were talking about this very family, and 'twas only last Purification Day in this very world, when the use-money is gied away to the second-best poor folk, you know, shepherd, and I can mind the day because they all had to traypse up to the vestry – yes, this very man's family.'

'Come, shepherd, and drink. 'Tis gape and swaller with us – a drap of sommit, but not of much account,' said the maltster, removing from the fire his eyes, which were vermillion-red and bleared by gazing into it for so many years. 'Take up the God-forgive-me, Jacob. See if 'tis warm, Jacob.'

Jacob stooped to the God-forgive-me, which was a two-handled tall mug standing in the ashes, cracked and charred with heat: it was rather furred with extraneous matter about the outside, especially in the crevices of the handles, the innermost curves of which may not have seen daylight for several years by reason of this encrustation thereon – formed of ashes accidentally wetted with cider and baked hard; but to the mind of any sensible drinker the cup was no worse for that, being incontestably clean on the inside and about the rim. It may be observed that such a class of mug is called a God-forgive-me in Weatherbury and its vicinity for uncertain reasons; probably because its size makes any given toper feel ashamed of himself when he sees its bottom in drinking it empty.

Jacob, on receiving the order to see if the liquor was warm enough, placidly dipped his forefinger into it by way of thermometer, and having pronounced it nearly of the proper degree, raised the cup and very civilly attempted to dust some of the ashes from the bottom with the skirt of his smock-frock, because Shepherd Oak was a stranger.

'A clane cup for the shepherd,' said the maltster commandingly.

'No – not at all,' said Gabriel, in a reproving tone of considerateness. 'I never fuss about dirt in its pure state, and when I know what sort it is.'

Taking the mug he drank an inch or more from the depth of its contents, and duly passed it to the next man. 'I wouldn't think of giving such trouble to neighbours in washing up when there's so much work to be done in the world already,' continued Oak in a moister tone, after recovering from the stoppage of breath which is occasioned by pulls at large mugs.

'A right sensible man,' said Jacob.

'True, true; it can't be gainsaid!' observed a brisk young man – Mark Clark by name, a genial and pleasant gentleman, whom to meet anywhere in your travels was to know, to know was to drink with, and to drink with was, unfortunately, to pay for.

'And here's a mouthful of bread and bacon that mis'ess have sent, shepherd. The cider will go down better with a bit of victuals. Don't ye chaw quite close, shepherd, for I let the bacon fall in the road outside as I was bringing it along, and may be 'tis rather gritty. There, 'tis clane dirt; and we all know what that is, as you say, and you bain't a particular man we see, shepherd.'

'True, true – not at all,' said the friendly Oak.

'Don't let your teeth quite meet, and you won't feel the sandiness at all. Ah! 'tis wonderful what can be done by contrivance!'

'My own mind exactly, neighbour.'

'Ah, he's his grandfer's own grandson! – his grandfer were just such a nice unparticular man!' said the maltster.

'Drink, Henry Fray – drink,' magnanimously said Jan Coggan, a person who held Saint-Simonian notions of share and share alike where liquor was concerned, as the vessel showed signs of approaching him in its gradual revolution among them.

Having at this moment reached the end of a wistful gaze into mid-air, Henry did not refuse. He was a man of more than middle age, with eyebrows high up in his forehead, who laid it down that the law of the world was bad, with a long-suffering look through his listeners at the world alluded to, as it presented itself to his imagination. He always signed his name 'Henery' – strenuously insisting upon that spelling, and if any passing schoolmaster ventured to remark that the second 'e' was superfluous and old-fashioned, he received the reply that 'H–e–n–e–r–y' was the name he was christened and the name he would stick to – in the tone of one to whom orthographical differences were matters which had a great deal to do with personal character.

Mr Jan Coggan, who had passed the cup to Henery, was a crimson man with a spacious countenance and private glimmer in his eye, whose name had appeared on the marriage register of Weatherbury and neighbouring parishes as best man and chief witness in countless unions of the previous twenty years; he also very frequently filled the post of head godfather in baptisms of the subtly-jovial kind.

'Come, Mark Clark – come. Ther's plenty more in the barrel,' said Jan.

'Ay – that I will; 'tis my only doctor,' replied Mr Clark, who, twenty years younger than Jan Coggan, revolved in the same orbit. He secreted mirth on all occasions for special discharge at popular parties.

'Why, Joseph Poorgrass, ye han't had a drop!' said Mr Coggan to a self-conscious man in the background, thrusting the cup towards him.

'Such a modest man as he is!' said Jacob Smallbury. 'Why, ye've hardly had strength of eye enough to look in our young mis'ess's face, so I hear, Joseph?'

All looked at Joseph Poorgrass with pitying reproach.

'No – I've hardly looked at her at all,' simpered Joseph, reducing his body smaller whilst talking, apparently from a meek sense of undue prominence. 'And when I seed her, 'twas nothing but blushes with me!'

'Poor feller,' said Mr Clark.

''Tis a curious nature for a man,' said Jan Coggan.

'Yes,' continued Joseph Poorgrass – his shyness, which was so painful as a defect, filling him with a mild complacency now that it was regarded as an interesting study. ''Twere blush, blush, blush with me every minute of the time, when she was speaking to me.'

'I believe ye, Joseph Poorgrass, for we all know ye to be a very bashful man.'

''Tis a' awkward gift for a man, poor soul,' said the maltster. 'And ye have suffered from it a long time, we know.'

'Ay, ever since I was a boy. Yes – mother was concerned to her heart about it – yes. But 'twas all for nought.'

'Did ye ever go into the world to try and stop it, Joseph Poorgrass?'

'Oh ay, tried all sorts o' company. They took me to Greenhill Fair, and into a great gay jerry-go-nimble show, where there were women-folk riding round – standing upon horses, with hardly anything on but their smocks; but it didn't cure me a morsel. And then I was put errand-man at the Women's Skittle Alley at the back of the Tailor's Arms in Casterbridge. 'Twas a horrible sinful situation, and a very curious place for a good man. I had to stand and look ba'dy people in the face from morning till night; but 'twas no use – I was just as bad as ever after all. Blushes hev been in the family for generations. There, 'tis a happy providence that I be no worse.'

'True,' said Jacob Smallbury, deepening his mind to a profounder view of the subject. ''Tis a thought to look at, that ye might have been worse; but even as you be, 'tis a very bad affliction for 'ee, Joseph. For ye see, shepherd, though 'tis very well for a woman, dang it all, 'tis awkward for a man like him, poor feller?'

''Tis – 'tis,' said Gabriel, recovering from a meditation. 'Yes, very awkward for the man.'

'Ay, and he's very timid, too,' observed Jan Coggan. 'Once he had been working late at Yalbury Bottom, and had had a drap of drink, and lost his way as he was coming home-along through Yalbury Wood, didn't ye, Master Poorgrass?'

'No, no, no; not that story!' expostulated the modest man, forcing a laugh to bury his concern.

' – And so 'a lost himself quite,' continued Mr Coggan, with an impassive face, implying that a true narrative, like time and tide, must run its course and would respect no man. 'And as he was coming along in the middle of the night, much afeared, and not able to find his way out of the trees nohow, 'a cried out, "Man-a-lost! man-a-lost!" A owl in a tree happened to be crying "Whoo-whoo-whoo!" as owls do, you know, shepherd' (Gabriel nodded), 'and Joseph, all in a tremble, said, "Joseph Poorgrass, of Weatherbury, sir!"'

'No, no, now – that's too much!' said the timid man, becoming a man of brazen courage all of a sudden. 'I didn't say *sir*. I'll take my oath I didn't say "Joseph Poorgrass o' Weatherbury, sir." No, no; what's right is right, and I never said sir to the bird, knowing very well that no man of a gentleman's rank would be hollering there at that time o' night. "Joseph Poorgrass of Weatherbury," – that's every word I said, and I shouldn't ha' said that if't hadn't been for Keeper Day's metheglin . . . There, 'twas a merciful thing it ended where it did'.

Far from the Madding Crowd

11

CHURCH AND CHAPEL

A 'churchy' man was Hardy's own description of himself. He was brought up strictly within the faith and practice of the Anglican church. By the age of fifteen he was well enough qualified to teach in the parish's Sunday School, and his knowledge of the Bible was such that his writings draw on it more readily and aptly than those of any other English author – so much so that his literary style, in cadence and phrasing, shows a clear biblical influence. Caught up as he was in early manhood in the great Victorian debate on Darwinian evolution and the enlargements of geological time and interstellar space, Hardy moved closer to his agnostic and rationalist friends; but the seminal power of his Anglican heritage persisted.

One of his childhood games was to play at being a parson, using a chair as a pulpit, a tablecloth as a surplice, and reading the morning service to a congregation consisting of his grandmother, with his cousin as the parson's clerk supplying loud 'Amens'. The thought that he might one day take holy orders persisted as a possibility in the later years of indecision about the career he should follow. The role of parson carried important advantages of book knowledge and social status which corresponded with Hardy's aspirations.

The local clergy of his youth often enjoyed a prestige in village life second only to that of the squire, with whom they were frequently related. It was common practice for a country living to be in the gift of one of the great landowners in the neighbourhood, acquired by him as a social niche and reliable income for one of his sons or the husband of one of his daughters. Such a parson would have his acknowledged rank

in the gentry of the county and would live in the style to which he had
been bred. A typical example was The Reverend Edward Murray,
presented in 1822 to the living of Stinsford by his kinsman the Earl of
Ilchester. Murray happened to be an ardent musician and encouraged
Hardy's father, uncle and grandfather to go to his house and practise
their string-playing with him. This long-established association of the
Hardys with their vicar and their parish church was deeply imprinted
on young Thomas.

When he came to write about Wessex life Hardy gave full weight to
the importance of the parson in the social pattern of events. Drawing
on his early experience he produced such a gallery of diverse portraits
that he must be counted a connoisseur of the clerical character. Where
the clergy are so often treated in a stereotyped manner Hardy, by
contrast, showed the range of their humanity, extending from the
almost saintly conduct of John Aumbry in 'A Changed Man' and Angel
Clare's father in *Tess of the d'Urbervilles* to the unlovable young clerics in
'A Tragedy of Two Ambitions' and 'The Son's Veto'. In between those
extremes we meet parsons who delight in hunting or pursue
antiquarian interests or catch our attention briefly by simple
kindnesses to the poor, like Parson Thirdly with his gift of seed
potatoes in *Far from the Madding Crowd*. And in his portrayals Hardy calls
on the leavening of rustic humour and ancient wisdom that informs the
parishioners' comfortable relationship with their pastors, in which so
much can be implied and left unsaid. When The Reverend Mr
Torkingham conducts a choir practice in *Two on a Tower* it is by no
means clear who is in charge.

The lesser officials of the church are not overlooked: the clerk and
the sexton are commemorated. So too is the church's annexe to
eternity, the graveyard – a place by no means as silent as your matter-
of-fact reader might expect. Within the church itself Hardy finds topics
for his pen in the view from the gallery of the congregation below, in a
confirmation service, and in the welcome distractions that accompany
an afternoon sermon. Even an unnamed memorial brass has its
moment of eloquence.

Though it was the church that provided Hardy with so rich a
subject-matter he did not overlook the other religious force in the rural
parishes of his native area. The various nonconformist persuasions
were strongly represented and he admired the dutiful attendance and
staunch conviction of the chapel-goers – and, not least, the ability, in
Jan Coggan's words, to 'lift up beautiful prayers out of their own heads,
all about their families and shipwracks in the newspaper'.

The stress of philosophical argument and lapsed belief belong to
the larger and later world that Hardy entered, when Reason made
meaningless 'the coded creeds of old-time godliness'; but there is one

early disputation, in *Desperate Remedies*, with which I can conclude this chapter. The postman's conviction that 'Goddymity' would soon be done away with is a typical reminder that some of the workfolk had also their own style of scepticism and gave no loyalty to either church or chapel.

I myself as a child, brought up according to strict Church principles, devoutly believed in the devil's pitchfork.

Letter to William Blackwood, 29 February 1892

'To succeed in the Church, people must believe in you, first of all, as a gentleman, secondly as a man of means, thirdly as a scholar, fourthly as a preacher, fifthly, perhaps, as a Christian – but always first as a gentleman, with all their heart and soul and strength.'

'A Tragedy of Two Ambitions'

'O, they [in Christminster] never look at anything that folks like we can understand,' the carter continued, by way of passing the time. 'On'y foreign tongues used in the days of the Tower of Babel, when no two families spoke alike. They read that sort of thing as fast as a night-hawk will whir. 'Tis all learning there – nothing but learning, except religion. And that's learning too, for I never could understand it. Yes, 'tis a serious-minded place. Not but there's wenches in the streets o' nights . . . You know, I suppose, that they raise pa'sons there like radishes in a bed? And though it do take – how many years, Bob? – five years to turn a lirruping hobble-de-hoy chap into a solemn preaching man with no corrupt passions, they'll do it, if it can be done, and polish un off like the workmen they be, and turn un out wi' a long face, and a long black coat and waistcoat, and a religious collar and hat, same as they used to wear in the Scriptures, so that his own mother wouldn't know un sometimes . . . There, 'tis their business, like anybody else's.'

Jude the Obscure

'We are thinking of making Joseph a parson,' said Mrs Chickerel.
    'Indeed! a parson.'
    'Yes; 'tis a genteel living for the boy. And he's talents that way. Since he has been under masters he knows all the strange sounds the old Romans and Greeks used to make by way of talking, and the love stories

of the ancient women as if they were his own. I assure you, Mr Julian, if
you could hear how beautiful the boy tells about little Cupid with his bow
and arrows, and the rows between that pagan apostle Jupiter and his wife
because of another woman, and the handsome young gods who kissed
Venus, you'd say he deserved to be made a bishop at once!'

The Hand of Ethelberta

'Now, we'll begin,' interrupted Mr Torkingham, his mind returning to
this world again on concluding his search for a hymn.

Thereupon the racket of chair-legs on the floor signified that they
were settling into their seats. The parson announced the tune, and his
voice burst forth with 'Onward Christian soldiers!' in notes of rigid
cheerfulness.

In this start, however, he was joined only by the girls and boys, the
men furnishing but an accompaniment of ahas and hems. Mr
Torkingham stopped, and Sammy Blore spoke, –

'Beg your pardon, sir, – if you'll deal mild with us a moment. What
with the wind and walking, my throat's as rough as a grater; and not
knowing you were going to hit up that minute, I hadn't hawked, and I
don't think Hezzy and Nat had, either, – had ye, souls?'

'I hadn't got thorough ready, that's true,' said Hezekiah.

'Quite right of you, then, to speak,' said Mr Torkingham. 'Don't
mind explaining; we are here for practice. Now clear your throats, then,
and at it again.'

There was a noise as of atmospheric hoes and scrapers, and the bass
contingent at last got under way with a time of its own:

'Honwerd, Christen sojers!'

'Ah, that's where we are so defective – the pronunciation,' interrupted
the parson. 'Now repeat after me: "On-ward, Christ-ian, sol-diers."'

The choir repeated like an exaggerative echo: 'On-wed, Chris-tine,
sol-jaws!'

'Better!' said the parson, in the strenuously sanguine tones of a man
who got his living by discovering a bright side in things where it was not
very perceptible to other people. 'But it should not be given with quite so
extreme an accent; or we may be called affected by other parishes. And,
Nathaniel Chapman, there's a jauntiness in your manner of singing
which is not quite becoming. Why don't you sing more earnestly?'

'My conscience won't let me, sir. They say every man for himself: but,
thank God, I'm not so mean as to lessen old fokes' chances by being
earnest at my time o' life, and they so much nearer the need o't.'

'It's bad reasoning, Nat, I fear. Now, perhaps we had better sol-fa the
tune. Eyes on your books, please. *Sol-sol! fa-fa! mi'* –

'I can't sing like that, not I!' said Sammy Blore, with condemnatory astonishment. 'I can sing genuine music, like F and G; but not anything so much out of the order of nater as that.'

'Perhaps you've brought the wrong book, sir?' chimed in Haymoss, kindly. 'I've knowed music early in life and late, – in short, ever since Luke Sneap broke his new fiddle-bow in the wedding psalm, when Pa'son Wilton brought home his bride (you can mind the time, Sammy? – when we sung "His wife, like a fair fertile vine, her lovely fruit shall bring," when the young woman turned as red as a rose, not knowing 'twas coming). I've knowed music ever since then, I say, sir, and never heard the like o' that. Every martel note had his name of A, B, C, at that time.'

'Yes, yes, men; but this is a more recent system!'

'Still, you can't alter a old-established note that's A or B by nater,' rejoined Haymoss, with yet deeper conviction that Mr Torkingham was getting off his head. 'Now sound A, neighbour Sammy, and let's have a slap at Christen sojers again, and show the Pa'son the true way!'

Two on a Tower

'"These hosses of yours, sir, will be much improved by this!" says the clerk as he rode along, just a neck behind the pa'son. "'Twas a happy thought of your reverent mind to bring 'em out to-day. Why, it may be frosty and slippery in a day or two, and then the poor things mid not be able to leave the stable for weeks."

'"They may not, they may not, it is true. A merciful man is merciful to his beast," says the pa'son.

'"Hee, hee!" says the clerk, glancing sly into the pa'son's eye.

'"Ha, ha!" says the pa'son, a-glancing back into the clerk's. "Halloo!" he shouts, as he sees the fox break cover at that moment.

'"Halloo!" cries the clerk. "There he goes! Why, dammy, there's two foxes –"

'"Hush, clerk, hush! Don't let me hear that word again! Remember our calling."

'"True, sir, true. But really, good sport do carry away a man so, that he's apt to forget his high persuasion!" And the next minute the corner of the clerk's eye shot again into the corner of the pa'son's, and the pa'son's back again to the clerk's "Hee, hee!" said the clerk.

'"Ha, ha!" said Pa'son Toogood.

'"Ah, sir," says the clerk again, "this is better than crying Amen to your Ever-and-ever on a winter's morning!"

'"Yes, indeed, clerk! To everything there's a season," says Pa'son Toogood, quite pat, for he was a learned Christian man when he liked, and had chapter and ve'se at his tongue's end, as a pa'son should.'

'Andrey Satchel and the Parson':
'A Few Crusted Characters'

'Ah, well do I bear in mind what I said to Pa'son Raunham, about thy
mother's family o' seven, Gad, the very first week of his comen here, when
I was just in my prime. "And how many daughters had that poor Weedy
got, clerk?" he says. "Six, sir," says I, "and every one of 'em has a
brother!" "Poor woman," says he, "a dozen children! – give her this half-
sovereign from me, clerk." 'A laughed a good five minutes afterwards,
when he found out my merry nater – 'a did. But there, 'tis over wi' me
now. Enteren the Church is the ruin of a man's wit for wit's nothen
without a faint shadder o' sin.'

Desperate Remedies

He passes down the churchyard track
        On his way to toll the bell;
And stops, and looks at the graves around,
And notes each finished and greening mound
                Complacently,
                As their shaper he,
        And one who can do it well,
And, with a prosperous sense of his doing,
                Thinks he'll not lack
Plenty such work in the long ensuing
                Futurity.
        For people will always die,
        And he will always be nigh
                To shape their cell.

'The Sexton at Longpuddle'

He often would ask us
That, when he died,
After playing so many
To their last rest,
If out of us any
Should here abide,
And it would not task us,
We would with our lutes
Play over him
By his grave-brim
The psalm he liked best –
The one whose sense suits
'Mount Ephraim' –
And perhaps we should seem
To him, in Death's dream,
Like the seraphim.

As soon as I knew
That his spirit was gone
I thought this his due,
And spoke thereupon.

'I think,' said the vicar,
'A read service quicker
Than viols out-of-doors
In these frosts and hoars.
That old-fashioned way
Requires a fine day,
And it seems to me
It had better not be.'

Hence, that afternoon,
Though his wish could not be,
To get through it faster
They buried the master
Without any tune.

But 'twas said that, when
At the dead of next night
The vicar looked out,
There struck on his ken
Thronged roundabout,
Where the frost was graying
The headstoned grass,
A band all in white
Like the saints in church-glass,
Singing and playing
The ancient stave
By the choirmaster's grave.

Such the tenor man told
When he had grown old.

'The Choirmaster's Burial'

'O Passenger, pray list and catch
    Our sighs and piteous groans,
Half stifled in this jumbled patch
    Of wrenched memorial stones!

'We late-lamented, resting here,
    Are mixed to human jam,
And each to each exclaims in fear,
    "I know not which I am!"

'The wicked people have annexed
    The verses on the good;
A roaring drunkard sports the text
    Teetotal Tommy should!

'Where we are huddled none can trace,
    And if our names remain,
They pave some path or porch or place
    Where we have never lain!

'Here's not a modest maiden elf
    But dreads the final Trumpet,
Lest half of her should rise herself,
    And half some sturdy strumpet!

'From restorations of Thy fane,
    From smoothings of Thy sward,
From zealous Churchmen's pick and plane
    Deliver us O Lord! Amen!'

'The Levelled Churchyard'

The gallery of Mellstock Church had a status and sentiment of its own. A stranger there was regarded with a feeling altogether differing from that of the congregation below towards him. Banished from the nave as an intruder whom no originality could make interesting, he was received above as a curiosity that no unfitness could render dull. The gallery, too, looked down upon and knew the habits of the nave to its remotest peculiarity, and had an extensive stock of exclusive information about it; whilst the nave knew nothing of the gallery folk, as gallery folk, beyond their loud-sounding minims and chest notes. Such topics as that the clerk was always chewing tobacco except at the moment of crying amen; that he had a dust-hole in his pew; that during the sermon certain young daughters of the village had left off caring to read anything so mild as the marriage service for some years, and now regularly studied the one which chronologically follows it; that a pair of lovers touched fingers through a knot-hole between their pews in the manner ordained by their great exemplars, Pyramus and Thisbe; that Mrs Ledlow, the farmer's wife, counted her money and reckoned her week's marketing expenses during the first lesson – all news to those below – were stale subjects here.

Under the Greenwood Tree

'Is there soon to be a confirmation?'

    'Yes. In this parish – the first time in Welland church for twenty years. As I say, I had told 'em that he was confirmed the same year that I went up to have it done, as I have very good cause to mind. When we went to be examined, the pa'son said to me, "Rehearse the articles of thy belief." Mr Blount (as he was then) was nighest me, and he whispered, "women and wine." "Women and wine," says I to the pa'son: and for that I was sent back till next confirmation, Sir Blount never owning that he was the rascal.'

'Confirmation was a sight different at that time,' mused Biles. 'The Bishops didn't lay it on so strong then as they do now. Now-a-days, yer Bishop gies both hands to every Jack-rag and Tom-straw that drops the knee afore him; but 'twas six chaps to one blessing when we was boys. The Bishop o' that time would stretch out his palms and run his fingers over our row of crowns as off-hand as a bank gentleman telling money. The great lords of the Church in them days wasn't particular to a soul or two more or less; and, for my part, I think living was easier for 't.'

Two on a Tower

The waggon-office was not far from All Saints' Church, and the church-windows being open, he could hear the afternoon service from where he lingered as distinctly as if he had been one of the congregation. Thus he was mentally conducted through the Psalms, through the first and second lessons, through the burst of fiddles and clarionets which announced the evening-hymn, and well into the sermon, before any signs of the waggon could be seen upon the London road.

The afternoon sermons at this church being of a dry and metaphysical nature at that date, it was by a special providence that the waggon-office was placed near the ancient fabric, so that whenever the Sunday waggon was late, which it always was in hot weather, in cold weather, in wet weather, and in weather of almost every other sort, the rattle, dismounting, and swearing outside completely drowned the parson's voice within, and sustained the flagging interest of the congregation at precisely the right moment. No sooner did the charity children begin to writhe on their benches, and adult snores grow audible, than the waggon arrived.

The Trumpet-Major

'Why do you weep there, O sweet lady,
    Why do you weep before that brass? –
(I'm a mere student sketching the mediaeval)
    Is some late death lined there, alas? –
Your father's? . . . Well, all pay the debt that paid he!'

'Young man, O must I tell! – My husband's! And under
   His name I set mine, and my death! –
Its date left vacant till my heirs should fill it,
   Stating me faithful till my last breath.'
– 'Madam, that you are a widow wakes my wonder!'

   'O wait! For last month I – remarried!
   And now I fear 'twas a deed amiss.
We've just come home. And I am sick and saddened
   At what the new one will say to this;
And will he think – think that I should have tarried?

   'I may add, surely, – with no wish to harm him –
   That he's a temper – yes, I fear!
And when he comes to church next Sunday morning,
   And sees that written . . . O dear, O dear!'
– 'Madam, I swear your beauty will disarm him!'

'The Memorial Brass: 186–'

'As for yourself, you are a Churchman at present, I presume?'
   'Yes; not but I was a Methodist once – ay, for a length of time. 'Twas owing to my taking a house next door to a chapel; so that what with hearing the organ bizz like a bee through the wall, and what with finding it saved umbrellas on wet Zundays, I went over to that faith for two years – though I believe I dropped money by it – I wouldn't be the man to say so if I hadn't. Howsomever, when I moved into this house I turned back again to my old religion. Faith, I don't zee much difference: be you one, or be you t'other, you've got to get your living.'

A Laodicean

There are two sorts of church people; those who go, and those who don't go: there is only one sort of chapel-people; those who go.

The Life of Thomas Hardy

On leaving the school Geoffrey went to the tranter's. Old William opened the door.
   'Is your grandson Dick in 'ithin, William?'
   'No, not just now, Mr Day. Though he've been at home a good deal lately.'
   'O, how's that?'
   'What wi' one thing, and what wi' t'other, he's all in a mope, as might

be said. Don't seem the feller he used to. Ay, 'a will sit studding and thinking as if 'a were going to turn chapel-member, and then do nothing but traypse and wamble about.'

Under the Greenwood Tree

'And I went to grand churches and chapels. And how the parson would pray! Yes; he would kneel down and put up his hands together, and make the holy gold rings on his fingers gleam and twinkle in yer eyes, that he'd earned by praying so excellent well! – Ah yes, I wish I lived there.'

'Our poor Parson Thirdly can't get no money to buy such rings,' said Matthew Moon thoughtfully. 'And as good a man as ever walked. I don't believe poor Thirdly have a single one, even of humblest tin or copper. Such a great ornament as they'd be to him on a dull a'ternoon, when he's up in the pulpit lighted by the wax candles! But 'tis impossible, poor man. Ah, to think how unequal things be.'

'Perhaps he's made of different stuff than to wear 'em,' said Gabriel grimly. 'Well, that's enough of this. Go on, Cainy – quick.'

'Oh – and the new style of pa'sons wear moustaches and long beards,' continued the illustrious traveller, 'and look like Moses and Aaron complete, and make we fokes in the congregation feel all over like the children of Israel.'

'A very right feeling – very,' said Joseph Poorgrass.

'And there's two religions going on in the nation now – High Church and High Chapel. And, thinks I, I'll play fair; so I went to High Church in the morning, and High Chapel in the afternoon.'

'A right and proper boy,' said Joseph Poorgrass.

'Well, at High Church they pray singing, and worship all the colours of the rainbow; and at High Chapel they pray preaching, and worship drab and whitewash only.'

Far from the Madding Crowd

It had so happened that Bastow, the other pupil (who, strangely enough for an architect mostly occupied with church-work, had been bred a Baptist), became very doctrinal during this time; he said he was going to be baptized, and in fact was baptized shortly after. He so impressed young Hardy with his earnestness and the necessity of doing likewise that, though the junior pupil had been brought up in High Church principles, he almost felt that he ought to be baptized again as an adult. He went to the vicar of his parish and stated the case. The vicar, an Oxford man, seemed bewildered, and said that the only book he possessed that might help Hardy was Hooker's Ecclesiastical Polity, which he lent his inquirer. Finding that this learned work did not help much in the peculiar circumstances, Hardy went to the curate of another

parish with whom he was acquainted. But all that the curate had was a
handbook on the Sacraments of an elementary kind.

However, he got hold of as many books and notes on Paedo-baptism
as he could, and though he was appalled at the feebleness of the
arguments for infant christening (assuming that New Testament practice
must be followed) he incontinently determined to 'stick to his own side',
as he considered the Church to be, at some costs of conscience.

The Life of Thomas Hardy

Going down into the kitchen of the inn, the floor of which was a step
below the passage, which in its turn was a step below the road outside,
what should Joseph see to gladden his eyes but two copper-coloured
discs, in the form of the countenances of Mr Jan Coggan and Mr Mark
Clark. These owners of the two most appreciative throats in the
neighbourhood, within the pale of respectability, were now sitting face to
face over a three-legged circular table, having an iron rim to keep cups
and pots from being accidentally elbowed off; they might have been said
to resemble the setting sun and the full moon shining *vis-à-vis* across the
globe.

'Why, 'tis neighbour Poorgrass!' said Mark Clark. 'I'm sure your face
don't praise your mistress's table, Joseph.'

'I've had a very pale companion for the last four miles,' said Joseph,
indulging in a shudder toned down by resignation. 'And to speak the
truth, 'twas beginning to tell upon me. I assure ye, I ha'n't seed the
colour of victuals or drink since breakfast time this morning, and that was
no more than a dew-bit afield.'

'Then drink, Joseph, and don't restrain yourself!' said Coggan,
handing him a hooped mug three-quarters full.

Joseph drank for a moderately long time, then for a longer time,
saying, as he lowered the jug, ''Tis pretty drinking – very pretty drinking,
and is more than cheerful on my melancholy errand, so to speak it.'

'True, drink is a pleasant delight,' said Jan, as one who repeated a
truism so familiar to his brain that he hardly noticed its passage over his
tongue; and, lifting the cup, Coggan tilted his head gradually backwards,
with closed eyes, that his expectant soul might not be diverted for one
instant from its bliss by irrelevant surroundings.

'Well, I must be on again,' said Poorgrass. 'Not but that I should like
another nip with ye; but the parish might lose confidence in me if I was
seed here.'

'Where be ye trading o't to to-day, then, Joseph?'

'Back to Weatherbury. I've got poor little Fanny Robin in my waggon
outside, and I must be at the churchyard gates at a quarter to five with
her.'

'Ay – I've heard of it. And so she's nailed up in parish boards after all, and nobody to pay the bell shilling and the grave half-crown.'

'The parish pays the grave half-crown, but not the bell shilling, because the bell's a luxery: but 'a can hardly do without the grave, poor body. However, I expect our mistress will pay all.'

'A pretty maid as ever I see! But what's yer hurry, Joseph? The poor woman's dead, and you can't bring her to life, and you may as well sit down comfortable, and finish another with us.'

'I don't mind taking just the least thimbleful ye can dream of more with ye, sonnies. But only a few minutes, because 'tis as 'tis.'

'Of course, you'll have another drop. A man's twice the man afterwards. You feel so warm and glorious, and you whop and slap at your work without any trouble, and everything goes on like sticks a-breaking. Too much liquor is bad, and leads us to that horned man in the smoky house; but after all, many people haven't the gift of enjoying a wet, and since we be highly favoured with a power that way, we should make the most o't.'

'True,' said Mark Clark. ''Tis a talent the Lord has mercifully bestowed upon us, and we ought not to neglect it. But, what with the parsons and clerks and school-people and serious tea parties, the merry old ways of good life have gone to the dogs – upon my carcase, they have!'

'Well, really, I must be onward again now,' said Joseph.

'Now, now, Joseph; nonsense! The poor woman is dead, isn't she, and what's your hurry?'

'Well, I hope Providence won't be in a way with me for my doings,' said Joseph, again sitting down. 'I've been troubled with weak moments lately, 'tis true. I've been drinky once this month already, and I did not go to church a-Sunday, and I dropped a curse or two yesterday; so I don't want to go too far for my safety. Your next world is your next world, and not to be squandered offhand.'

'I believe ye to be a chapel-member, Joseph. That I do.'

'Oh, no, no! I don't go so far as that.'

'For my part,' said Coggan, 'I'm staunch Church of England.'

'Ay, and faith, so be I,' said Mark Clark.

'I won't say much for myself; I don't wish to,' Coggan continued, with that tendency to talk on principles which is characteristic of the barley-corn. 'But I've never changed a single doctrine: I've stuck like a plaster to the old faith I was born in. Yes; there's this to be said for the Church, a man can belong to the Church and bide in his cheerful old inn, and never trouble or worry his mind about doctrines at all. But to be a meetinger, you must go to chapel in all winds and weathers, and make yerself as frantic as a skit. Not but that chapel-members be clever chaps enough in their way. They can lift up beautiful prayers out of their own heads, all about their families and shipwracks in the newspaper.'

'They can – they can,' said Mark Clark, with corroborative feeling; 'but we Churchmen, you see, must have it all printed aforehand, or, dang it all, we should no more know what to say to a great gaffer like the Lord than babes unborn.'

'Chapel-folk be more hand-in-glove with them above than we,' said Joseph thoughtfully.

'Yes,' said Coggan. 'We know very well that if anybody do go to heaven, they will. They've worked hard for it, and they deserve to have it, such as 'tis. I bain't such a fool as to pretend that we who stick to the Church have the same chance as they, because we know we have not. But I hate a feller who'll change his old ancient doctrines for the sake of getting to heaven. I'd as soon turn king's-evidence for the few pounds you get. Why, neighbours, when every one of my taties were frosted, our Pa'son Thirdly were the man who gave me a sack for seed, though he hardly had one for his own use, and no money to buy 'em. If it hadn't been for him, I shouldn't hae had a tatie to put in my garden. D'ye think I'd turn after that? No, I'll stick to my side; and if we be in the wrong, so be it: I'll fall with the fallen!'

Far from the Madding Crowd

Thus the conversation was begun, and the postman proceeded to narrate the different strange events that marked his experience. Manston grew very friendly.

'Postman, I don't know what your custom is,' he said, after a while; 'but between you and me, I always carry a drop of something warm in my pocket when I am out on such a morning as this. Try it.' He handed the bottle of brandy.

'If you'll excuse me, please. I haven't took no stimmilents these five years.'

''Tis never too late to mend.'

'Against the regulations, I be afraid.'

'Who'll know it?'

'That's true – nobody will know it. Still, honesty's the best policy.'

'Ah – it is certainly. But, thank God, I've been able to get on without it yet. You'll surely drink with me?'

'Really, 'tis a'most too early for that sort o' thing – however, to oblige a friend, I don't object to the faintest shadder of a drop.' The postman drank, and Manston did the same to a very slight degree. Five minutes later, when they came to a gate, the flask was pulled out again.

'Well done!' said the postman, beginning to feel its effect; 'but guide my soul, I be afraid 'twill hardly do!'

'Not unless 'tis well followed, like any other line you take up,' said Manston. 'Besides, there's a way of liking a drop of liquor, and of being good – even religious – at the same time.'

'Ay, for some thimble-and-button in-an-out fellers; but I could never get into the knack o' it; not I.'

'Well, you needn't be troubled; it isn't necessary for the higher class of mind to be religious – they have so much common-sense that they can risk playing with fire.'

'That hits me exactly.'

'In fact, a man I know, who always had no other god but "Me;" and devoutly loved his neighbour's wife, says now that believing is a mistake.'

'Well, to be sure! However, believing in God is a mistake made by very few people, after all.'

'A true remark.'

'Not one Christian in our parish would walk half a mile in a rain like this to know whether the Scripture had concluded him under sin or grace.'

'Nor in mine.'

'Ah, you may depend upon it they'll do away wi' Goddymity altogether afore long, although we've had him over us so many years.'

'There's no knowing.'

'And I suppose the Queen 'ill be done away wi' then. A pretty concern that'll be! Nobody's head to put on your letters; and then your honest man who do pay his penny will never be known from your scamp who don't. O, 'tis a nation!'

Desperate Remedies

12

THE RUINED MAID

In Hardy's Wessex, as elsewhere, the ruined maid – seduced and betrayed by a faithless lover – is an archetypal figure of drama in folk song, ballad and parish anecdote. Cautionary tales of local girls 'in trouble' must have been one of the familiar themes of conversation in Hardy's youth: it was from the raw material of their obscure lives that he drew Fanny Robin and ultimately Tess. Illicit unions and illegitimate births – to use the jargon of public morality – were a subject for continuing meditation during his life and provided themes for much of his writing. In some circumstances he called in question the word 'ruined'. Tess, after all, was for him 'a pure woman'; and Selina Paddock, in the story 'Enter a Dragoon', considers herself a married woman and her son legitimate despite the fact that the calling of the banns for her marriage was not completed. Hardy's conviction that life sometimes threw up greater realities than were contained in social codes was expressed with beautiful simplicity in a sentence, probably jotted down in a notebook in 1889 and not published until after his death, in *The Life of Thomas Hardy*:

> That which, socially, is a great tragedy, may be in Nature no alarming circumstance.

He was compassionately interested in the varying ways these social tragedies might be interpreted by the young women themselves and by others. The extracts from his writings, brought together in this section, make a remarkably comprehensive survey of what was largely omitted, or only hinted at, in the works of his contemporaries. The almost ludicrous anguish in George Eliot's attempts, in *Adam Bede*, to get Hetty Sorrel into focus emphasizes the broad advance that Hardy achieved.

In the villages of Stinsford and Puddletown and Melbury Osmond there was a widespread acceptance of the view – shared with many another peasant community – that marriage was for those who could demonstrate the ability to breed. It was therefore customary for a bride to come to the altar in a decently early stage of pregnancy. Hardy himself attended his mother's wedding *in utero*. In *The Well-Beloved* he hinted discreetly that, on the Isle of Portland, a formal betrothal required by custom a sexual ratification. In *Jude the Obscure* Arabella's secret discussion with her friends on the advisability of pregnancy as a sure way to gain a man as a husband ends with the worldly-wise comment, 'Lots of girls do it; or do you think they'd get married at all?'

The ruined maid emerges therefore as the loser in a gamble. She may have misjudged the honourable commitment of a lover whose promises proved to be false; or some unforeseen intervention, some act of God or Fate or human agency, may have frustrated the best intentions. The bald story is stereotyped but the personalities involved are far from being so, as their responses show in the composite record that Hardy provides.

Some have a light-hearted easygoing wantonness, doing what comes naturally with little concern for what might follow. Suke Damson in *The Woodlanders*, enjoying her midsummer tumble in the hay with Dr Fitzpiers, is one such. Another is Jenny in the poem 'The Dance at the Phoenix' – a sixteen-year-old who favoured the troopers of the King's Own Cavalry when they occupied the barracks at Casterbridge. The transient figure of the redcoat, the soldier in his splendid regimentals, is a fascinating and dangerous presence in the background of such tales of intemperate and ill-judged romances, with Sergeant Troy as the supreme example. Tragedy might follow, and Hardy never shied away from tragedy, but he also captured the exuberance and gaiety and generous spirit of young love in the character of Julie-Jane, that 'girl of joy'.

More enigmatic is the unnamed girl in the poem 'The Mound', telling the poet

> The history of her undoing,
> (As I saw it), but she called 'comradeship'. . . .

She was not prepared to be bound for life to one man, but I wonder if she kept that vow. The prominence given to the word 'comradeship' suggests a link with another poem, 'I Rose Up as My Custom Is', in which the poet – now in an imagined after-life – revisits his love who

lies beside her husband and who begins to explain her change of mind
with the words:

> 'Old comrade, is that you?
> Well, on the whole, I like my life, –
> I know I swore I'd be no wife,
>   But what was I to do?

A respectable marriage was no unusual sequel to 'ruin' of the more
discreet sort. Suke Damson had no difficulty in becoming Mrs Timothy
Tangs and Jenny of the Phoenix became a good and loyal wife. Tess's
mother, that fund of worldly wisdom, was well aware of the importance
of discretion – not least in her own case.

The traditional price to be paid for the public disgrace of a
maiden's ruin was her banishment from the family home and the
community, with the expectation that she would probably turn
prostitute in some town or city. Hardy's satire on this cliché of moral
downfall inspired one of his best-known poems, 'The Ruined Maid'.
The method of turning an argument upside down in order to show it in
a new light appealed to Hardy and he used it here with mischievous
effect – tongue in cheek perhaps – to suggest that the fashionable
courtesan had bettered her lot in ways that a visiting country cousin
could only envy.

An alternative remedy was to contrive an abortion, by magic
potions or crude surgery. Did any poet before Hardy attempt a poem
on the dark-toned theme of 'A Sunday Morning Tragedy'? It is a
graphic reminder that his writings encompassed everything that was
enacted and talked about in his native surroundings. He touched the
deepest chord of tragedy in that terrible cry of the mother, 'O women!
scourged the worst are we'; but tragedy is not the whole story of the
ruined maid. There is the other extreme of broad and bawdy comedy,
even farce, in the different patterns of sexual behaviour. Dairyman
Crick's anecdote of Jack Dollop's philanderings in *Tess of the d'Urbervilles*
makes a telling counterpoint to the main theme of Tess's distress.

Faced with what 'A Sunday Morning Tragedy' speaks of as 'ill-
mothering', the obviously preferred remedy was marriage without
delay, whether accompanied or not by the traditional shot-gun.
Abortion, infanticide and banishment alike resorted to a callousness
and violence incompatible with normally natural feelings. The
remaining option was one of stoical acceptance, of resignation to what
Mrs Durbeyfield saw as simple human nature 'and what do please
God'.

Acceptance, however, is not necessarily accompanied by
resignation. Hardy, with his keen sense of the injustices suffered by

women, responded positively to what we now define as 'one-parent' families. Confronting the word 'bastard', he turned it neatly upside down in *A Laodicean*, where Dare remarks: 'I have an illegitimate father to support'. Anecdotes of spirited unmarried mothers went into Hardy's notebooks and took literary shape in the short story 'For Conscience Sake': here the tardily repentant seducer, offering a belated marriage, is shown as a harmful intruder pestering the woman with his conscience and endangering the satisfactory life she has built up with their daughter.

Such ironies were relished by Hardy and celebrated nowhere more happily than in the final poem here, 'The Dark-Eyed Gentleman'.

Bayonets and firelocks!
    I wouldn't my mammy should know't,
But I've been kissed in a sentry-box,
    Wrapped up in a soldier's coat!

The Dynasts

Now Jenny's life had hardly been
    A life of modesty;
And few in Casterbridge had seen
    More loves of sorts than she
From scarcely sixteen years above;
    Among them sundry troopers of
    The King's-Own Cavalry.

'The Dance at the Phoenix'

Sing; how 'a would sing!
    How 'a would raise the tune
When we rode in the waggon from harvesting
    By the light o' the moon!

Dance; how 'a would dance!
    If a fiddlestring did but sound
She would hold out her coats, give a slanting glance,
    And go round and round.

Laugh; how 'a would laugh!
    Her peony lips would part
As if none such a place for a lover to quaff
    At the deeps of a heart.

Julie, O girl of joy,
　　Soon, soon that lover he came.
Ah, yes; and gave thee a baby-boy,
　　But never his name. . . .

　　－ Tolling for her, as you guess;
　　And the baby too. . . . 'Tis well.
You knew her in maidhood likewise? － Yes,
　　That's her burial bell.

'I suppose,' with a laugh, she said,
　　'I should blush that I'm not a wife;
But how can it matter, so soon to be dead,
　　What one does in life!'

When we sat making the mourning
　　By her death-bed side, said she,
'Dears, how can you keep from your lovers, adorning
　　In honour of me!'

Bubbling and brightsome eyed!
　　But now － O never again.
She chose her bearers before she died
　　From her fancy-men.

　　　　　　　　　　　　　　　　　　'Julie-Jane'

NOTE. – It is, or was, a common custom in Wessex, and probably other country places, to prepare the mourning beside the death-bed, the dying person sometimes assisting, who also selects his or her bearers on such occasions.

　　'Coats' (line 7), old name for petticoats.

Tess wrote a most touching and urgent letter to her mother the very next day, and by the end of the week a response to her communication arrived in Joan Durbeyfield's wandering last-century hand.

　　Dear Tess, – J write these few lines Hoping they will find you well, as they leave me at Present, thank God for it. Dear Tess, we are all glad to Hear that you are going really to be married soon. But with respect to your question, Tess, J say between ourselves, quite private but very strong, that on no account do you say a word of your Bygone Trouble to him. J did not tell everything to your Father, he being so Proud on account of his Respectability, which, perhaps, your Intended is the same. Many a woman – some of the Highest in the Land – have had a Trouble in their time; and why should you Trumpet yours when others don't

Trumpet theirs? No girl would be such a Fool, specially as it is so long ago, and not your Fault at all. J shall answer the same if you ask me fifty times.

Tess of the d'Urbervilles

For a moment pause: –
　　Just here it was;
And through the thin thorn hedge, by the rays of the moon,
I can see the tree in the field, and beside it the mound –
Now sheeted with snow – whereon we sat that June
　　When it was green and round,
And she crazed my mind by what she coolly told –
　　The history of her undoing,
(As I saw it), but she called 'comradeship',
　　That bred in her no rueing:
　　And saying she'd not be bound
For life to one man, young, ripe-yeared, or old,
Left me – an innocent simpleton to her viewing;
For, though my accompt of years outscored her own,
　　Hers had more hotly flown. . . .
We never met again by this green mound,
To press as once so often lip on lip,
　　　And palter, and pause: –
　　　Yes; here it was!

'The Mound'

'O 'Melia, my dear, this does everything crown!
Who could have supposed I should meet you in Town?
And whence such fair garments, such prosperi-ty?' –
'O didn't you know I'd been ruined?' said she.

– 'You left us in tatters, without shoes or socks,
Tired of digging potatoes, and spudding up docks;
And now you've gay bracelets and bright feathers three!' –
'Yes: that's how we dress when we're ruined,' said she.

– 'At home in the barton you said "thee" and "thou",
And "thick oon", and "theäs oon", and "t'other"; but now
Your talking quite fits 'ee for high compa-ny!' –
'Some polish is gained with one's ruin,' said she.

– 'Your hands were like paws then, your face blue and bleak
But now I'm bewitched by your delicate cheek,
And your little gloves fit as on any la-dy!' –
'We never do work when we're ruined,' said she.

– 'You used to call home-life a hag-ridden dream,
And you'd sigh, and you'd sock; but at present you seem
To know not of megrims or melancho-ly!' –
'True. One's pretty lively when ruined,' said she.

– 'I wish I had feathers, a fine sweeping gown,
And a delicate face, and could strut about Town!' –
'My dear – a raw country girl, such as you be,
Cannot quite expect that. You ain't ruined,' said she.

'The Ruined Maid'

I bore a daughter flower-fair,
In Pydel Vale, alas for me;
I joyed to mother one so rare,
But dead and gone I now would be.

Men looked and loved her as she grew,
And she was won, alas for me;
She told me nothing, but I knew,
And saw that sorrow was to be.

I knew that one had made her thrall,
A thrall to him, alas for me;
And then, at last, she told me all,
And wondered what her end would be.

She owned that she had loved too well,
Had loved too well, unhappy she,
And bore a secret time would tell,
Though in her shroud she'd sooner be.

I plodded to her sweetheart's door
In Pydel Vale, alas for me;
I pleaded with him, pleaded sore,
To save her from her misery.

He frowned, and swore he could not wed,
Seven times he swore it could not be;
'Poverty's worse than shame,' he said,
Till all my hope went out of me.

'I've packed my traps to sail the main'
Roughly he spake, alas did he –
'Wessex beholds me not again,
'Tis worse than any jail would be!'

– There was a shepherd whom I knew,
A subtle man, alas for me:
I sought him all the pastures through,
Though better I had ceased to be.

I traced him by his lantern light,
And gave him hint, alas for me,
Of how she found her in the plight
That is so scorned in Christendie.

'Is there an herb . . . ?' I asked. 'Or none?'
Yes, thus I asked him desperately.
' – There is,' he said; 'a certain one. . . .'
Would he had sworn that none knew he!

'To-morrow I will walk your way,'
He hinted low, alas for me. –
Fieldwards I gazed throughout next day;
Now fields I never more would see!

The sunset-shine, as curfew strook,
As curfew strook beyond the lea,
Lit his white smock and gleaming crook,
While slowly he drew near to me.

He pulled from underneath his smock
The herb I sought, my curse to be –
'At times I use it in my flock,'
He said, and hope waxed strong in me.

''Tis meant to balk ill-motherings' –
(Ill-motherings! Why should they be?) –
'If not, would God have sent such things?'
So spoke the shepherd unto me.

That night I watched the poppling brew,
With bended back and hand on knee:
I stirred it till the dawnlight grew,
And the wind whiffled wailfully.

'This scandal shall be slain,' said I,
'That lours upon her innocency:
I'll give all whispering tongues the lie;' –
But worse than whispers was to be.

'Here's physic for untimely fruit,'
I said to her, alas for me,
Early that morn in fond salute;
And in my grave I now would be.

– Next Sunday came, with sweet church chimes
In Pydel Vale, alas for me:
I went into her room betimes;
No more may such a Sunday be!

'Mother, instead of rescue nigh,'
She faintly breathed, alas for me,
'I feel as I were like to die,
And underground soon, soon should be.'

From church that noon the people walked
In twos and threes, alas for me,
Showed their new raiment – smiled and talked,
Though sackcloth-clad I longed to be.

Came to my door her lover's friends,
And cheerly cried, alas for me,
'Right glad are we he makes amends,
For never a sweeter bride can be.'

My mouth dried, as 'twere scorched within,
Dried at their words, alas for me:
More and more neighbours crowded in,
(O why should mothers ever be!)

'Ha-ha! Such well-kept news!' laughed they,
Yes – so they laughed, alas for me.
'Whose banns were called in church to-day?' –
Christ, how I wished my soul could flee!

'Where is she? O the stealthy miss,'
Still bantered they, alas for me,
'To keep a wedding close as this. . . .'
Ay, Fortune worked thus wantonly!

'But you are pale – you did not know?'
They archly asked, alas for me,
I stammered, 'Yes – some days – ago,'
While coffined clay I wished to be.

''Twas done to please her, we surmise?'
(They spoke quite lightly in their glee)
'Done by him as a fond surprise?'
I thought their words would madden me.

Her love entered. 'Where's my bird? –
My bird – my flower – my picotee?
First time of asking, soon the third!'
Ah, in my grave I well may be.

To me he whispered: 'Since your call – '
So spoke he then, alas for me –
'I've felt for her, and righted all.'
– I think of it to agony.

'She's faint to-day – tired – nothing more –'
Thus did I lie, alas for me. . . .
I called her at her chamber door
As one who scarce had strength to be.

No voice replied. I went within –
O women! scourged the worst are we. . . .
I shrieked. The others hastened in
And saw the stroke there dealt on me.

There she lay – silent, breathless, dead,
Stone dead she lay   wronged, sinless she!
Ghost-white the cheeks once rosy-red:
Death had took her. Death took not me.

I kissed her colding face and hair,
I kissed her corpse – the bride to be! –
My punishment I cannot bear,
But pray God not to pity me.

                          'A Sunday Morning Tragedy'

'Jack Dollop, a 'hore's-bird of a fellow we had here as milker at one time,
sir, courted a young woman over at Mellstock, and deceived her as he
had deceived many afore. But he had another sort o' woman to reckon wi'
this time, and it was not the girl herself. One Holy Thursday of all days in
the almanack, we was here as we mid be now, only there was no churning
in hand, when we zid the girl's mother coming up to the door, wi' a great
brass-mounted umbrella in her hand that would ha' felled an ox, and
saying "Do Jack Dollop work here? – because I want him! I have a big
bone to pick with he, I can assure 'n!" And some way behind her mother
walked Jack's young woman, crying bitterly into her handkercher. "O
Lard, here's a time!" said Jack, looking out o' winder at 'em. "She'll
murder me! Where shall I get – where shall I – ? Don't tell her where I
be!" And with that he scrambled into the churn through the trap-door,
and shut himself inside, just as the young woman's mother busted into
the milk-house. "The villain – where is he?" says she, "I'll claw his face
for'n, let me only catch him!" Well, she hunted about everywhere,
ballyragging Jack by side and by seam, Jack lying a'most stifled inside
the churn, and the poor maid – or young woman rather – standing at the
door crying her eyes out. I shall never forget it, never! 'Twould have

melted a marble stone! But she couldn't find him nowhere at all.'

The dairyman paused, and one or two words of comment came from the listeners.

Dairyman Crick's stories often seemed to be ended when they were not really so, and strangers were betrayed into premature interjections of finality; though old friends knew better. The narrator went on –

'Well, how the old woman should have had the wit to guess it I could never tell, but she found out that he was inside that there churn. Without saying a word she took hold of the winch (it was turned by handpower then), and round she swung him, and Jack began to flop about inside. "O Lard! stop the churn! let me out!" says he, popping out his head, "I shall be churned into a pummy!" (he was a cowardly chap in his heart, as such men mostly be). "Not till ye make amends for ravaging her virgin innocence!" says the old woman. "Stop the churn, you old witch!" screams he. "You call me old witch, do ye, you deceiver!" says she, "when ye ought to ha' been calling me mother-law these last five months!" And on went the churn, and Jack's bones rattled round again. Well, none of us ventured to interfere; and at last 'a promised to make it right wi' her. "Yes – I'll be as good as my word!" he said. And so it ended that day.'

Tess of the d'Urbervilles

'Well! – my dear Tess!' exclaimed her surprised mother, jumping up and kissing the girl. 'How be ye? I didn't see you till you was in upon me! Have you come home to be married?'

'No, I have not come for that, mother.'

'Then for a holiday?'

'Yes – for a holiday; for a long holiday,' said Tess.

'What, isn't your cousin going to do the handsome thing?'

'He's not my cousin, and he's not going to marry me.'

Her mother eyed her narrowly.

'Come, you have not told me all,' she said.

Then Tess went up to her mother, put her face upon Joan's neck, and told.

'And yet th'st not got him to marry 'ee!' reiterated her mother. 'Any woman would have done it but you, after that!'

'Perhaps any woman would except me.'

'You ought to have been more careful if you didn't mean to get him to make you his wife!'

'O mother, my mother!' cried the agonized girl, turning passionately upon her parent as if her poor heart would break. 'How could I be expected to know? I was a child when I left this house four months ago. Why didn't you tell me there was danger in men-folk? Why didn't you warn me? Ladies know what to fend hands against, because they read novels that tell them of these tricks; but I never had the chance o' learning in that way, and you did not help me!'

Her mother was subdued.

'I thought if I spoke of his fond feelings and what they might lead to, you would be hontish wi' him and lose your chance,' she murmured, wiping her eyes with her apron. 'Well, we must make the best of it, I suppose. 'Tis nater, after all, and what do please God!'

Tess of the d'Urbervilles

I do not know if the rule is general, but in this county the girls who have made the mistake of Tess almost invariably lead chaste lives thereafter, even under strong temptation.

Letter to Frederic Harrison, 1 January 1892

He [Lord Portsmouth] showed me a bridge over which bastards were thrown and drowned, even down to quite recent times.

The Life of Thomas Hardy

> Many and many a time I thought,
> 'Would my child were in its grave!'
> Such the trouble and shame it brought.
>
> Now 'tis there. And now I'd brave
> Opinion's worst, in word or act,
> To have that child alive; yes, slave
>
> To dress and flaunt it to attract;
> Show it the gossips brazenly
> And let as nothing be the fact
> That never its father married me.

'The Dead Bastard'

Heard another curious story. Mil (Amelia) C – had an illegitimate child by the parish doctor. She christened him all the doctor's names, which happened to be a mouthful – Frederick Washington Ingen – and always called him by the three names complete. Moreover the doctor had a squint, and to identify him still more fully as the father she hung a bobbin from the baby's cap between his eyes, and so trained him to squint likewise.

The Life of Thomas Hardy

In December Hardy was told a story by a Mrs Cross, a very old country-woman he met, of a girl she had known who had been betrayed and deserted by a lover. She kept her child by her own exertions, and lived bravely and throve. After a time the man returned poorer than she, and wanted to marry her; but she refused. He ultimately went into the Union workhouse. The young woman's conduct in not caring to be 'made respectable' won the novelist-poet's admiration, and he wished to know her name; but the old narrator said, 'Oh, never mind their names! they be dead and rotted by now'.

The Life of Thomas Hardy

'How do you do, Mr Millborne?' she said cheerfully, as to any chance caller. 'I am obliged to receive you here because my daughter has a friend downstairs.'

'Your daughter – and mine.'

'Ah – yes, yes,' she replied hastily, as if the addition had escaped her memory. 'But perhaps the less said about that the better, in fairness to me. You will consider me a widow, please.'

'Certainly, Leonora . . .' He could not get on, her manner was so cold and indifferent. The expected scene of sad reproach, subdued to delicacy by the run of years, was absent altogether. He was obliged to come to the point without preamble.

'You are quite free, Leonora – I mean as to marriage? There is nobody who has your promise, or –'

'O yes; quite free, Mr Millborne,' she said, somewhat surprised.

'Then I will tell you why I have come. Twenty years ago I promised to make you my wife; and I am here to fulfil that promise. Heaven forgive my tardiness!'

Her surprise was increased, but she was not agitated. She seemed to become gloomy, disapproving. 'I – fear I could not entertain such an idea at this time of life,' she said after a moment or two. 'It would complicate matters too greatly. I have a very fair income, and require no help of any sort. I have no wish to marry . . . What could have induced you to come on such an errand now? It seems quite extraordinary, if I may say so!'

'It must – I daresay it does,' Millborne replied vaguely, 'and I must tell you that impulse – I mean in the sense of passion – has little to do with it. I wish to marry you, Leonora; I much desire to marry you. But it is an affair of conscience, a case of fulfilment. I promised you, and it was dishonourable of me to go away. I want to remove that sense of dishonour before I die. No doubt we might get to love each other as warmly as we did in old times?'

She dubiously shook her head. 'I appreciate your motives, Mr Millborne; but you must consider my position; and you will see that,

short of the personal wish to marry, which I don't feel, there is no reason
why I should change my state, even though by so doing I should ease
your conscience. My position in this town is a respected one; I have built
it up by my own hard labours, and in short, I don't wish to alter it.'

'For Conscience Sake':
Life's Little Ironies

I pitched my day's leazings in Crimmercrock Lane,
To tie up my garter and jog on again,
When a dear dark-eyed gentleman passed there and said,
In a way that made all o' me colour rose-red,
        'What do I see –
        O pretty knee!'
And he came and he tied up my garter for me.

'Twixt sunset and moonrise it was I can mind:
Ah, 'tis easy to lose what we nevermore find! –
Of the dear stranger's home, of his name, I knew nought,
But I soon knew his nature and all that it brought.
        Then bitterly
        Sobbed I that he
Should ever have tied up my garter for me!

Yet now I've beside me a fine lissom lad,
And my slip's nigh forgot, and my days are not sad;
My own dearest joy is he, comrade, and friend,
He it is who safe-guards me, on him I depend;
        No sorrow brings he,
        And thankful I be
That his daddy once tied up my garter for me!

'The Dark-Eyed Gentleman'

13

'FRESH AS PEACHES':
the Fair Maids of Wessex

The disturbing presence of the soldiery, in Casterbridge and Budmouth, undoubtedly sent a thrill of dangerous adventure among the fair maids of Wessex, to the prejudice of their chastity; but of course there was also a deal of harmless flirtation, which sometimes led to the pledging of hearts as transparently honest as Trumpet-Major Loveday's. Shyness and reserve were not exclusively feminine attributes, nor audacity male: the Hussars strolling on Budmouth Esplanade when they were encamped on the downs above the town met their match in the high spirited local girls, as did the King's Own Cavalry and 'the Fifth' in Casterbridge with the girls who sat and sang on Grey's Bridge. For them all the pleasures of the moment carried the bitter-sweet knowledge that, when their regiments embarked for foreign service, the girls must be left behind in dreams of a reunion in some shadowy future. Meanwhile, in the here and now, they were 'fresh as peaches'.

Hardy's own youthful encounters have come down to us richer in speculation than in fact. All his life he was susceptible to the charms of women and found an inexhaustible interest in them. That his feelings were aroused in adolescence is certain but he dismissed the topic in *The Life* as a triviality. Not until much later did he begin to recall the village beauties who had captivated him, and to add their portraits in verse to his great collection of poems inspired by the women in his life. Louisa Harding and the gamekeeper's daughter named by Hardy's invention as 'Lizbie Browne' have known identities, but I wonder who were Retty and Carrey Clavel – two endearing young girls who pass so swiftly through these pages and vanish. Tranter Reuben might argue that 'they be all alike in the groundwork; 'tis only in the flourishes there's a difference', but it was precisely the 'flourishes' that Hardy caught so perceptively.

He was also aware of the chilling disappointments that sometimes blighted the freshness and fair countenance of a maid denied marriage to her sweetheart by reason of poverty or the enforced absence that employment demanded. The sad figure of Patty Beech at Casterbridge Fair, hoping to speak to someone from the village of Hermitage, has a moving eloquence that seems to spring directly from a moment of real life. In the consideration of a village wedding money was a factor to be weighed with great care. When Dick Dewey asked his father's opinion of Fancy Day as a prospective bride in *Under the Greenwood Tree*, the tranter's favourable view of her was influenced by 'her father being rather better in the pocket than we'. It was poor Patty's tragedy that her lover failed to thrive well enough to make her his bride.

The group of poems inspired by Casterbridge Fair reflect the personal sadness and nostalgia of Hardy himself when he realized that the middle-aged, unattractive market-women were the present forms of the 'muslined pink young things' he and his contemporaries had courted in their prime. It was that deep nostalgia which drew him back again and again in his poetry to celebrate his fair prizes, as he thought of them – the unnamed girls of Weymouth and his home villages, together with cousin Phena and the 'West of Wessex' girl whom he married and who 'opened the door of Romance' for him.

When we lay where Budmouth Beach is,
   O, the girls were fresh as peaches,
With their tall and tossing figures and their eyes of blue and brown!
   And our hearts would ache with longing
   As we paced from our sing-songing,
With a sharp *Clink! Clink!* up the Esplanade and down.

   They distracted and delayed us
   By the pleasant pranks they played us,
And what marvel, then, if troopers, even of regiments of renown,
   On whom flashed those eyes divine, O,
   Should forget the countersign, O,
As we tore *Clink! Clink!* back to camp above the town.

Do they miss us much, I wonder,
Now that war has swept us sunder,
And we roam from where the faces smile to where the faces frown?
And no more behold the features
Of the fair fantastic creatures,
And no more *Clink! Clink!* past the parlours of the town?

Shall we once again there meet them?
Falter fond attempts to greet them?
Will the gay sling-jacket glow again beside the muslin gown? –
Will they archly quiz and con us
With a sideway glance upon us,
While our spurs *Clink! Clink!* up the Esplanade and down?

'Budmouth Dears' (Hussar's Song):
The Dynasts

Sitting on the bridge
Past the barracks, town and ridge,
At once the spirit seized us
To sing a song that pleased us –
As 'The Fifth' were much in rumour;
It was 'Whilst I'm in the humour,
Take me, Paddy, will you now?'
And a lancer soon drew nigh,
And his Royal Irish eye
Said, 'Willing, faith, am I,
O, to take you anyhow, dears,
To take you anyhow.'

But, lo! – dad walking by,
Cried, 'What, you lightheels! Fie!
Is this the way you roam
And mock the sunset gleam?'
And he marched us straightway home
Though we said, 'We are only, daddy,
Singing, "Will you take me, Paddy?"'
– Well, we never saw from then,
If we sang there anywhen,
The soldier dear again,
Except at night in dream-time,
Except at night in dream.

Perhaps that soldier's fighting
   In a land that's far away,
Or he may be idly plighting
   Some foreign hussy gay;
Or perhaps his bones are whiting
   In the wind to their decay! . . .
   Ah! – does he mind him how
   The girls he saw that day
On the bridge, were sitting singing
At the time of curfew-ringing,
'Take me, Paddy; will you now, dear?
   Paddy, will you now?'

     'Sitting on the Bridge' (Echo of an old song)

Grey's Bridge, Dorchester

My Love's gone a-fighting
   Where war-trumpets call,
The wrongs o' men righting
   Wi' carbine and ball,
And sabre for smiting,
   And charger, and all!

Of whom does he think there
   Where war-trumpets call?
To whom does he drink there,
   Wi' carbine and ball
On battle's red brink there,
   And charger, and all?

Her, whose voice he hears humming
   Where war-trumpets call,
'I wait, Love, thy coming
   Wi' carbine and ball,
And bandsmen a-drumming
   Thee, charger and all!'

'My Love's Gone a-Fighting' (Country-Girl's Song):
                    The Dynasts

Somewhat later, though it may as well be mentioned here among other such trivialities, he lost his heart for a few days to a young girl who had come from Windsor just after he had been reading Ainsworth's *Windsor Castle*. But she disappointed him on his finding that she took no interest in Herne the Hunter or Anne Boleyn. In this kind there was another young girl, a game-keeper's pretty daughter, who won Hardy's boyish admiration because of her beautiful bay-red hair. But she despised him, as being two or three years her junior, and married early. He celebrated her later on as 'Lizbie Browne'. Yet another attachment, somewhat later, which went deeper, was to a well-to-do farmer's daughter named Louisa. There were more probably. They all appear, however, to have been quite fugitive, except perhaps the one for Louisa.

The Life of Thomas Hardy

He used to pass, well-trimmed and brushed,
    My window every day,
And when I smiled on him he blushed,
That youth, quite as a girl might; aye,
    In the shyest way.

Thus often did he pass hereby,
    That youth of bounding gait,
Until the one who blushed was I,
And he became, as here I sate,
    My joy, my fate.

And now he passes by no more,
    That youth I loved too true!
I grieve should he, as here of yore,
Pass elsewhere, seated in his view,
    Some maiden new!

If such should be, alas for her!
    He'll make her feel him dear,
Become her daily comforter,
Then tire him of her beauteous gear,
    And disappear!

'The Passer-By' (L.H. Recalls Her Romance)

March 1. Youthful recollections of four village beauties:
1. Elizabeth B—, and her red hair. [She seems to appear in the poem called 'To Lizbie Browne', and was a gamekeeper's daughter, a year or two older than Hardy himself.]
2. Emily D—, and her mere prettiness.
3. Rachel H—, and her rich colour, and vanity, and frailty, and clever

artificial dimple-making. [She is probably in some respects the original of Arabella in Jude the Obscure.]
4. Alice P— and her mass of flaxen curls.

The Life of Thomas Hardy

Dear Lizbie Browne,
Where are you now?
In sun, in rain? –
Or is your brow
Past joy, past pain,
Dear Lizbie Browne?

Sweet Lizbie Browne,
How you could smile,
How you could sing! –
How archly wile
In glance-giving,
Sweet Lizbie Browne!

And, Lizbie Browne,
Who else had hair
Bay-red as yours,
Or flesh so fair
Bred out of doors,
Sweet Lizbie Browne?

When, Lizbie Browne,
You had just begun
To be endeared
By stealth to one,
You disappeared
My Lizbie Browne!

Ay, Lizbie Browne,
So swift your life,
And mine so slow,
You were a wife
Ere I could show
Love, Lizbie Browne.

Still, Lizbie Browne,
You won, they said,
The best of men
When you were wed . . .
Where went you then,
O Lizbie Browne?

Dear Lizbie Browne,
I should have thought,
'Girls ripen fast,'
And coaxed and caught
You ere you passed,
Dear Lizbie Browne!

But, Lizbie Browne,
I let you slip;
Shaped not a sign;
Touched never your lip
With lip of mine,
Lost Lizbie Browne!

So, Lizbie Browne,
When on a day
Men speak of me
As not, you'll say,
'And who was he?' –
Yes, Lizbie Browne!

                    'To Lizbie Browne'

You turn your back, you turn your back,
    And never your face to me,
Alone you take your homeward track,
    And scorn my company.

What will you do when Charley's seen
    Dewbeating down this way?
– You'll turn your back as now, you mean?
    Nay, Carrey Clavel, nay!

You'll see none's looking; put your lip
    Up like a tulip, so;
And he will coll you, bend, and sip:
    Yes, Carrey, yes; I know!

                    'To Carrey Clavel'

    Retty used to shake her head,
        Look with wicked eye;
    Say, 'I'd tease you, simple Ned,
        If I cared to try!'
    Then she'd hot-up scarlet red,
        Stilly step away,
    Much afraid that what she'd said
        Sounded bold to say.

Retty used to think she loved
  (Just a little) me.
Not untruly, as it proved
  Afterwards to be.
For, when weakness forced her rest
  If she walked a mile
She would whisper she was blest
  By my clasp awhile.

Retty used at last to say
  When she neared the Vale,
'Mind that you, Dear, on that day
  Ring my wedding peal!'
And we all, with pulsing pride,
  Vigorous sounding gave
Those six bells, the while outside
  John filled in her grave.

Retty used to draw me down
  To the turfy heaps,
Where, with yeoman, squire, and clown
  Noticeless she sleeps.
Now her silent slumber-place
  Seldom do I know,
For when last I saw her face
  Was so long ago!

                                              'Retty's Phases'

From an old draft of 1868

NOTE: – In many villages it was customary after the funeral of an unmarried young woman to ring a peal as for her wedding while the grave was being filled in, as if Death were not to be allowed to balk her of bridal honours. Young unmarried men were always her bearers.

And are ye one of Hermitage –
Of Hermitage, by Ivel Road,
And do ye know, in Hermitage
A thatch-roofed house where sengreens grow?
And does John Waywood live there still –
He of the name that there abode
When father hurdled on the hill
  Some fifteen years ago?

> Does he now speak o' Patty Beech
> The Patty Beech he used to – see,
> Or ask at all if Patty Beech
> Is known or heard of out this way?
> – Ask ever if she's living yet,
> And where her present home may be,
> And how she bears life's fag and fret
>   After so long a day?
>
> In years agone at Hermitage
> This faded face was counted fair,
> None fairer; and at Hermitage
> We swore to wed when he should thrive.
> But never a chance had he or I,
> And waiting made his wish outwear,
> And Time, that dooms man's love to die,
>   Preserves a maid's alive.

'The Inquiry'

Dick looked into the distance at a vast expanse of mortgaged estate. 'I wish I was as rich as a squire when he's as poor as a crow,' he murmured; 'I'd soon ask Fancy something.'

'I wish so too, wi' all my heart, sonny; that I do. Well, mind what beest about, that's all.'

Smart moved on a step or two. 'Supposing now, father, – We-hey, Smart! – I did think a little about her, and I had a chance, which I ha'n't; don't you think she's a very good sort of – of – one?'

'Ay, good; she's good enough. When you've made up your mind to marry, take the first respectable body that comes to hand – she's as good as any other; they be all alike in the groundwork; 'tis only in the flourishes there's a difference. She's good enough; but I can't see what the nation a young feller like you – wi' a comfortable house and home, and father and mother to take care o' thee, and who sent 'ee to a school so good that 'twas hardly fair to the other children – should want to go hollering after a young woman for, when she's quietly making a husband in her pocket, and not troubled by chick nor chiel, to make a poverty-stric' wife and family of her, and neither hat, cap, wig, nor waistcoat to set 'em up with: be drowned if I can see it, and that's the long and short o't, my sonny!'

Dick looked at Smart's ears, then up the hill; but no reason was suggested by any object that met his gaze.

'For about the same reason that you did, father, I suppose.'

'Dang it, my sonny, thou'st got me there!' And the tranter gave vent to a grim admiration, with the mien of a man who was too magnanimous not to appreciate artistically a slight rap on the knuckles, even if they were his own.

'Whether or no,' said Dick, 'I asked her a thing going along the road.'

'Come to that, is it? Turk! won't thy mother be in a taking! Well, she's ready, I don't doubt?'

'I didn't ask her anything about having me; and if you'll let me speak, I'll tell 'ee what I want to know. I just said, Did she care about me?'

'Piph–ph–ph!'

'And then she said nothing for a quarter of a mile, and then she said she didn't know. Now, what I want to know is, what was the meaning of that speech?' The latter words were spoken resolutely, as if he didn't care for the ridicule of all the fathers in creation.

'The meaning of that speech is,' the tranter replied deliberately, 'that the meaning is meant to be rather hid at present. Well, Dick, as an honest father to thee, I don't pretend to deny what you d'know well enough; that is, that her father being rather better in the pocket than we, I should welcome her ready enough if it must be somebody.'

'But what d'ye think she really did mean?' said the unsatisfied Dick.

'I'm afeard I am not o'much account in guessing, especially as I was not there when she said it, and seeing that your mother was the only 'ooman I ever cam' into such close quarters as that with.'

'And what did mother say to you when you asked her?' said Dick musingly.

'I don't see that that will help 'ee.'

'The principle is the same.'

'Well – ay: what did she say? Let's see. I was oiling my working-day boots without taking 'em off, and wi' my head hanging down when she just brushed on by the garden hatch like a flittering leaf. "Ann," I said says I, and then, – but Dick, I'm afeard 'twill be no help to thee; for we were such a rum couple, your mother and I, leastways one half was, that is myself – and your mother's charms was more in the manner than the material.'

'Never mind! "Ann," said you.'

'"Ann," said I, as I was saying . . . "Ann," I said to her when I was oiling my working-day boots wi' my head hanging down, "Woot hae me?" . . . What came next I can't quite call up at this distance o' time. Perhaps your mother would know, – she's got a better memory for her little triumphs than I. However, the long and the short o' the story is that we were married somehow, as I found afterwards.'

Under the Greenwood Tree

These market-dames, mid-aged, with lips thin-drawn
    And tissues sere,
Are they the ones we loved in years agone,
    And courted here?

Are these the muslined pink young things to whom
    We vowed and swore
In nooks on summer Sundays by the Froom,
    Or Budmouth shore?

Do they remember those gay tunes we trod
    Clasped on the green;
Aye; trod till moonlight set on the beaten sod
    A satin sheen?

They must forget, forget! They cannot know
    What once they were,
Or memory would transfigure them, and show
    Them always fair.

                              'Former Beauties'

Not a line of her writing have I,
    Not a thread of her hair,
No mark of her late time as dame in her dwelling, whereby
    I may picture her there;
    And in vain do I urge my unsight
    To conceive my lost prize
At her close, whom I knew when her dreams were upbrimming with
    light,
    And with laughter her eyes.

What scenes spread around her last days,
    Sad, shining, or dim?
Did her gifts and compassions enray and enarch her sweet ways
    With an aureate nimb?
    Or did life-light decline from her years,
    And mischances control
Her full day-star; unease, or regret, or forebodings, or fears
    Disennoble her soul?

Thus I do but the phantom retain
    Of the maiden of yore
As my relic; yet haply the best of her – fined in my brain
    It may be the more
    That no line of her writing have I,
    Nor a thread of her hair,
No mark of her late time as dame in her dwelling, whereby
    I may picture her there.

              'Thoughts of Phena' (At News of Her Death)

March 1890

She opened the door of the West to me,
  With its loud sea-lashings,
  And cliff-side clashings
Of waters rife with revelry.

She opened the door of Romance to me,
  The door from a cell
  I had known too well,
Too long, till then, and was fain to flee.

She opened the door of a Love to me,
  That passed the wry
  World-welters by
As far as the arching blue the lea.

She opens the door of the Past to me,
  Its magic lights,
  Its heavenly heights,
When forward little is to see!

                              'She Opened the Door'

1913

14

SUPERSTITION AND WITCHCRAFT

In his description of Blackmore Vale Hardy commented: 'Superstitions linger longest on these heavy soils'. The lighter sands and gravels of the heaths and the chalk of the downlands, however, did also appear to sustain a mysterious array of occult and supernatural powers which cast their shadows on the conventional surfaces of daily life. Though Hardy might be regarded as an intellectual ally by the editor of the Rationalist Press, his imagination was richly stored with tales of ghosts and divinations, exponents of both black and white witchcraft, hauntings and the casting of spells. Such matters must have figured prominently in the general gossip of his home circle and neighbours. They added an extra ingredient of drama to an otherwise humdrum chronicle and they did so with the force of authentic feeling. Time and again as an author Hardy drew on his own early memories or the entries he made in his notebooks of strange folk tales that he heard locally. What we can discern in the background is a community of villagers frequently preoccupied with supernatural forces of a non-Christian or even satanic nature. Their attitude to these forces varied greatly: at times deadly serious, at others sceptical, occasionally even jocularly, depending on personal circumstances.

Llewelyn Powys recalled Hardy telling him that, in his boyhood, it was common practice for people to bless themselves if a raven flew over their cottage (an ill omen, mentioned in the poem 'Premonitions'). Such observances were necessary to ward off the menace of hostile powers, which had not been conjured up by some malevolent person but were universally active and impenetrable. Of the same nature were the hauntings of places, or the omens and portents touching individuals. These were seemingly capricious interventions, lingering in a stable where a man was killed or startling the wedding of Tess and Angel Clare with the ominous crowing of a cock. No human agency contrived them: they were drawn to the location of some crime or sin as lightning is drawn to a conductor.

To be perpetually confronted with such an impalpable adversary was cause enough for a pervasive fear. The ghost in the dark lane, the threatening portent, the aimless stroke of ill luck – these, told and retold to superstitious ears, created an undertone of always impending danger. How understandable and revealing becomes the conviction of Tess's mother that her fortune-telling book contains a dangerously magical power which should not be kept in the house at night! Old-fashioned she might be, but she was surely one of the majority who would see in ghostly apparitions much more than the 'walking vapours' that Hezekiah Biles rejected so scornfully in *Two on a Tower*.

Where a human agency was added, the mood changed. Some forms of magic were suitable for a do-it-yourself technique, using a simple and widely known formula. Other forms needed the more professional skill of a conjuror, astrologer or witch. The purposes ranged from a harmless desire to foretell a future event or cure an ailment to a secret mode of maiming or even murdering.

A practice associated with Midsummer Eve and favoured by village girls was an act of divination which revealed the identity of a future husband; or if not his identity, at least his trade – an important clue in a small community. This would often be a group activity, a half-serious game accompanied by giggling, teasing and conflicting expressions of belief and disbelief. It forms a pleasant and amusing interlude in *Under the Greenwood Tree*. Later, in *The Woodlanders*, Hardy developed it as an important part of the action. In *Far from the Madding Crowd* the combination of a lock-key and a verse in the biblical Book of Ruth, as used by Bathsheba, was another well-known method of achieving the same end.

More serious were the uses of homologous magic to gain secret control over another person or an animal. In the furtherance of 'ill-wishing', a pigeon's heart became the symbol of a particular human heart or a crudely modelled wax effigy became the body of one's enemy. By inserting pins or exposing to fire it was thought possible to transfer appropriate pains and injuries to the intended victim. The scene in *The Return of the Native* when Susan Nunsuch makes an effigy of Eustacia for such a purpose conveys a sinister power that no reader is likely to forget.

Susan's action is of course premeditated and malevolent. Not so the

weird relationship in *The Woodlanders* between John South and the elm
tree that he believes has always been destined to kill him. His
involuntary terror has a passive ambiguity about it. Is he himself in
some way motivating the tree or is it the agent of some supernatural
force that has singled out poor South for this mental torment? Has his
mind fallen prey to the woodland ambience of superstition and black
magic? The enigma remains, and this is no isolated case. His
daughter's comment is plain enough – 'Others have been like it afore
in Hintock'.

The whole subject becomes more orderly in the hands of the
professionals, the various masters of necromancy, conjuration of
spirits, veterinary lore, weather forecasting and witchcraft in all its
degrees. Like Gilbert's John Wellington Wells these 'dealers in magic
and spells' radiate confidence in themselves and inspire faith in others.
During his boyhood Hardy must have heard many a discussion of the
rival merits of those conjurors who became local celebrities as a result
of their uncanny ability to remove warts, cure sick animals, raise up a
cloudy human image in a tumbler of water, provide a shield against an
enemy's dastardly spell and generally handle with apparent ease those
supernatural forces that plagued the rest of mankind. Many a
desperate voice must have echoed Dairyman Crick's recognition that
his last resort was to go to a conjuror – 'O yes, I shall have to go to 'n, if
this sort of thing continnys!'

In such matters it is not easy to draw a line between the magic
powers of witchcraft and the practical wisdom of an empirical kind that
included a knowledge of herbally derived medicines. In the poem 'A
Sunday Morning Tragedy' the shepherd who provides a herb which
can abort a pregnancy and prevent 'ill-motherings' scarcely qualifies as
a conjuror since he is merely applying the traditional herbal lore that
has developed among generations of shepherds. Admittedly, though,
much of the apparently magical skill of the conjurors derived similarly
from herbal medicine. It is a grey area.

In the further reaches of this black art there can be no doubt that
the conjurors were practising witchcraft, or a fraudulent pretence of it.
To conjure up in a glass of water a vision of some future event or
identifiable person was a potent act. Its dramatic possibilities were
applied by Hardy in his most complete and haunting story in this *genre*:
'The Withered Arm' contains also the possession of a sleeping woman
by an incubus and the pursuit of a macabre cure for the bewitched
maiming of a limb. The entire story might well have been included
here. I have limited my selection to a single episode.

The winding road downwards became just visible to her under the wan starlight as she followed it, and soon she paced a soil so contrasting with that above it that the difference was perceptible to the tread and to the smell. It was the heavy clay land of Blackmore Vale, and a part of the Vale to which turnpike-roads had never penetrated. Superstitions linger longer on these heavy soils. Having once been forest, at this shadowy time it seemed to assert something of its old character, the far and the near being blended and every tree and tall hedge making the most of its presence. The harts that had been hunted here, the witches that had been pricked and ducked, the green-spangled fairies that 'whickered' at you as you passed; – the place teemed with beliefs in them still, and they formed an impish multitude now.

Tess of the d'Urbervilles

Marty prepared her a comfortable place and she sat down in the circle and listened to Fitzpiers while he drew from her father and the bark-rippers sundry narratives of their fathers', their grandfathers', and their own adventures in these woods; of the mysterious sights they had seen – only to be accounted for by supernatural agency; of white witches and black witches: and the standard story of the spirits of the Two Brothers who had fought and fallen and had haunted King's Hintock Court a few miles off till they were exorcised by the priest, and compelled to retreat to a swamp whence they were returning to their old quarters at the Court at the rate of a cock's stride every New Year's Day, Old Style; hence the local saying, 'On new-year's tide, a cock's stride'.

The Woodlanders

Passed a lonely old house formerly an inn. The road-contractor now living there showed us into the stable, and drew our attention to the furthest stall. When the place was an inn, he said, it was the haunt of smugglers, and in a quarrel there one night a man was killed in that stall. If an old horse is put there on certain nights, at about two in the morning (when the smuggler died) the horse cries like a child, and on entering you find him in a lather of sweat.

The Life of Thomas Hardy

'William, as you may know, was a curious, silent man; you could feel when he came near 'ee; and if he was in the house or anywhere behind your back without your seeing him, there seemed to be something clammy in the air, as if a cellar door was opened close by your elbow. Well, one Sunday, at a time that William was in very good health to all

appearance, the bell that was ringing for church went very heavy all of a
sudden; the sexton, who told me o't, said he'd not known the bell go so
heavy in his hand for years – and he feared it meant a death in the parish.
That was on the Sunday, as I say. During the week after, it chanced that
William's wife was staying up late one night to finish her ironing, she
doing the washing for Mr and Mrs Hardcome. Her husband had finished
his supper and gone to bed as usual some hour or two before. While she
ironed she heard him coming down-stairs; he stopped to put on his boots
at the stair-foot, where he always left them, and then came on into the
living-room, where she was ironing, passing through it towards the door,
this being the only way from the stair-case to the outside of the house. No
word was said on either side, William not being a man given to much
speaking, and his wife being occupied with her work. He went out and
closed the door behind him. As her husband had now and then gone out
in this way at night before when unwell, or unable to sleep for want of a
pipe, she took no particular notice, and continued at her ironing. This she
finished shortly after, and as he had not come in she waited a while for
him, putting away the irons and things, and preparing the table for his
breakfast in the morning. Still he did not return, and supposing him not
far off, and wanting to get to bed herself, tired as she was, she left the door
unbarred and went to the stairs, after writing on the back of the door with
chalk: *Mind and do the door* (because he was a forgetful man).

'To her great surprise, and I might say alarm, on reaching the foot of
the stairs his boots were standing there as they always stood when he had
gone to rest; going up to their chamber she found him in bed sleeping as
soundly as a rock. How he could have got back again without her seeing
or hearing him was beyond her comprehension. It could only have been
by passing behind her very quietly while she was bumping with the iron.
But this notion did not satisfy her: it was surely impossible that she
should not have seen him come in through a room so small. She could not
unravel the mystery, and felt very queer and uncomfortable about it.
However, she would not disturb him to question him then, and went to
bed herself.

'He rose and left for his work very early the next morning, before she
was awake, and she waited his return to breakfast with much anxiety for
an explanation, for thinking over the matter by daylight made it seem
only the more startling. When he came in to the meal he said, before she
could put her question, "What's the meaning of them words chalked on
the door?"

'She told him, and asked him about his going out the night before.
William declared that he had never left the bedroom after entering it,
having in fact undressed, lain down, and fallen asleep directly, never once
waking till the clock struck five, and he rose up to go to his labour.

'Betty Privett was as certain in her own mind that he did go out as she was of her own existence, and was little less certain that he did not return. She felt too disturbed to argue with him, and let the subject drop as though she must have been mistaken. When she was walking down Longpuddle street later in the day she met Jim Weedle's daughter Nancy, and said, "Well, Nancy, you do look sleepy today!"

'"Yes, Mrs Privett," says Nancy. "Now don't tell anybody, but I don't mind letting you know what the reason o't is. Last night, being Old Midsummer Eve, some of us went to church porch, and didn't get home till near one."

'"Did ye?" says Mrs Privett. "Old Midsummer yesterday, was it? Faith I didn't think whe'r t'was Midsummer or Michaelmas; I'd too much work to do."

'"Yes. And we were frightened enough, I can tell 'ee, by what we saw."

'"What did ye see?"

'(You may not remember, sir, having gone off to foreign parts so young, that on Midsummer night it is believed hereabout that the faint shapes of all the folk in the parish who are going to be at death's door within the year can be seen entering the church. Those who get over their illness come out again after a while; those that are doomed to die do not return.)

'"What did you see?" asked William's wife.

'"Well," says Nancy, backwardly – "we needn't tell what we saw or who we saw."

'"You saw my husband," says Betty Privett, in a quiet way.

'"Well, since you put it so," says Nancy, hanging fire, "we – thought we did see him; but it was darkish, and we was frightened, and of course it might not have been he."

'"Nancy, you needn't mind letting it out, though 'tis kept back in kindness. And he didn't come out of church again: I know it as well as you."

'Nancy did not answer yes or no to that, and no more was said. But three days after, William Privett was mowing with John Chiles in Mr Hardcome's meadow, and in the heat of the day they sat down to eat their bit o' nunch under a tree, and empty their flagon. Afterwards both of 'em fell asleep as they sat. John Chiles was the first to wake, and as he looked towards his fellow-mower he saw one of those great white miller's-souls as we call 'em – that is to say, a miller-moth – come from William's open mouth while he slept, and fly straight away. John thought it odd enough, as William had worked in a mill for several years when he was a boy. He then looked at the sun and found by the place o't that they had slept a long while, and as William did not wake, John called to him and said it was high time to begin work again. He took no notice, and then John went up and shook him, and found he was dead.

Now on that very day old Philip Hookhorn was down at Longpuddle Spring dipping up a pitcher of water; and as he turned away, who should he see coming down to the spring on the other side but William, looking very pale and odd. This surprised Philip Hookhorn very much, for years before that time William's little son – his only child – had been drowned in that spring while at play there, and this had so preyed on William's mind that he'd never been seen near the spring afterwards, and had been known to go half a mile out of his way to avoid the place. On inquiry, it was found that William in body could not have stood by the spring, being in the mead two miles off; and it also came out that the time at which he was seen at the spring was the very time when he had died.

'The Superstitious Man's Story':
Life's Little Ironies

She [Lizzy D—] used to tell a story of a woman who came to her to consult her about the ghost of another woman she declared she had seen, and who 'troubled her' – the deceased wife of the man who was courting her.

'How long hev' the woman been dead' I said.

'Many years!'

'Oh, that were no ghost. Now if she'd only been dead a month or two, and you were making her husband your fancy-man, there might have been something in your story. But Lord, much can she care about him after years and years in better company!'

The Life of Thomas Hardy

Afternoon came, and with it the hour for departure. They had decided to fulfil the plan of going for a few days to the lodgings in the old farmhouse near Wellbridge Mill, at which he meant to reside during his investigation of flour processes. At two o'clock there was nothing left to do but to start. All the servantry of the dairy were standing in the red-brick entry to see them go out, the dairyman and his wife following to the door. Tess saw her three chamber-mates in a row against the wall, pensively inclining their heads. She had much questioned if they would appear at the parting moment; but there they were, stoical and staunch to the last. She knew why the delicate Retty looked so fragile, and Izz so tragically sorrowful, and Marian so blank; and she forgot her own dogging shadow for a moment in contemplating theirs.

She impulsively whispered to him –

'Will you kiss 'em all, once, poor things, for the first and last time?'

Clare had not the least objection to such a farewell formality – which was all that it was to him – as he passed them he kissed them in succession where they stood, saying 'Good-bye' to each as he did so. When they reached the door Tess femininely glanced back to discern the effect of that kiss of charity; there was no triumph in her glance, as there might have been. If there had it would have disappeared when she saw how moved the girls all were. The kiss had obviously done harm by awakening feelings they were trying to subdue.

Of all this Clare was unconscious. Passing on to the wicket-gate he shook hands with the dairyman and his wife, and expressed his last thanks to them for their attentions; after which there was a moment of silence before they had moved off. It was interrupted by the crowing of a cock. The white one with the rose comb had come and settled on the palings in front of the house, within a few yards of them, and his notes thrilled their ears through, dwindling away like echoes down a valley of rocks.

'Oh?' said Mrs Crick. 'An afternoon crow!'

Two men were standing by the yard gate, holding it open.

'That's bad,' one murmured to the other, not thinking that the words could be heard by the group at the door-wicket.

The cock crew again – straight towards Clare.

'Well!' said the dairyman.

'I don't like to hear him!' said Tess to her husband. 'Tell the man to drive on. Good-bye, good-bye!'

The cock crew again.

'Hoosh! Just you be off, sir, or I'll twist your neck!' said the dairyman with some irritation, turning to the bird and driving him away. And to his wife as they went indoors: 'Now, to think o' that just to-day! I've not heard his crow of an afternoon all the year afore.'

'It only means a change in the weather,' said she; 'not what you think: 'tis impossible!'

Tess of the d'Urbervilles

April 20. Vagg Hollow, on the way to Load Bridge (Somerset) is a place where 'things' used to be seen – usually taking the form of a wool-pack in the middle of the road. Teams and other horses always stopped on the brow of the hollow, and could only be made to go on by whipping. A waggoner once cut at the pack with his whip; it opened in two, and smoke and a hoofed figure rose out of it.

The Life of Thomas Hardy

'What do you see in Vagg Hollow,
Little boy, when you go
In the morning at five on your lonely drive?'
' – I see men's souls, who follow
Till we've passed where the road lies low,
When they vanish at our creaking!

'They are like white faces speaking
Beside and behind the waggon –
One just as father's was when here.
The waggoner drinks from his flagon,
(Or he'd flinch when the Hollow is near)
But he does not give me any.

'Sometimes the faces are many;
But I walk along by the horses,
He asleep on the straw as we jog;
And I hear the loud water-courses,
And the drops from the trees in the fog,
And watch till the day is breaking.

'And the wind out by Tintinhull waking;
I hear in it father's call
As he called when I saw him dying,
As he sat by the fire last Fall,
And mother stood by sighing;
But I'm not afraid at all!'

'Vagg Hollow'

Vagg Hollow is a marshy spot on the old Roman Road near Ilchester
where 'things' are seen. Merchandise was formerly fetched inland from
the canal-boats at Load-Bridge by waggons this way.

Tess, being left alone with the younger children, went first to the
outhouse with the fortune-telling book, and stuffed it into the thatch. A
curious fetichistic fear of this grimy volume on the part of her mother
prevented her ever allowing it to stay in the house all night, and hither it
was brought back whenever it had been consulted. Between the mother,
with her fast-perishing lumber of superstitions, folk-lore, dialect and
orally transmitted ballads, and the daughter, with her trained National
teachings and Standard knowledge under an infinitely Revised Code,
there was a gap of two hundred years as ordinarily understood. When
they were together the Jacobean and the Victorian ages were juxtaposed.

Tess of the d'Urbervilles

'Well, well; I've not held out against the figure o' starvation these five-
and-twenty year, on nine shillings a week, to be afeard of a walking
vapour, sweet or savoury,' said Hezzy. 'So here's home-along.'

Two on a Tower

October 1888. A game that used to be played at Bockhampton. All kinds of materials are put down in a circle (wood, iron, brick, etc): girls blindfolded, turned round, & made to crawl from centre Whichever material they crawl to will bear upon their future husband's vocation.

Personal Notebooks of Thomas Hardy

The dance ended. 'Piph–h–h–h!' said tranter Dewy, blowing out his breath in the very finest stream of vapour that a man's lips could form. 'A regular tightener, that one, sonnies!' He wiped his forehead, and went to the cider and ale mugs on the table.

'Well!' said Mrs Penny, flopping into a chair, 'my heart haven't been in such a thumping state of uproar since I used to sit up on old Midsummer-eves to see who my husband was going to be.'

'And that's getting on for a good few years ago now, from what I've heard you tell,' said the tranter without lifting his eyes from the cup he was filling. Being now engaged in the business of handing round refreshments he was warranted in keeping his coat off still though the other heavy men had resumed theirs.

'And a thing I never expected would come to pass, if you'll believe me, came to pass then,' continued Mrs Penny. 'Ah, the first spirit ever I see on a Midsummer-eve was a puzzle to me when he appeared, a hard puzzle, so say I!'

'So I should have fancied,' said Elias Spinks.

'Yes,' said Mrs Penny, throwing her glance into past times and talking on in a running tone of complacent abstraction, as if a listener were not a necessity. 'Yes; never was I in such a taking as on that Midsummer-eve! I sat up, quite determined to see if John Wildway was going to marry me or no. I put the bread-and-cheese and beer quite ready, as the witch's book ordered, and I opened the door, and I waited till the clock struck twelve, my nerves all alive and so strained that I could feel every one of 'em twitching like bell-wires. Yes, sure! and when the clock had struck, lo and behold I could see through the door a *little small* man in the lane wi' a shoemaker's apron on.'

Here Mr Penny stealthily enlarged himself half an inch.

'Now, John Wildway,' Mrs Penny continued, 'who courted me at that time, was a shoemaker, you see, but he was a very fair-sized man, and I couldn't believe that any such a little small man had anything to do wi' me, as anybody might. But on he came, and crossed the threshold – not John, but actually the same little small man in the shoemaker's apron –'

'You needn't be so mighty particular about little and small!' said her husband.

'In he walks and down he sits, and O my goodness me, didn't I flee upstairs, body and sould hardly hanging together! Well, to cut a long

story short, by-long and by-late John Wildway and I had a miff and
parted; and lo and behold, the coming man came! Penny asked me if I'd
go snacks with him, and afore I knew what I was about a'most, the thing
was done.'

'I've fancied you never knew better in your life; but I mid be
mistaken,' said Mr Penny in a murmur.

Under the Greenwood Tree

Fitzpiers having heard a voice or voices, was looking over his garden gate
(where he now looked more frequently than into his books) fancying that
Grace might be abroad with some friends. He was irretrievably
committed in heart to Grace Melbury, though he was by no means sure
that she was so far committed to him. It was not Grace who had passed,
however, but several of the ordinary village girls in a group; some steadily
walking, some in a mood of wild gaiety. He quietly asked his landlady,
who was also in the garden, what these girls were intending, and she
informed him that it being old Midsummer eve, they were about to
attempt some spell or enchantment which would afford them a glimpse of
their future partners for life. She declared it to be an ungodly
performance, and one that she for her part would never countenance;
saying which she entered her house and retired to bed.

The young man lit a cigar, and followed the bevy of maidens slowly
up the road. They had turned into the wood at an opening between
Melbury's and Marty South's; but Fitzpiers could easily track them by
their voices, low as they endeavoured to keep their tones.

In the meantime other inhabitants of Little Hintock had become
aware of the nocturnal experiment about to be tried, and were also
sauntering stealthily after the frisky maidens. Miss Melbury had been
informed by Marty South during the day of the proposed peep into
futurity, and, being only a girl like the rest, she was sufficiently interested
to wish to see the issue. The moon was so bright and the night so calm
that she had no difficulty in persuading Mrs Melbury to accompany her;
and thus, joined by Marty, these went onward in the same direction.

When they had proceeded a little further Marty was joined by
Grammer Oliver (who was as young as the youngest in such matters),
and Grace and Mrs Melbury went on by themselves till they had arrived
at the spot chosen by the village daughters, whose primary intention of
keeping their expedition a secret had been quite defeated. Grace and her
stepmother paused by a holly tree; and at a little distance stood Fitzpiers
under the shade of a young oak, intently observing Grace, who was in the
full rays of the moon.

He watched her without speaking, and unperceived by any but Marty
and Grammer, who had drawn up on the dark side of the same holly

which sheltered Mrs and Miss Melbury on its bright side. The two former conversed in low tones; and at that minute the girls, some of whom were from Great Hintock, were seen advancing to work the incantation, it being now about midnight.

'Directly we see anything we'll run home as fast as we can,' said one, whose courage had begun to fail her. To this the rest assented, not knowing that a dozen neighbours lurked in the bushes around.

'I wish we had not thought of trying this,' said another 'but had contented ourselves with the hole digging tomorrow at twelve, and hearing our husband's trades. It is too much like having dealings with the evil one to try to raise their forms.'

However, they had gone too far to recede, and slowly began to march forward in a skirmishing line through the trees, each intending to plunge alone into a deep recess of the wood. As far as the listeners could gather, the particular form of black art to be practised on this occasion was one connected with the sowing of hempseed, a handful of which was carried by each girl.

The Woodlanders

Old Midsummer custom: On old Midsr. eve, at going to bed:

> I put my shoes in the form of a T,
> And trust my true love for to see

Another:

On old Midsr. noon dig a hole in the grass plot, and place your ear thereon precisely at 12. The occupation of your future husband will be revealed by the noises heard.

Another old custom. Allhallows eve. Kill a pigeon: stick its heart full of pins. Roast the heart in the candle flame. Faithless lover will twist and toss with nightmare in his sleep.

Personal Notebooks of Thomas Hardy

Among the many stories of spell-working that I have been told, the following is one of how it was done by two girls about 1830. They killed a pigeon, stuck its heart full of pins, made a tripod of three knitting-needles, and suspended the heart on them over a lamp, murmuring an incantation while it roasted, and using the name of the young man in whom one or both were interested. The said young man felt racking pains about the region of the heart, and suspecting something went to the constables. The girls were sent to prison.

The Life of Thomas Hardy

The distant light which Eustacia had cursorily observed in leaving the house came, as she had divined, from the cottage-window of Susan Nunsuch. What Eustacia did not divine was the occupation of the woman within at that moment. Susan's sight of her passing figure earlier in the evening, not five minutes after the sick boy's exclamation, 'Mother, I do feel so bad!' persuaded the matron that an evil influence was certainly exercised by Eustacia's propinquity.

On this account Susan did not go to bed as soon as the evening's work was over, as she would have done at ordinary times. To counteract the malign spell which she imagined poor Eustacia to be working, the boy's mother busied herself with a ghastly invention of superstition, calculated to bring powerlessness, atrophy, and annihilation on any human being against whom it was directed. It was a practice well known on Egdon at that date, and one that is not quite extinct at the present day.

She passed with her candle into an inner room, where, among other utensils, were two large brown pans, containing together perhaps a hundredweight of liquid honey, the produce of the bees during the foregoing summer. On a shelf over the pans was a smooth and solid yellow mass of a hemispherical form, consisting of beeswax from the same take of honey. Susan took down the lump, and, cutting off several thin slices, heaped them in an iron ladle, with which she returned to the living-room, and placed the vessel in the hot ashes of the fireplace. As soon as the wax had softened to the plasticity of dough she kneaded the pieces together. And now her face became more intent. She began moulding the wax; and it was evident from her manner of manipulation that she was endeavouring to give it some preconceived form. The form was human.

By warming and kneading, cutting and twisting, dismembering and re-joining the incipient image she had in about a quarter of an hour produced a shape which tolerably well resembled a woman, and was about six inches high. She laid it on the table to get cold and hard. Meanwhile she took the candle and went upstairs to where the boy was lying.

'Did you notice, my dear, what Mrs Eustacia wore this afternoon besides the dark dress?'

'A red ribbon round her neck.'

'Anything else?'

'No – except sandal-shoes.'

'A red ribbon and sandal-shoes,' she said to herself.

Mrs Nunsuch went and searched till she found a fragment of the narrowest red ribbon, which she took downstairs and tied round the neck of the image. Then fetching ink and a quill from the rickety bureau by the window, she blackened the feet of the image to the extent presumably covered by shoes; and on the instep of each foot marked cross-lines in the shape taken by the sandal-strings of those days. Finally she tied a bit of black thread round the upper part of the head, in faint resemblance to a snood worn for confining the hair.

Susan held the object at arm's length and contemplated it with a satisfaction in which there was no smile. To anybody acquainted with the inhabitants of Egdon Heath the image would have suggested Eustacia Yeobright.

From her work-basket in the window seat the woman took a paper of pins, of the old long and yellow sort, whose heads were disposed to come off at their first usage. These she began to thrust into the image in all directions with apparently excruciating energy. Probably as many as fifty were thus inserted, some into the head of the wax model, some into the shoulders, some into the trunk, some upwards through the soles of the feet, till the figure was completely permeated with pins.

She turned to the fire. It had been of turf; and though the high heap of ashes which turf fires produce was somewhat dark and dead on the outside, upon raking it abroad with the shovel the inside of the mass showed a glow of red heat. She took a few pieces of fresh turf from the chimney-corner and built them together over the glow, upon which the fire brightened. Seizing with the tongs the image that she had made of Eustacia, she held it in the heat, and watched as it began to waste slowly away. And while she stood thus engaged there came from between her lips a murmur of words.

It was a strange jargon – the Lord's Prayer repeated backwards – the incantation usual in proceedings for obtaining unhallowed assistance against an enemy. Susan uttered the lugubrious discourse three times slowly, and when it was completed the image had considerably diminished. As the wax dropped into the fire a long flame arose from the spot, and curling its tongue round the figure ate still further into its substance. A pin occasionally dropped with the wax, and the embers heated it red as it lay.

The Return of the Native

If Henchard had only waited long enough he might at least have avoided loss, though he had not made a profit. But the momentum of his character knew no patience. At this turn of the scales he remained silent. The movements of his mind seemed to tend to the thought that some power was working against him.

'I wonder,' he asked himself with eerie misgiving; 'I wonder if it can be that somebody has been roasting a waxen image of me, or stirring an unholy brew to confound me! I don't believe in such power; and yet – what if they should ha' been doing it!' These isolated hours of superstition came to Henchard in time of moody depression, when all his practical largeness of view had oozed out of him.

The Mayor of Casterbridge

Mr Warry says that a farmer who was a tenant of a friend of his used to take the heart of every calf that died, and, sticking it full of black thorns, hang it on the cotterel, or cross-bar, of his chimney: this was done to prevent the spread of the disease that had killed the calf. When the next tenant came the chimney smoked very much, and examining it, they found it choked with hearts treated in the manner described – by that time dry and parched.

The Life of Thomas Hardy

'Father is still so much troubled in his mind about that tree,' Marty said. 'You know the tree I mean, Mr Winterborne? the tall one in front of the house that he thinks will blow down and kill us. Can you come and see if you can persuade him out of his notion? I can do nothing.'

He accompanied her to the cottage, and she conducted him upstairs. John South was pillowed up in a chair between the bed and the window, exactly opposite the latter, towards which his face was turned.

'Ah, neighbour Winterborne,' he said. 'I could bear up, I know I could, if it were not for the tree – yes, the tree 'tis that's killing me. There he stands, threatening my life every minute that the wind do blow. He'll come down upon us, and squat us dead.'

Giles looked out of the window in the direction of the woodman's gaze. The tree was a tall elm, familiar to him from childhood, which stood at a distance of two-thirds its own height from the front of South's dwelling. Whenever the wind blew, as it did now, the tree rocked, naturally enough; and the sight of its motion, and sound of its sighs, had gradually bred the terrifying illusion in the woodman's mind. Thus he would sit all day, in spite of persuasion, watching its every sway and listening to the melancholy Gregorian melodies which the air wrung out of it. This fear it apparently was, rather than any organic disease, which was eating away the health of John South.

As the tree waved South waved his head, making it his fugleman with abject obedience. 'Ah, when it was quite a small tree,' he said 'and I was a little boy, I thought one day of chopping it off with my hook to make a clothes-line prop with. But I put off doing it, and then I again thought that I would; but I forgot it and didn't. At last it got too big, and now 'tis my enemy, and will be the death of me. Little did I think, when I let that sapling stay, that a time would come when it would torment me, and dash me into my grave.'

'No, no,' said Winterborne and Marty soothingly. But they thought it possible that it might hasten him into his grave, though in another way than by falling.

. . .

They heard footsteps – a man's, but of a lighter weight than usual. 'There is Dr Fitzpiers again,' she said, and descended. Presently his tread was heard on the naked stairs.

Mr Fitzpiers entered the sick chamber as a doctor is wont to do on such occasions and pre-eminently when the room is that of the humble cottager; looking round towards the patient with a preoccupied gaze which so plainly reveals that he has well-nigh forgotten all about the case and the circumstances since he dismissed them from his mind at his last exit from the same apartment. He nodded to Winterborne, recalled the case to his thoughts, and went leisurely on to where South sat.

'This is an extraordinary case,' he said at last to Winterborne, after examining South by conversation, look and touch, and learning that the craze about the elm was stronger than ever. 'Come downstairs, and I'll tell you what I think.'

They accordingly descended, and the doctor continued 'The tree must be cut down; or I won't answer for his life.'

''Tis Mrs Charmond's tree; and I suppose we must get permission?' said Giles.

'O, never mind whose tree it is – what's a tree beside a life! Cut it down. I have not the honour of knowing Mrs Charmond as yet; but I am disposed to risk that much with her.'

''Tis timber,' rejoined Giles. 'They never fell a stick about here without its being marked first, either by her or the agent.'

'Then we'll inaugurate a new era forthwith. How long has he complained of the tree?' asked the doctor of Marty.

'Weeks and weeks, sir. The shape of it seems to haunt him like an evil spirit. He says that it is exactly his age, that it has got human sense, and sprouted up when he was born on purpose to rule him, and keep him as its slave. Others have been like it afore in Hintock.'

The Woodlanders

An old man, a wizard, used to bring toads' legs in little bags to Bagber Bridge (close to where Hardy was living), where he was met by crowds of people who came in vehicles and on foot, and bought them as charms to cure scrofula by wearing them round the neck. These legs were supposed to twitch occasionally in the bag, and probably did, when it gave the wearer's blood a 'turn,' and changed the course of the disease.

The Life of Thomas Hardy

Dec. 'The Planet Ruler'

He used to come his rounds like a pedlar, passing through M—y about every month. He carried a little bundle in his hand – a 'fardlet' it was called – wore shoes, white stockings, old black coat and trousers. Had a room at Beaminster, into which some people had seen. His method of telling your fortune was to do it religiously, his first greeting being 'The Lord hath sent us a fine morning: the Lord hath thought proper to send us rain.' At the end, 'The Lord will bless you,' etc. People used to tell him the day and hour they were born; and the next time he came he would bring the ruling of the planets – a half-sheet of letter-paper written over. He told A. Sh—, whose planet he ruled, that she would have a large family, travel, etc. His charge was sixpence: some would get him to do it for fourpence.

Diana Chester was the opposite. She used to work her spells by the Devil.

The above planet-ruler or astrologer was said to have astrological diagrams in his room at Beaminster.

Another man of the sort was called a conjuror; he lived in Blackmoor Vale. He would cause your enemy to rise in a glass of water. He did not himself know your enemy's name, but the bewitched person did, of course, recognising the form as the one he had expected.

Personal Notebooks of Thomas Hardy

Elizabeth Endorfield had a repute among women which was in its nature something between distinction and notoriety. It was founded on the following items of character. She was shrewd and penetrating; her house stood in a lonely place; she never went to church; she wore a red cloak; she always retained her bonnet indoors; and she had a pointed chin. Thus far her attributes were distinctly Satanic; and those who looked no further called her, in plain terms, a witch. But she was not gaunt, nor ugly in the upper part of her face, nor particularly strange in manner; so that, when her more intimate acquaintances spoke of her the term was softened, and she became simply a Deep Body, who was as long-headed as she was high. It may be stated that Elizabeth belonged to a class of suspects who were gradually losing their mysterious characteristics under the administration of the young vicar; though during the long reign of Mr Grinham the parish of Mellstock had proved extremely favourable to the growth of witches.

Under the Greenwood Tree

Heard a story of a farmer who was 'over-looked' [malignly affected] by *himself*. He used to go and examine his stock every morning before breakfast with anxious scrutiny. The animals pined away. He went to a conjuror or white witch, who told him he had no enemy; that the evil was of his own causing, the eye of a fasting man being very blasting: that he should eat a 'dew-bit' before going to survey any possession about which he had hopes.

The Life of Thomas Hardy

There was a great stir in the milk-house just after breakfast. The churn revolved as usual, but the butter would not come. Whenever this happened the dairy was paralyzed. Squish, squash, echoed the milk in the great cylinder, but never arose the sound they waited for.

Dairyman Crick and his wife, the milkmaids, Tess, Marian, Retty Priddle, Izz Huett, and the married ones from the cottages; also Mr Clare, Jonathan Kail, old Deborah, and the rest, stood gazing hopelessly at the churn; and the boy who kept the horse going outside put on moon-like eyes to show his sense of the situation. Even the melancholy horse himself seemed to look in at the window in inquiring despair at each walk round.

"'Tis years since I went to Conjuror Trendle's son in Egdon – years!' said the dairyman bitterly. 'And he was nothing to what his father had been. I have said fifty times, if I have said once, that I don't believe in en; though he do cast folks' waters very true. But I shall have to go to 'n if he's alive. O yes, I shall have to go to 'n, if this sort of thing continnys!'

Even Mr Clare began to feel tragical at the dairyman's desperation.

'Conjuror Fall, t'other side of Casterbridge, that they used to call 'Wide-O', was a very good man when I was a boy,' said Jonathan Kail. 'But he's rotten as touchwood by now.'

'My grandfather used to go to Conjuror Mynterne out at Owlscombe, and a clever man a' were, so I've heard grandf'er say,' continued Mr Crick. 'But there's no such genuine folk about nowadays!'

Mrs Crick's mind kept nearer to the matter in hand. 'Perhaps somebody in the house is in love,' she said tentatively. 'I've heard tell in my younger days that that will cause it. Why, Crick – that maid we had years ago, do ye mind, and how the butter didn't come then – '

'Ah, yes, yes! – but that isn't the rights o't. It had nothing to do with the love-making'.

Tess of the d'Urbervilles

We went to bed early that night, on account of our long walk; but we were far too excited to sleep at once. It was scarcely dark as yet, and the nights being still warm the window was left open as it had been left during the summer. Thus we could hear everything that passed without. People were continually coming to dip water from my aunt's well; they gathered round it in groups, and discussed the remarkable event which had latterly occurred for the first time in parish history.

'My belief is that witchcraft have done it,' said the shoe-maker, 'and the only remedy that I can think o', is for one of us to cut across to Bartholomew Gann, the white wizard, and get him to tell us how to counteract it. 'Tis a long pull to his house for a little man, such as I be, but I'll walk it if nobody else will.'

Our Exploits at West Poley

Conjuror Mynterne when consulted by Patt P— (a strapping handsome woman), told her that her husband would die on a certain day, and showed her the funeral in a glass of water. She said she could see the bearers moving along. She made her mourning. She used to impress all this on her inoffensive husband, and assure him that he would go to hell if he made the conjuror a liar. He didn't, but died on the day foretold. Oddly enough she never married again.

The Life of Thomas Hardy

In a lonely hamlet a few miles from the town – so lonely, that what are called lonely villages were teeming by comparison – there lived a man of curious repute as a forecaster or weather-prophet. The way to his house was crooked and miry – even difficult in the present unpropitious season. One evening when it was raining so heavily that ivy and laurel resounded like distant musketry, and an out-door man could be excused for shrouding himself to his ears and eyes, such a shrouded figure on foot might have been perceived travelling in the direction of the hazel-copse which dripped over the prophet's cot. The turnpike-road became a lane, the lane a cart-track, the cart-track a bridle-path, the bridle-path a foot-way, the foot-way overgrown. The solitary walker slipped here and there, and stumbled over the natural springes formed by the brambles, till at length he reached the house, which, with its garden, was surrounded with a high, dense hedge. The cottage, comparatively a large one, had been built of mud by the occupier's own hands, and thatched also by himself. Here he had always lived, and here it was assumed he would die.

He existed on unseen supplies; for it was an anomalous thing that while there was hardly a soul in the neighbourhood but affected to laugh at this man's assertions, uttering the formula, 'There's nothing in 'em,' with full assurance on the surface of their faces, very few of them were unbelievers in their secret hearts. Whenever they consulted him they did it 'for a fancy'. When they paid him they said, 'Just a trifle for Christmas,' or 'Candlemas,' as the case might be.

He would have preferred more honesty in his clients, and less sham ridicule; but fundamental belief consoled him for superficial irony. As stated, he was enabled to live; people supported him with their backs turned. He was sometimes astonished that men could profess so little and believe so much at his house, when at church they professed so much and believed so little.

Behind his back he was called 'Wide-Oh,' on account of his reputation; to his face 'Mr' Fall.

The hedge of his garden formed an arch over the entrance, and a door was inserted as in a wall. Outside the door the tall traveller stopped, bandaged his face with a handkerchief as if he were suffering from tooth-ache, and went up the path. The window shutters were not closed, and he could see the prophet within, preparing his supper.

In answer to the knock Fall came to the door, candle in hand. The visitor stepped back a little from the light, and said, 'Can I speak to 'ee?' in significant tones. The other's invitation to come in was responded to by the country formula, 'This will do, thank ye,' after which the householder has no alternative but to come out. He placed the candle on the corner of the dresser, took his hat from a nail, and joined the stranger in the porch, shutting the door behind him.

'I've long heard that you can – do things of a sort?' began the other, repressing his individuality as much as he could.

'Maybe so, Mr Henchard,' said the weather-caster.

'Ah – why do you call me that?' asked the visitor with a start.

'Because it's your name. Feeling you'd come, I've waited for ye; and thinking you might be leery from your walk, I laid two supper plates – look ye here.' He threw open the door and disclosed the supper-table, at which appeared a second chair, knife, fork, plate and mug, as he had declared.

Henchard felt like Saul at his reception by Samuel; he remained in silence for a few moments, then throwing off the disguise of frigidity which he had hitherto preserved, he said, 'Then I have not come in vain ... Now, for instance, can ye charm away warts?'

'Without trouble.'

'Cure the evil?'

'That I've done – with consideration – if they will wear the toad-bag by night as well as by day.'

'Forecast the weather?'

'With labour and time.'

'Then take this,' said Henchard. ''Tis a crown-piece. Now, what is the harvest fortnight to be? When can I know?'

'I've worked it out already, and you can know at once.' (The fact was that five farmers had already been there on the same errand from different parts of the country.) 'By the sun, moon and stars, by the clouds,

the winds, the trees, and grass, the candle-flame and swallows, the smell
of the herbs; likewise by the cats' eyes, the ravens, the leeches, the
spiders, and the dung-mixen, the last fortnight in August will be – rain
and tempest.'

'You are not certain, of course?'

'As one can be in a world where all's unsure. 'Twill be more like living
in Revelations this autumn than in England. Shall I sketch it out for ye in
a scheme?'

'O no, no,' said Henchard. 'I don't altogether believe in forecasts,
come to second thoughts on such. But I – '

'You don't – you don't – 'tis quite understood,' said Wide-oh, without
a sound of scorn. 'You have given me a crown because you've one too
many. But won't you join me at supper, now 'tis waiting and all?'

Henchard would gladly have joined; for the savour of the stew had
floated from the cottage into the porch with such appetizing distinctness,
that the meat, the onions, the pepper, and the herbs could be severally
recognized by his nose. But as sitting down to hob-and-nob there would
have seemed to mark him too implicitly as the weather-caster's apostle,
he declined, and went his way.

The Mayor of Casterbridge

Half a dozen years passed away, and Mr and Mrs Lodge's married
experience sank into prosiness, and worse. The farmer was usually
gloomy and silent; the woman whom he had wooed for her grace and
beauty was contorted and disfigured in the left limb; moreover she had
brought him no child, which rendered it likely that he would be the last of
a family who had occupied that valley for some two hundred years.

The once blithe-hearted and enlightened Gertrude was changing into
an irritable, superstitious woman, whose whole time was given to
experimenting upon her ailment with every quack remedy she came
across. She was honestly attached to her husband, and was ever secretly
hoping against hope to win back his heart again by regaining some at
least of her personal beauty. Hence it arose that her closet was lined with
bottles, packets and ointment-pots of every description – nay, bunches of
mystic herbs, charms, and books of necromancy, which in her schoolgirl
time she would have ridiculed as folly.

'Damned if you won't poison yourself with these apothecary messes
and witch mixtures some time or other,' said her husband, when his eye
chanced to fall upon the multitudinous array.

She did not reply, but turned her sad, soft glance upon him in such
heart-swollen reproach that he looked sorry for his words, and added, 'I
only meant it for your good, you know, Gertrude.'

'I'll clear out the whole lot, and destroy them,' said she huskily, 'and try such remedies no more!'

She was now five-and-twenty; but she seemed older. 'Six years of marriage, and only a few months of love,' she sometimes whispered to herself. And then she thought of the apparent cause, and said, with a tragic glance at her withering limb, 'If I could only again be as I was when he first saw me!'

She obediently destroyed her nostrums and charms; but there remained a hankering wish to try something else – some other sort of cure altogether. She had never revisited Trendle since she had been conducted to the house of the solitary by Rhoda against her will; but it now suddenly occurred to Gertrude that she would, in a last desperate effort at deliverance from this seeming curse, again seek out the man, if he yet lived. He was entitled to a certain credence, for the indistinct form he had raised in the glass had undoubtedly resembled the only woman in the world who – as she now knew, though not then – could have a reason for bearing her ill-will. The visit should be paid.

This time she went alone, though she nearly got lost on the heath, and roamed a considerable distance out of her way. Trendle's house was reached at last, however; he was not indoors, and instead of waiting at the cottage, she went to where his bent figure was pointed out to her at work a long way off. Trendle remembered her, and laying down the handful of furze-roots which he was gathering and throwing into a heap, he offered to accompany her in her homeward direction, as the distance was considerable and the days were short. So they walked together, his head bowed nearly to the earth, and his form of a colour with it.

'You can send away warts and other excrescences, I know,' she said; 'why can't you send away this?' And the arm was uncovered.

'You think too much of my powers!' said Trendle; 'and I am old and weak now, too. No, no; it is too much for me to attempt in my own person. What have ye tried?'

She named to him some of the hundred medicaments and counter-spells which she had adopted from time to time. He shook his head.

'Some were good enough,' he said approvingly; 'but not many of them for such as this. This is of the nature of a blight, not of the nature of a wound, and if you ever do throw it off, it will be all at once.'

'If only I could!'

'There is only one chance of doing it known to me. It has never failed in kindred afflictions – that I can declare. But it is hard to carry out, and especially for a woman.'

'Tell me!' said she.

'You must touch with the limb the neck of a man who's been hanged.'

She started a little at the image he had raised.

'Before he's cold – just after he's cut down,' continued the conjuror impassively.

'How can that do good?'

'It will turn the blood and change the constitution. But, as I say, to do
it is hard. You must go to the jail when there's a hanging, and wait for
him when he's brought off the gallows. Lots have done it, though perhaps
not such pretty women as you. I used to send dozens for skin complaints.
But that was in former times. The last I sent was in '13 – near twelve
years ago.'

He had no more to tell her, and, when he had put her into a straight
track homeward, turned and left her, refusing all money as at first.

A RIDE

The communication sank deep into Gertrude's mind. Her nature was
rather a timid one; and probably of all remedies that the white wizard
could have suggested there was not one which would have filled her with
so much aversion as this, not to speak of the immense obstacles in the way
of its adoption.

Casterbridge, the county-town, was a dozen or fifteen miles off; and
though in those days, when men were executed for horse-stealing, arson
and burglary, an assize seldom passed without a hanging, it was not
likely that she could get access to the body of the criminal unaided. And
the fear of her husband's anger made her reluctant to breathe a word of
Trendle's suggestion to him or to anybody about him.

She did nothing for months, and patiently bore her disfigurement as
before. But her woman's nature, craving for renewed love, through the
medium of renewed beauty (she was but twenty-five), was ever
stimulating her to try what, at any rate, could hardly do her any harm.
'What came by a spell will go by a spell surely,' she would say.

Whenever her imagination pictured the act she shrank in terror from
the possibility of it; then the words of the conjuror, 'It will turn your
blood,' were seen to be capable of a scientific no less than a ghastly
interpretation; the mastering desire returned, and urged her on again.

There was at this time but one county paper, and that her husband
only occasionally borrowed. But old-fashioned days had old-fashioned
means, and news was extensively conveyed by word of mouth from
market to market, or from fair to fair, so that, whenever such an event as
an execution was about to take place, few within a radius of twenty miles
were ignorant of the coming sight; and, so far as Holmstoke was
concerned, some enthusiasts had been known to walk all the way to
Casterbridge and back in one day, solely to witness the spectacle. The
next assizes were in March; and when Gertrude Lodge heard that they
had been held, she inquired stealthily at the inn as to the result, as soon
as she could find opportunity.

She was, however, too late. The time at which the sentences were to
be carried out had arrived, and to make the journey and obtain admission

at such short notice required at least her husband's assistance. She dared not tell him, for she had found by delicate experiment that these smouldering village beliefs made him furious if mentioned, partly because he half entertained them himself. It was therefore necessary to wait for another opportunity.

Her determination received a fillip from learning that two epileptic children had attended from this very village of Holmstoke many years before with beneficial results, though the experiment had been strongly condemned by the neighbouring clergy. April, May, June passed; and it is no overstatement to say that by the end of the last-named month Gertrude wellnigh longed for the death of a fellow-creature. Instead of her formal prayers each night, her unconscious prayer was, 'O Lord, hang some guilty or innocent person soon!'

This time she made earlier enquiries and was altogether more systematic in her proceedings. Moreover the season was summer, between haymaking and the harvest, and in the leisure thus afforded him her husband had been holiday-taking away from home.

The assizes were in July, and she went to the inn as before. There was to be one execution – only one – for arson.

Her greatest problem was not how to get to Casterbridge, but what means she should adopt for obtaining admission to the jail. Though access for such purposes had never formerly been denied, the custom had fallen into desuetude; and in contemplating her possible difficulties, she was again almost driven to fall back upon her husband. But, on sounding him out about the assizes, he was so uncommunicative, so more than usually cold, that she did not proceed, and decided that whatever she did she would do alone.

Fortune, obdurate hitherto, showed her unexpected favour. On the Thursday before the Saturday fixed for the execution, Lodge remarked to her that he was going away from home for another day or two on business at a fair, and that he was sorry he could not take her with him.

She exhibited on this occasion so much readiness to stay at home that he looked at her in surprise. Time had been when she would have shown deep disappointment at the loss of such a jaunt. However, he lapsed into his usual taciturnity, and on the day named left Holmstoke.

It was now her turn. She at first had thought of driving, but on reflection held that driving would not do, since it would necessitate her keeping to the turnpike-road, and so increase by tenfold the risk of her ghastly errand being found out. She decided to ride, and avoid the beaten track, notwithstanding that in her husband's stables there was no animal just at present which by any stretch of imagination could be considered a lady's mount, in spite of his promise before marriage to always keep a mare for her. He had, however, many cart-horses, fine ones of their kind; and among the rest was a serviceable creature, an equine Amazon, with a back as broad as a sofa, on which Gertrude had occasionally taken on airing when unwell. This horse she chose.

On Friday afternoon one of the men brought it round. She was dressed, and before going down looked at her shrivelled arm. 'Ah!' she said to it, 'if it had not been for you this terrible ordeal would have been saved me!'

When strapping up the bundle in which she carried a few articles of clothing, she took occasion to say to the servant, 'I take these in case I should not get back tonight from the person I am going to visit. Don't be alarmed if I am not in by ten, and close up the house as usual. I shall be at home tomorrow for certain.' She meant then to tell her husband privately; the deed accomplished was not like the deed projected. He would almost certainly forgive her.

And then the pretty palpitating Gertrude Lodge went from her husband's homestead; but though her goal was Casterbridge she did not take the direct route thither through Stickleford. Her cunning course at first was in precisely the opposite direction. As soon as she was out of sight, however, she turned to the left, by a road which led into Egdon, and on entering the heath wheeled round, and set out in the true course, due westerly. A more private way down the county could not be imagined; and as to direction she had merely to keep her horse's head to a point a little to the right of the sun. She knew that she would light upon a furze-cutter or cottager of some sort from time to time, from whom she might correct her bearing.

Though the date was comparatively recent, Egdon was much less fragmentary in character than now. The attempts – successful and otherwise – at cultivation on the lower slopes, which intrude and break up the original heath into small detached heaths, had not been carried far; Enclosure Acts had not taken effect, and the banks and fences which now exclude the cattle of those villagers who formerly enjoyed rights of commonage thereon, and the carts of those who had turbary privileges which kept them in firing all the year round, were not erected. Gertrude, therefore, rode along with no other obstacles than the prickly furze-bushes, the mats of heather, the white water-courses, and the natural steeps and declivities of the ground.

Her horse was sure, if heavy-footed and slow, and though a draught animal, was easy-paced; had it been otherwise, she was not a woman who could have ventured to ride over such a bit of country with a half-dead arm. It was therefore nearly eight o'clock when she drew rein to breathe her bearer on the last outlying high point of heath-land towards Casterbridge, previous to leaving Egdon for the cultivated valleys.

She halted before a pool called Rushy-pond, flanked by the ends of two hedges; a railing ran through the centre of the pond, dividing it in half. Over the railing she saw the low green country; over the green trees the roofs of the town; over the roofs a white flat façade, denoting the entrance to the county jail. On the roof of this front specks were moving about; they seemed to be workmen erecting something. Her flesh crept. She descended slowly, and was soon amid corn-fields and pastures. In another half-hour, when it was almost dusk, Gertrude reached the White Hart, the first inn of the town on that side.

Little surprise was excited by her arrival; farmers' wives rode on horseback then more than they do now; though, for that matter, Mrs Lodge was not imagined to be a wife at all; the inn-keeper supposed her some harum-skarum young woman who had come to attend 'hang-fair' next day. Neither her husband nor herself ever dealt in Casterbridge market, so that she was unknown. While dismounting she beheld a crowd of boys standing at the door of a harness-maker's shop just above the inn, looking inside it with deep interest.

'What is going on there?' she asked of the ostler.

'Making the rope for to-morrow.'

She throbbed responsively, and contracted her arm.

''Tis sold by the inch afterwards,' the man continued. 'I could get you a bit, miss, for nothing, if you'd like?'

She hastily repudiated any such wish, all the more from a curious creeping feeling that the condemned wretch's destiny was becoming interwoven with her own; and having engaged a room for the night, sat down to think.

Up to this time she had formed but the vaguest notions about her means of obtaining access to the prison. The words of the cunning-man returned to her mind. He had implied that she should use her beauty, impaired though it was, as a pass-key. In her inexperience she knew little about jail functionaries; she had heard of a high-sheriff and an under-sheriff, but dimly only. She knew, however, that there must be a hangman, and to the hangman she determined to apply.

A WATER-SIDE HERMIT

At this date, and for several years after, there was a hangman to almost every jail. Gertrude found, on inquiry, that the Casterbridge official dwelt in a lonely cottage by a deep slow river flowing under the cliff on which the prison buildings were situate – the stream being the self-same one, though she did not know it, which watered the Stickleford and Holmstoke meads lower down in its course.

Having changed her dress, and before she had eaten or drunk – for she could not take her ease till she had ascertained some particulars – Gertrude pursued her way by a path along the water-side to the cottage indicated. Passing thus the outskirts of the jail, she discerned on the level roof over the gateway three rectangular lines against the sky, where the specks had been moving in her distant view; she recognised what the erection was, and passed quickly on. Another hundred yards brought her to the executioner's house, which a boy pointed out. It stood close to the same stream, and was hard by a weir, the waters of which emitted a steady roar.

While she stood hesitating the door opened, and an old man came forth, shading a candle with one hand. Locking the door on the outside, he turned to a flight of wooden steps fixed against the end of the cottage, and began to ascend them, this being evidently the staircase to his bedroom. Gertrude hastened forward, but by the time she reached the foot of the ladder he was at the top. She called to him loudly enough to be heard above the roar of the weir; he looked down and said, 'What d'ye want here?'

'To speak to you a minute'.

The candle-light, such as it was, fell upon her imploring, pale, upturned face, and Davies (as the hangman was called) backed down the ladder. 'I was just going to bed,' he said. '"Early to bed and early to rise," but I don't mind stopping a minute for such a one as you. Come into house.' He reopened the door, and preceded her to the room within.

The implements of his daily work, which was that of a jobbing gardener, stood in a corner, and seeing probably that she looked rural, he said, 'If you want me to undertake country work I can't come, for I never leave Casterbridge for gentle nor simple – not I. My real calling is officer of justice,' he added formally.

'Yes, yes! That's it. Tomorrow!'

'Ah! I thought so. Well, what's the matter about that? 'Tis no use to come here about the knot – folks do come continually, but I tell 'em one knot is as merciful as another if ye keep it under the ear. Is the unfortunate man a relation; or, I should say, perhaps' (looking at her dress) 'a person who's been in your employ?'

'No. What time is the execution?'

'The same as usual – twelve o'clock, or as soon after as the London mail-coach gets in. We always wait for that, in case of a reprieve.'

'O – a reprieve – I hope not!' she said involuntarily.

'Well, – hee, hee! – as a matter of business, so do I! But still, if ever a young fellow deserved to be let off, this one does; only just turned eighteen, and only present by chance when the rick was fired. Howsomever, there's not much risk of it, as they are obliged to make an example of him, there having been so much destruction of property that way lately.'

'I mean,' she explained, 'that I want to touch him for a charm, a cure of an affliction, by the advice of a man who has proved the virtue of the remedy.'

'O yes, miss! Now I understand. I've had such people come in past years. But it didn't strike me that you looked of a sort to require blood-turning. What's the complaint? The wrong kind for this, I'll be bound.'

'My arm.' She reluctantly showed the withered skin.

'Ah! – 'tis all a-scram!' said the hangman, examining it.

'Yes,' said she.

'Well,' he continued, with interest, 'that *is* the class o' subject, I'm bound to admit! I like the look of the wownd; it is truly as suitable for the cure as any I ever saw. 'Twas a knowing-man that sent 'ee, whoever he was.'

'You can contrive for me all that's necessary?' she said breathlessly.

'You should really have gone to the governor of the jail, and your doctor with 'ee, and given your name and address – that's how it used to be done, if I recollect. Still, perhaps, I can manage it for a trifling fee.'

'O, thank you! I would rather do it this way, as I should like it kept private.'

'Lover not to know, eh?'

'No – husband.'

'Aha! Very well. I'll get 'ee a touch of the corpse.'

'Where is it now?' she said, shuddering.

'It? – *he*, you mean; he's living yet. Just inside that little small winder up there in the glum.' He signified the jail on the cliff above.

She thought of her husband and her friends. 'Yes, of course,' she said; 'and how am I to proceed?'

He took her to the door. 'Now, do you be waiting at the little wicket in the wall, that you'll find up there in the lane, not later than one o'clock. I will open it from the inside, as I shan't come home to dinner till he's cut down. Good-night. Be punctual; and if you don't want anybody to know 'ee, wear a veil. Ah – once I had such a daughter as you!'

She went away, and climbed the path above, to assure herself that she would be able to find the wicket next day. Its outline was soon visible to her – a narrow opening in the outer wall of the prison precincts. The steep was so great that, having reached the wicket, she stopped a moment to breathe; and, looking back upon the water-side cot, saw the hangman again ascending his outdoor staircase. He entered the loft or chamber to which it led, and in a few minutes extinguished his light.

The town clock struck ten, and she returned to the White Hart as she had come.

'The Withered Arm'

15

UPSTAIRS, DOWNSTAIRS

Nobody who recalls the scene in *Jude the Obscure* where Jude, exploring the colleges of Christminster, stands outside the wall that divides him from the undergraduates whom he yearns to join, will forget the intensity of Hardy's comment – 'Only a wall – but what a wall!'

It was that wall, of class and privilege, which bulked so large and for so long in Hardy's own life. The community into which he was born had its traditional class structure, distinctly perceived and generally respected. In their appropriate grades were the landowning aristocracy; the professional gentry composed of the clergy, naval and military officers, senior legal figures and their like; the tenant farmers and merchants; the independent craftsmen and tradesmen; and the workfolk, the labouring class. Each preserved an almost tribal separateness from the rest in their social activities and their *mores*. In *The Woodlanders* Dr Fitzpiers, of aristocratic lineage, admits frankly that he thinks of himself as belonging to a different species from the manual labourers whose work he is watching.

Hardy, in his lifetime, started near the bottom of the social heap and finished near the top. The older Hardy men, as master masons and occasional employers of others, were a cut above the 'workfolk'. They had secure tenure of the cottage at Bockhampton, by lifehold, and therefore enjoyed an economic independence at a modest level; but in other respects they were on the wrong side of the culture gap – in education and social etiquette, in speech and pedigree and the prevailing ideas of good taste and gentlemanly conduct. At best they were in the worthy yeoman tradition. Domestic service was a familiar world to their womenfolk, who thus penetrated the upper reaches of society, learned their codes and shibboleths and brought into their own marriages the niceties and aspirations they had picked up from their observation posts below stairs, at table and in the boudoir.

Like any cottage child Hardy would have learned early on how he was expected to behave in public to the squire and his lady, and what were the ways by which he might 'better' himself. One noble dame of his later acquaintance upbraided the mother of a five-year-old because the little girl had not already been taught to curtsey to her superiors. Among the cottagers themselves the correctly genteel pronunciation of an everyday word like 'potatoes' could be a burning topic, and for a woman to 'keep herself up' at all times was a matter of great concern. Old habits of speech, like the use of 'thee' and 'thou', were frowned on. Even in quite humble homes there were status symbols, as specific to their class as a shield to a nobleman: the little digression on coffin stools in *The Woodlanders* is a revealing instance.

Noble pedigree stands out as the chief bulwark of the class system as Hardy knew it. With sufficient application a commoner could acquire the wealth that opened many doors and could school himself in the manners of high society, but he could not change his ancestry. At most he could – like Mr Simon Stoke – buy a dignified and ancient name like d'Urberville, but he remained a fraud. The unqualified respect for titled personages, in which Hardy was nurtured, never fell entirely away from him though he satirized it in the person of Mr Melbury in *The Woodlanders*. Moreover, though he poked fun at the man, he also understood Melbury's bitter anguish when he was snubbed in his daughter's presence by a gentleman riding to hounds. It is not so surprising that Melbury should hope to see his daughter making a 'romantical' marriage that linked her with 'history'. The forceful influence of high-born names would not have been doubted or underrated in the family circle at Bockhampton. To be 'kin to a coach' had a solid and negotiable value, as Tess's mother knew; and Hardy used the phrase more than once.

Always in Hardy, though, there is a sense of longer perspectives; and never more so than here, in this matter of noble lineage which is subject, as is all else, to the rise and fall, the flowering and the decline of the passing generations. It is this which liberalizes the apparently rigid system and finds superb expression in the ultimately decayed aristocrat, Tess's father – Sir John d'Urberville, no less, with 'grander and nobler skillentons' in the family vault than anyone else could boast of. And to add to the disrepute of this aristocratic descent Tess's mother says: 'Thank God, I was never of no family, and have nothing to be ashamed of in that way!' to which her husband replies: 'Don't you

be so sure o' that. From your nater 'tis my belief you've disgraced
yourselves more than any o' us, and was Kings and Queens outright at
one time'. The partly chaffing, partly satirical tone is characteristic of
Hardy.

In his first published novel, *Desperate Remedies*, he made a
straightforward statement of his own conception of himself in class
terms when he described the attitude of a haughty lady of the manor
towards a young man of lowly origins: she was unable to understand
how this son of one of her tenants could have become 'an educated
man' whose attitude to society was 'Bohemian'. There could be no
apter description of the young Hardy. He was an indefatigable self-
educator, and Bohemian was a key-word with him – describing the
artists, novelists, poets and philosophers who stood apart from the
class system and transgressed its demarcations at will.

In order to become a Bohemian and an author writing about
something more than the quaintness of village life Hardy had to train
himself to pass as a man of the world, at ease in the several levels of
society. His early difficulties were reflected in his first novel, 'The Poor
Man and the Lady', which was not published or even preserved intact;
but some parts of it were salvaged and embodied later in *An Indiscretion
in the Life of an Heiress*. Geraldine, the heiress, in her thoughts about the
humble background of her lover, Egbert, is sometimes 'a trifle vexed
that their experiences contained so little in common – that he had
never dressed for dinner, or made use of a carriage in his life'. To help
him to acquire an air of sophistication she tells Egbert: 'You must get
to talk authoritatively about vintages and their dates'. The same idea
of the cryptic vocabulary of class signals recurs in *A Pair of Blue Eyes*,
when the rector, Mr Swancourt, expresses his doubt of 'a man's being a
gentleman if his palate had no acquired tastes'. As late as January 1874,
in a letter to Genevieve Smith, Hardy described himself as 'having
been denied until very lately the society of educated womankind,
which teaches men what cannot be acquired from books'.

What his Bohemian standpoint gave Hardy was the objective
blending of satire in the scenes of accepted rural snobberies as he so
intimately knew them. Miller Loveday's conventional apology, in *The
Trumpet-Major*, for allowing the workfolk into the parlour in Mrs
Garland's presence carries a sly hint that these uncouth persons
happen also to be the brave volunteers preparing to defend Mrs
Garland from an imminent invasion by the French army. And when
Haymoss, in *Two on a Tower*, suggests that a comet is an ill omen, to be
feared, his companion dismisses it scornfully on the ground that such a
remarkable phenomenon would not be wasted on the lower classes but
must be intended exclusively for the manor house.

As a further step Hardy designed a novel, *The Hand of Ethelberta*, to reverse the customary social perspective so that 'the drawing-room was sketched in many cases from the point of view of the servants' hall'. Ethelberta herself is a fascinating character – a butler's daughter who swiftly and conveniently becomes Mrs Petherwin, the widow of the heir to a baronetcy, and is therefore equally at home upstairs or downstairs. She also writes poetry of a rather advanced and even *risqué* kind, which clearly classifies her as a Bohemian. The identification of her social ambivalence with Hardy's is abundantly clear and gives added point to her 'sense of disloyalty to her class and kin'.

To someone who, in today's jargon, was as upwardly mobile as Hardy in the prime of his manhood, that sense of disloyalty was a secret burden of guilt that he himself gradually purged. In his early novels he claims little more for the village folk than that their quaintness will amuse the educated reading public. The centre of his stage is given mainly to the inhabitants of the manor house, the rectory, the professional office, the garrison quarters. It is by degrees, as his command of the novel develops, that the obscure folk of Wessex shed their humorous oddities and take over the leading roles. In that sense Ethelberta is a transitional figure. It is she, the butler's daughter, who takes charge of the estate of her decadent aristocratic husband and becomes the efficient manager. Through her ambiguous world of above and below stairs she leads the way to the epic figures of Henchard, the itinerant hay-trusser; Tess the dairymaid; Marty South the spar-maker and bark-cutter; and Jude the stonemason.

When Hardy, in 1895, at the end of his career as novelist, wrote a preface for a new edition of *The Hand of Ethelberta* he could claim with justice that 'such a reversal of the social foreground has, perhaps, since grown more welcome'. At that moment he might well have called to mind the splendid lampoon of the pedigree that even the least of us share with Miller Loveday, as it is enunciated in *The Trumpet-Major*.

'I dare say I am inhuman, and supercilious, and contemptibly proud of my poor old ramshackle family; but I do honestly confess to you that I feel as if I belonged to a different species from the people who are working in that yard'.

Edred Fitzpiers in *The Woodlanders*

Mrs Dewy sighed and appended a remark (ostensibly behind her husband's back, though that the words should reach his ears distinctly was understood by both): 'Such a man as Dewy is! Nobody do know the trouble I have to keep that man barely respectable. And did you ever hear too – just now at supper-time – talking about "taties" with Michael in such a work-folk way. Well, 'tis what I was never brought up to! With our family 'twas never less than "taters", and very often "pertatoes" outright; mother was so particular and nice with us girls: there was no family in the parish that kept themselves up more than we.'

Under the Greenwood Tree

'Mother,' exclaimed Stephen, 'how absurdly you speak! Criticizing whether she's fit for me or no, as if there were room for doubt on the matter! Why, to marry her would be the great blessing of my life – socially and practically, as well as in other respects. No such good fortune as that, I'm afraid; she's too far above me. Her family doesn't want such country lads as I in it.'

'Then if they don't want you, I'd see them dead corpses before I'd want them, and go to families who do want you.'

'Ah, yes; but I could never put up with the distaste of being welcomed among such people as you mean, whilst I could get indifference among such people as hers.'

'What crazy twist of thinking will enter your head next?' said his mother. 'And come to that, she's not a bit too high for you, or you too low for her. See how careful I am to keep myself up. I'm sure I never stop for more than a minute together to talk to any journeymen people; and I never invite anybody to our party o' Christmases who are not in business for themselves. And I talk to several toppermost carriage people that come to my lord's without saying ma'am or sir to 'em, and they take it as quiet as lambs.'

'You curtseyed to the vicar, mother; and I wish you hadn't.'

A Pair of Blue Eyes

'You'd be surprised to see how vain the girls about here be getting. Little rascals, why they won't curtsey to the loftiest lady in the land; no, not if you were to pay 'em to do it. Now, the men be different. Any man will touch his hat for a pint of beer.'

The Hand of Ethelberta

As the afternoon advanced the guests gathered on the spot, where music, dancing, and the singing of songs went forward with great spirit throughout the evening. The propriety of every one was intense, by reason of the influence of Fancy, who, as an additional precaution in this direction had strictly charged her father and the tranter to carefully avoid saying 'thee' and 'thou' in their conversation, on the plea that those ancient words sounded so very humiliating to persons of newer taste; also that they were never to be seen drawing the back of the hand across the mouth after drinking – a local English custom of extraordinary antiquity, but stated by Fancy to be decidedly dying out among the better classes of society.

Under the Greenwood Tree

Beside her, in case she might require more light, a brass candlestick stood on a little round table, curiously formed of an old coffin-stool, with a deal top nailed on, the white surface of the latter contrasting oddly with the black carved oak of the sub-structure. The social position of the household in the past was almost as definitively shown by the presence of this article as that of an esquire or nobleman by his old helmets or shields. It had been customary for every well-to-do villager, whose tenure was by copy of court-roll, or in any way more permanent than that of the mere cotter, to keep a pair of these stools for the use of his own dead; but changes had led to the discontinuance of the custom, and the stools were frequently made use of in the manner described.

The Woodlanders

A few weeks later there was a friendly dinner-party at the house of a gentleman called Doncastle, who lived in a moderately fashionable square of west London. All the friends and relatives present were nice people, who exhibited becoming signs of pleasure and gaiety at being there; but as regards the vigour with which these emotions were expressed, it may be stated that a slight laugh from far down the throat and a slight narrowing of the eye were equivalent as indices of the degree of mirth felt to a Ha-ha-ha! and a shaking of the shoulders among the minor traders of the kingdom; and to a Ho-ho-ho! contorted features, purple face, and stamping foot among the gentlemen in corduroy and fustian who adorn the remoter provinces.

The Hand of Ethelberta

Melbury's respect for Fitzpiers was based less on his professional position, which was not much, than on the standing of his family in the county in bygone days. That touching faith in members of long-established families as such, irrespective of their personal condition or character, which is still found among old-fashioned people in the rural districts, reached its full perfection in Melbury. His daughter's suitor was descended from a line he had heard of in his grand-father's time as being once among the greatest, a family which had conferred its name upon a neighbouring village; how then could anything be amiss in this betrothal?

The Woodlanders

It was a day of rather bright weather for the season. Miss Melbury went out for a morning walk, and her ever-regardful father, having an hour's leisure, offered to walk with her.

The breeze was fresh and quite steady, filtering itself through the denuded mass of twigs without swaying them, but making the point of each ivy-leaf on the trunks scratch its underlying neighbour restlessly. Grace's lips sucked in this native air of hers like milk. They soon reached a place where the wood ran down into a corner, and they went outside it towards comparatively open ground. Having looked round, they were intending to re-enter the copse when a panting fox emerged with a dragging brush, trotted past them tamely as a domestic cat, and disappeared amid some dead fern. They walked on, her father merely observing, after watching the animal, 'They are hunting somewhere near.'

Further up they saw in the mid-distance the hounds running hither and thither, as if the scent lay cold that day. Soon members of the hunt appeared on the scene, and it was evident that the chase had been stultified by general puzzle-headedness as to the whereabouts of the intended victim. In a minute a gentleman-farmer, panting with Actaeonic excitement, rode up to the two pedestrians, and Grace being a few steps in advance he asked her if she had seen the fox.

'Yes,' said she. 'I saw him some time ago – just out there.'

'Did you cry Halloo?'

'I said nothing'.

'Then why the devil didn't you, or get the old buffer to do it for you?' said the man as he cantered away.

She looked rather disconcerted, and observing her father's face saw that it was quite red.

'He ought not to have spoken to 'ee like that!' said the old man in the tone of one whose heart was bruised, though it was not by the epithet applied to himself. 'And he wouldn't if he had been a gentleman. 'Twas not the language to use to a woman of any niceness. You so well read and cultivated – how could he expect ye to go shouting a view-halloo like a farm tomboy! Hasn't it cost me near a hundred a year to lift you out of all that, so as to show an example to the neighbourhood of what a woman can be? Grace, shall I tell you the secret of it? 'Twas because I was in your company. If a black-coated squire or pa'son had been walking with you instead of me he wouldn't have spoken so.'

'No, no, father; there's nothing in you rough or ill-mannered!'

'I tell you it is that! I've noticed, and I've noticed it many times, that a woman takes her colour from the man she's walking with. The woman who looks an unquestionable lady when she's with a polished-up fellow, looks a tawdry imitation article when she's hobbing and nobbing with a homely blade. You sha'nt be treated like that for long, or at least your children shan't. You shall have somebody to walk with you who looks more of a dandy than I – please God you shall!'

'But, my dear father,' she said, much distressed, 'I don't mind at all. I don't wish for more honour than I already have!'

'A perplexing and ticklish possession is a daughter,' according to the Greek poet, and to nobody was one ever more so than to Melbury.

'You would like to have more honour, if it pleases me?' asked her father, in continuation of the subject.

Despite her feeling she assented to this. His reasoning had not been without weight upon her.

'Grace,' he said, just before they had reached the house, 'if it costs me my life you shall marry well! To-day has shown me that whatever a young woman's niceness she stands for nothing alone. You shall marry well.'

The Woodlanders

'There,' he said. 'You see that hill rising out of the level like a great whale, and just behind the hill a particularly green sheltered bottom? That's where Mr Fitzpiers's family were lords of the manor for I don't know how many hundred years, and there stands the village of Oakbury Fitzpiers. A wonderful property 'twas – wonderful!'

'But they are not lords of the manor there now.'

'Why, no. But good and great folk fall as well as humble and foolish. The only ones representing the family now, I believe, are our doctor and a maiden lady living I don't know where. You can't help being happy, Grace, in allying yourself with such a romantical family. Why, on the mother's side he's connected with the long line of the Lords Baxby of Sherton. You'll feel as if you've stepped into history.

'We've been at Hintock as long as they were at Oakbury; is it not so? You say our name occurs in old deeds, continually.'

'O yes – as yeomen, copyholders, and such like. But think how much better this will be for 'ee. You'll be living a high, perusing life, such as has now become natural to you; and though the doctor's practice is small here he'll no doubt go to a dashing town when he's got his hand in, and keep a stylish carriage, and you'll be brought to know a good many ladies of excellent society. If you should ever meet me then, Grace, you can drive past me, looking the other way. I shouldn't expect you to speak to me, or wish such a thing – unless it happened to be in some lonely private place where 'twouldn't lower 'ee at all.'

The Woodlanders

'However, it is well to be kin to a coach though you never ride in it'.

The Hand of Ethelberta

'However, 'tis well to be kin to a coach, even if you don't ride in 'en'.

Tess of the d'Urbervilles

'Well, Fred, I don't mind telling you that the secret is that I'm one of a noble race – it has been just found out by me this present afternoon, P.M.' And as he made the announcement, Durbeyfield, declining from his sitting position, luxuriously stretched himself out upon the bank among the daisies.

The lad stood before Durbeyfield, and contemplated his length from crown to toe.

'Sir John d'Urberville – that's who I am,' continued the prostrate man. 'That is if knights were baronets – which they be. 'Tis recorded in history all about me. Dost know of such a place, lad, as Kingsbere-sub-Greenhill?'

'Ees. I've been there to Greenhill Fair.'

'Well, under the church of that city there lie – '

''Tisn't a city, the place I mean; leastwise 'twaddn' when I was there – 'twas a little one-eyed, blinking sort o' place.'

'Never you mind the place, boy, that's not the question before us. Under the church of that there parish lie my ancestors – hundreds of 'em – in coats of mail and jewels, in gr't lead coffins weighing tons and tons. There's not a man in the county o' South-Wessex that's got grander and nobler skillentons in his family than I.'

Tess of the d'Urbervilles

Miss Aldclyffe, like a good many others in her position, had plainly not realized that a son of her tenant and inferior could have become an educated man, who had learnt to feel his individuality, to view society from a Bohemian standpoint, far outside the farming grade in Carriford parish, and that hence he had all a developed man's unorthodox opinion about the subordination of classes.

Desperate Remedies

'I was inclined to suspect him, because he didn't care about sauces of any kind. I always did doubt a man's being a gentleman if his palate had no acquired tastes. An unedified palate is the irrepressible cloven foot of the upstart. The idea of my bringing out a bottle of my '40 Martinez – only eleven of them left now – to a man who didn't know it from eighteenpenny!'

A Pair of Blue Eyes

The elder Loveday apologized in a whisper to Mrs Garland for the presence of the inferior villagers. 'But as they are learning to be brave defenders of their home and country, ma'am, as fast as they can master the drill, and have worked for me off and on these many years, I've asked 'em in, and thought you'd excuse it'.

The Trumpet-Major

'And what do this comet mean?' asked Haymoss. 'That some great tumult is going to happen, or that we shall die of a famine?'

'Famine – no!' said Nat Chapman. 'That only touches such as we, and the Lord only consarns himself with born gentlemen. It isn't to be supposed that a strange fiery lantern like that would be lighted up for folks with ten or a dozen shillings a week and their gristing, and a load o' thorn faggots when we can get 'em. If 'tis a token that he's getting hot about the ways of anybody in this parish, 'tis about my Lady Constantine's, since she is the only one of a figure worth such a hint.'

Two on a Tower

On its first appearance the novel suffered, perhaps deservedly, for what was involved in these intentions – for its quality of unexpectedness in particular – that unforgivable sin in the critic's sight – the immediate precursor of 'Ethelberta' having been a purely rural tale. Moreover, in its choice of medium, and line of perspective, it undertook a delicate task: to excite interest in a drama – if such a dignified word may be used in the connection – wherein servants were as important as, or more important than, their masters; wherein the drawing-room was sketched in many cases from the point of view of the servants' hall. Such a reversal of the social foreground has, perhaps, since grown more welcome, and readers even of the finer crusted kind may now be disposed to pardon a writer for presenting the sons and daughters of Mr and Mrs Chickerel as beings who come within the scope of a congenial regard.

T.H.

December 1895

Preface to The Hand of Ethelberta

It was an ordinary family dinner that day, but their nephew Neigh happened to be present. Just as they were sitting down Mrs Doncastle said to her husband 'Why have you not told me of the wedding to-morrow; – or don't you know anything about it?'

'Wedding?' said Mr Doncastle.

'Lord Mountclere is to be married to Mrs Petherwin quite privately.'

'Good God!' said some person.

Mr Doncastle did not speak the words; they were not spoken by Neigh: they seemed to float over the room and round the walls, as if originating in some spiritualistic source. Yet Mrs Doncastle, remembering the symptoms of attachment between Ethelberta and her nephew which had appeared during the summer, looked towards Neigh instantly, as if she thought the words must have come from him after all; but Neigh's face was perfectly calm; he, together with her husband, was sitting with his eyes fixed in the direction of the sideboard; and turning to the same spot she beheld Chickerel standing pale as death, his lips being parted as if he did not know where he was.

'Did you speak?' said Mrs Doncastle, looking with astonishment at the butler.

'Chickerel, what's the matter – are you ill?' said Mr Doncastle simultaneously. 'Was it you who said that?'

'I did, sir,' said Chickerel in a husky voice, scarcely above a whisper. 'I could not help it.'

'Why?'

'She is my daughter, and it shall be known at once!'

'Who is your daughter?'

He paused a few moments nervously. 'Mrs Petherwin,' he said.

Upon this announcement Neigh looked at poor Chickerel as if he saw through him into the wall. Mrs Doncastle uttered a faint exclamation and leant back in her chair; the bare possibility of the truth of Chickerel's claims to such paternity shook her to pieces when she viewed her intimacies with Ethelberta during the past season – the court she had paid her, the arrangements she had entered into to please her; above all, the dinner-party which she had contrived and carried out solely to gratify Lord Mountclere and bring him into personal communication with the general favourite; thus making herself probably the chief though unconscious instrument in promoting a match by which her butler was to become father-in-law to a peer she delighted to honour. The crowd of perceptions almost took away her life; she closed her eyes in a white shiver.

'Do you mean to say that the lady who sat here at dinner at the same time that Lord Mountclere was present, is your daughter?' asked Doncastle.

'Yes, sir,' said Chickerel respectfully.

'How did she come to be your daughter?'

'I – Well, she is my daughter, sir.'

'Did you educate her?'

'Not altogether, sir. She was a very clever child. Lady Petherwin took a deal of trouble about her education. They were both left widows about the same time: the son died, then the father. My daughter was only seventeen then. But though she's older now, her marriage with Lord Mountclere means misery. He ought to marry another woman.'

'It is very extraordinary,' Mr Doncastle murmured. 'If you are ill you had better go and rest yourself, Chickerel. Send in Thomas '

Chickerel, who seemed to be much disturbed, then very gladly left the room, and dinner proceeded. But such was the peculiarity of the case, that, though there was in it neither murder, robbery, illness, accident, fire, or any other of the tragic and legitimate shakers of human nerves, two of the three who were gathered there sat through the meal without the least consciousness of what viands had composed it. Impressiveness depends as much upon propinquity as upon magnitude; and to have honoured unawares the daughter of the vilest Antipodean miscreant and murderer would have been less discomfiting to Mrs Doncastle than it was to make the same blunder with the daughter of a respectable servant who happened to live in her own house. To Neigh the announcement was as the catastrophe of a story already begun, rather than as an isolated wonder. Ethelberta's words had prepared him for something, though the nature of that thing was unknown.

'Chickerel ought not to have kept us in ignorance of this – of course he ought not!' said Mrs Doncastle, as soon as they were left alone.

'I don't see why not,' replied Mr Doncastle, who took the matter very coolly, as was his custom.

'Then she herself should have let it be known.'

'Nor does that follow. You didn't tell Mrs Petherwin that your grandfather narrowly escaped hanging for shooting his rival in a duel.'

'Of course not. There was no reason why I should give extraneous information.'

'Nor was there any reason why she should. As for Chickerel, he doubtless felt how unbecoming it would be to make personal remarks upon one of your guests – Ha-ha-ha! Well, well – Ha-ha-ha-ha!'

'I know this,' said Mrs Doncastle, in great anger, 'that if my father had been in the room, I should not have let the fact pass unnoticed, and treated him like a stranger!'

'Would you have had her introduce Chickerel to us all round? My dear Margaret, it was a complicated position for a woman.'

'Then she ought not to have come!'

'There may be something in that, though she was dining out at other houses as good as ours. Well, I should have done just as she did, for the joke of the thing. Ha-ha-ha! – It is very good   very. It was a case in which the appetite for a jest would overpower the sting of conscience in any well-constituted being – that, my dear, I must maintain.'

'I say she should not have come!' answered Mrs Doncastle firmly. 'Of course I shall dismiss Chickerel.'

'Of course you will do no such thing. I have never had a butler in the

house before who suited me so well. It is a great credit to the man to have
such a daughter, and I am not sure that we do not derive some lustre of a
humble kind from his presence in the house. But, seriously, I wonder at
your short-sightedness, when you know the troubles we have had through
getting new men from nobody knows where.'

The Hand of Ethelberta

'Lord Mountclere is still alive and well, I am told?'

'O ay. He'll live to be a hundred. Never such a change as has come
over the man of late years.'

'Indeed!'

'O, 'tis my lady. She's a one to put up with! Still, 'tis said here and
there that marrying her was the best day's work that he ever did in his
life, although she's got to be my lord and my lady both.'

'Is she happy with him?'

'She is very sharp with the pore man – about happy I don't know. He
was a good-natured old man, for all his sins, and would sooner any day
lay out money in new presents than pay it in old debts. But 'tis altered
now. 'Tisn't the same place. Ah, in the old times I have seen the floor of
the servants' hall over the vamp of your boot in solid beer that we had
poured aside from the horns because we couldn't see straight enough to
pour it in. See? No, we couldn't see a hole in a ladder! And now, even at
Christmas or Whitsuntide, when a man, if ever he desires to be overcome
with a drop, would naturally wish it to be, you can walk out of Enckworth
as straight as you walked in. All her doings.'

'Then she holds the reins?'

'She do! There was a little tussle at first; but how could a old man
hold his own against such a spry young body as that! She threatened to
run away from him, and kicked up Bob's-a-dying, and I don't know what
all; and being the woman, of course she was sure to beat in the long run.
Pore old nobleman, she marches him off to church every Sunday as
regular as a clock, makes him read family prayers that haven't been read
in Enckworth for the last thirty years to my certain knowledge, and keeps
him down to three glasses of wine a day, strict, so that you never see him
any the more generous for liquor or a bit elevated at all, as it used to be.
There, 'tis true, it has done him good in one sense, for they say he'd have
been dead in five years if he had gone on as he was going.'

'So that she's a good wife to him, after all.'

'Well, if she had been a little worse 'twould have been a little better
for him in one sense, for he would have had his own way more. But he
was a curious feller at one time, as we all know and I suppose 'tis as much
as he can expect; but 'tis a strange reverse for him. It is said that when
he's asked out to dine, or to anything in the way of a jaunt, his eye flies

across to hers afore he answers: and if her eye says yes, he says yes: and if her eye says no, he says no. 'Tis a sad condition for one who ruled womankind as he, that a woman should lead him in a string whether he will or no.'

'Sad indeed!'

'She's steward, and agent, and everything. She has got a room called "my lady's office," and great ledgers and cash-books you never see the like. In old times there were bailiffs to look after the workfolk, foremen to look after the tradesmen, a building-steward to look after the foremen, a land-steward to look after the building-steward, and a dashing grand agent to look after the land-steward: fine times they had then, I assure ye. My lady said they were eating out the property like a honeycomb, and then there was a terrible row. Half of 'em were sent flying; and now there's only the agent, and the viscountess, and a sort of surveyor man, and of the three she does most work so 'tis said. She marks the trees to be felled, settles what horses are to be sold and bought, and is out in all winds and weathers. There, if somebody hadn't looked into things 'twould soon have been all up with his lordship, he was so very extravagant. In one sense 'twas lucky for him that she was born in humble life, because owing to it she knows the ins and outs of contriving, which he never did.'

The Hand of Ethelberta

Miller Loveday was the representative of an ancient family of corn-grinders whose history is lost in the mists of antiquity. His ancestral line was contemporaneous with that of De Ros, Howard, and De La Zouche; but, owing to some trifling deficiency in the possessions of the house of Loveday, the individual names and intermarriages of its members were not recorded during the Middle Ages, and thus their private lives in any given century were uncertain. But it was known that the family had formed matrimonial alliances with farmers not so very small, and once with a gentleman-tanner, who had for many years purchased after their death the horses of the most aristocratic persons in the county – fiery steeds that earlier in their career had been valued at many hundred guineas.

It was also ascertained that Mr Loveday's great-grandparents had been eight in number, and his great-great-grandparents sixteen, every one of whom reached to years of discretion: at every stage backwards his sires and gammers thus doubled and doubled till they became a vast body of Gothic ladies and gentlemen of the rank known as ceorls or villeins, full of importance to the country at large, and ramifying throughout the unwritten history of England.

The Trumpet-Major

16

LAW AND ORDER

The public face of the law in Britain today is almost featureless. Accused persons make fleeting appearances concealed under blankets. No punishments are administered publicly and no cameras are permitted in trial courts. Convicts disappear in an unseen world of imprisonment. None is executed or flogged.

It is all so different from the home world of Hardy's youth and from the testimony of his parents and grandparents. To them the countenance of the law was a constantly present one of great severity. In conspicuous roadside locations gibbets were still standing as a reminder of the Bloody Assize after the battle of Sedgemoor when John Whiting, a Quaker, protested at 'this forcing poor men to hale about men's quarters, like horse-flesh or carrion, to boil and hang them up as monuments of their cruelty and inhumanity'. Hardy himself witnessed two hangings. The public whipping of men, women and children had been a commonplace sight to his parents and grandparents. One of today's more 'romantic' relics, the village stocks, was in general use.

To these traditional displays of the law's power to punish and deter there was a more recent addition – transportation to the colonies. After Sedgemoor James II's Queen made a handsome profit from the transportation to the West Indies of the hundred rebels given to her, at her request; but it was not until the settlement of Australia that transportation became a regular and widely feared punishment, and the words 'Botany Bay' acquired that sinister ring which echoed for long after the penalty fell into disuse.

These matters were prominent topics of conversation at

Bockhampton. How could they not be, in the light of local events in the
1830s? The revolt of the farm labourers against deepening poverty,
which swept across southern England, has come to be symbolized in
the story of the Tolpuddle Martyrs: and Tolpuddle is only about five
miles from Bockhampton. Even nearer was the outbreak of arson and
destruction at Puddletown. Memories of those days lingered for a long
time in the popular consciousness. I once heard a labourer, speaking of
some wrongdoers in his village, recall a stern magistrate of his younger
days and remark, 'If the old 'un 'ad bin alive, 'e'd 'a' transported 'n.'

The hangings that Hardy saw in his youth made a deep and lasting
impression on him. Near the end of his life he could still write with a
morbid fascination of the 'fine figure' of the hanged woman, Martha
Brown, and how her tight silk gown 'set off her shape as she wheeled
half-round and back'. The excuse he made for his presence – that he
had to be in the vicinity anyway – is disingenuous: on the other
occasion he went to rising ground behind his home and focused a
telescope on the gallows in front of Dorchester gaol in order to see a
man hanged.

There were rougher forms of law enforcement, when the interests of
the landed gentry and the government were threatened by lawless men
in confrontations of unrestrained violence. Poachers, deer-stealers and
smugglers were ranged against the gins and spring-guns and the
keepers of the game preserves, and the excise men or revenue men who
patrolled the Channel coast. Episodes of this sort have acquired a
patina of romance as they recede into the past, but often they were
bloody affrays in which men were maimed for life and sometimes
killed. Cranborne Chase was not disfranchised until ten years before
Hardy's birth: the legendary battles there – only a score of miles from
Bockhampton – must have been in the family's repertoire of anecdotes.
Of his grandfather's association with local smugglers Hardy was
aware, and it was from an ex-smuggler latterly employed by his father
that Hardy acquired the background knowledge that he used to good
effect in 'The Distracted Preacher'.

There are obvious elements of class warfare here. A separate
working-class culture with its alternative form of law shows even more
clearly in the practice of wife-selling. While it may sometimes have
been a brutal degradation of a woman's status, it was probably in the
main a poor person's divorce by consent. The cost of a legal divorce
made that a privilege of the wealthy. The alternative of a public wife
sale satisfied the need to publish a change of relationship with the tacit
approval of the community. Purchase by the woman's lover might
often have been agreed beforehand. The scene in the market place was
the working-class equivalent of the divorce court – sharing with the
neighbouring folk in an open and above-board way what would

otherwise have been a furtive act. It was of course illegal but the official
response varied greatly. In one recorded case a prosecution led to
imprisonment, while in another the worst that happened was that the
lord of the manor demanded payment of the toll due to him on all sales
in the market.

The 'skimmington ride' could similarly be regarded as a piece of
alternative folk law, in which neighbours of fellow-townsmen sought to
redress a wrong by taking the law into their own hands and imposing
their own penalty in forms of ridicule and satire. It was not the role of
the official law courts to punish the bullying wife or the adulterous
husband. For such purposes the skimmington was a last resort.

In his notebooks and in correspondence Hardy revealed his intense
interest in the rigours of the law in the earlier decades of the
nineteenth century, but when he began his career as an author he
judged the taste of his readers to favour a countryman figure, a Hodge,
who exhibited a quaintness and a whimsicality – even a cheerfulness –
rather than a blend of revolutionary fervour and abject misery. By the
1880s, at the height of his powers as a novelist, he might have written
the following, which he was well equipped to do –

> Towards the end of the year [1816] wheat rose to 103 shillings a
> quarter, and incendiarism was common all over England. A sense of
> insecurity and terror took possession of everybody. Secret outrages,
> especially fires at night, chill the courage of the bravest, as those know
> well enough who have lived in an agricultural county, when, just
> before going to bed, great lights are seen on the horizon.

That is not from Hardy's pen, however, but from Mark Rutherford's
The Revolution in Tanner's Lane, published in 1887. Hardy made little
direct use of material of that kind, probably feeling that it was like the
milk from Talbothays farm which needed the judicious addition of
water before it reached Londoners, to lower its strength 'so that it may
not get up into their heads'. The confrontation between law-officers
and smugglers in 'The Distracted Preacher' has a gently bowdlerized
tone to it for which Hardy felt obliged to add an extenuating postscript
thirty years later. In *The Mayor of Casterbridge* the deeply felt animosities
of gamekeeper and poacher mellow into reminiscent bonhomie among
the retired combatants at The Peter's Finger in Mixen Lane. The
village stocks occur only fleetingly in a poem of such indifferent quality
that I have omitted it. In the stories which contain hangings the reader
is not permitted to witness the event.

From whatever motive, Hardy chose not to exploit, in a
documentary way, the grim store of anecdote and local history that he
had gathered and might have used to illuminate the style of social

repression and punishment that prevailed in his heritage. Some of it perhaps was too recent, too personal, too near the bone. Occasionally, in a low key, a harsh and bitter cry breaks through. The poem 'The Fight on Durnover Moor' has a brutal realism transmitted with unrelieved accuracy from its time and place: its final climactic words are 'Botany Bay'. And the same sudden shock comes when Farfrae is singing his sentimental love of Scotland, in *The Mayor of Casterbridge*, and Christopher Coney listens incredulously and exclaims: 'I have no more love for my country than I have for Botany Bay'.

That undercurrent is an unemphasized part of the sustained murmuring of rustic voices which accompanies Hardy's writing. His preferred technique was to transform it into an ironical humour in which the glint of satire is inescapable. To that extent he took a civilized revenge for what others had suffered, but the core of early impressions stayed with him and maintained its potency. When his imagination took wing it was the lingering brutalities of man-trap, wife sale, skimmington, hangman and the like which were transformed into the masterpieces of his fiction.

My grandmother told me that when she was a girl – 1785 to 1790 – she used to pass a gibbet in Berkshire with great terror.

Letter to Frederic Harrison, 20 June 1918

Brine says that Jack White's gibbet (near Wincanton) was standing as late as 1835 – i.e. the oak-post with the iron arm sticking out, and a portion of the cage in which the body had formerly hung.

The Life of Thomas Hardy

In the neighbourhood of county-towns hanging matters used to form a large proportion of the local tradition; and though never personally acquainted with any chief operator at such scenes, the writer of these pages had as a boy the privilege of being on speaking terms with a man who applied for the office, and who sank into an incurable melancholy because he failed to get it, some slight mitigation of his grief being to dwell upon striking episodes in the lives of those happier ones who had held it with success and renown. His tale of disappointment used to cause his listener some wonder why his ambition should have taken such an unfortunate form, by limiting itself to a profession of which there could be only one practitioner in England at one time, when it might have aimed at something more common-place – that would have afforded him more chances – such as the office of a judge, a bishop, or even a member of Parliament – but its nobleness was never questioned. In those days, too, there was still living an old woman who, for the cure of some eating disease, had been taken in her youth to have her 'blood turned' by a convict's corpse, in the manner described in 'The Withered Arm.'

Preface to *Wessex Tales*

My dear Lady Pinney,

My sincere thanks for the details you have been so indefatigable as to obtain about that unhappy woman Martha Brown, whom I am ashamed to say I saw hanged, my only excuse being that I was but a youth, & had to be in the town at the time for other reasons . . . I remember what a fine figure she showed against the sky as she hung in the misty rain, & how the tight black silk gown set off her shape as she wheeled half-round & back.

Letter to Lady Hester Pinney, 20 January 1926

One summer morning at Bockhampton, just before he sat down to breakfast, he remembered that a man was to be hanged at eight o'clock at Dorchester. He took up the big brass telescope that had been handed on in the family, and hastened to a hill on the heath a quarter of a mile from the house, whence he looked towards the town. The sun behind his back shone straight on the white stone façade of the gaol, the gallows upon it, and the form of the murderer in white fustian, the executioner and officials in dark clothing, and the crowd below, being invisible at this distance of three miles. At the moment of his placing the glass to his eye the white figure dropped downwards, and the faint note of the town clock struck eight.

The whole thing had been so sudden that the glass nearly fell from Hardy's hands. He seemed alone on the heath with the hanged man; and he crept homeward wishing he had not been so curious. It was the second and last execution he witnessed, the first having been that of a woman two or three years earlier, when he stood close to the gallows.

The Life of Thomas Hardy

Father says that when there was a hanging at Dorchester in his boyhood it was carried out at one o'clock, it being the custom to wait till the mail-coach came in from London in case of a reprieve.

The Life of Thomas Hardy

T. Voss used to take casts of heads of executed convicts. He took those of Preedy and Stone. Dan Pouncy held the heads while it was being done. Voss oiled the faces, and took them in halves, afterwards making casts from the masks. There was a groove where the rope went, and Voss saw a little blood in the case of Stone, where the skin had been broken, – not in Preedy's.

The Life of Thomas Hardy

'I am told that when Jack Ketch had done whipping by the Town Pump [Dorchester] the prisoners' coats were thrown over their bleeding backs, and, guarded by the town-constables with their long staves, they were conducted back to prison. Close at their heels came J.K., the cats held erect – there was one cat to each man – the lashes were of knotted whipcord.

The Life of Thomas Hardy

Culprits were whipped in the market place continually: here it was done on Saturdays, in a farmer's waggon by the town-pump. My mother when a girl saw a child whipped at the cart-tail round Yeovil for stealing a book from a stall.

Letter to Frederic Harrison, 20 June 1918

February 6th. Sunday. To see my father. It was three men whom he last saw flogged in Dorchester by the Town-pump – about 1830. He happened to go in from Stinsford about mid-day. Some soldiers coming down the street from the barracks interfered, and swore at Davis [Jack Ketch] because he did not 'flog fair'; that is to say he waited between each lash for the flesh to recover sensation, whereas, as they knew from experience, by striking quickly the flesh remained numb through several strokes.

The Life of Thomas Hardy

September 9. My Father says that Dick Facey used to rivet on the fetters of criminals when they were going off by coach (Facey was journeyman for Clare the smith). He was always sent for secretly, that people might not know and congregate at the gaol entrance. They were carried away at night, a stage-coach being specially ordered. One K. of Troytown, on the London Road, a poacher, who was in the great fray at Westwood Barn near Lulworth Castle about 1825, was brought past his own door thus, on his way to transportation: he called to his wife and family; they heard his shout and ran out to bid him good-bye as he sat in chains. He was never heard of again by them.

The Life of Thomas Hardy

'My husband was a connoisseur in man-traps and spring-guns and such articles, collecting them from all his neighbours. He knew the histories of all these – which gin had broken a man's leg, which gun had killed a man'.

Mrs Charmond in The Woodlanders

Were the inventors of automatic machines to be ranged according to the excellence of their devices for producing sound artistic torture, the creator of the man-trap would occupy a very respectable, if not a very high, place.

It should rather, however, be said, the inventor of the particular form of man-trap of which this found in the keeper's outhouse was a specimen. For there were other shapes and other sizes, instruments which, if placed in a row beside one of the type disinterred by Tim, would have worn the subordinate aspect of the bears, wild boars, or wolves in a travelling menagerie as compared with the leading lion or tiger. In short, though many varieties had been in use during those centuries which we are accustomed to look back upon as the true and only period of merry England – in the rural districts more especially – and onward down to the third decade of the nineteenth century, this model had borne the palm, and had been most usually followed when the orchards and estates required new ones.

There had been the toothless variety used by the softer-hearted landlords – quite contemptible in their clemency. The jaws of these resembled the jaws of an old woman to whom time has left nothing but gums. There were also the intermediate or half-toothed sorts, probably devised by the middle-natured squires, or those under the influence of their wives: two inches of mercy, two inches of cruelty, two inches of mere nip, two inches of probe, and so on, through the whole extent of the jaws. There were also, as a class apart, the bruisers, which did not lacerate the flesh, but only crushed the bone.

The sight of one of these gins, when set, produced a vivid impression that it was endowed with life. It exhibited the combined aspects of a shark, a crocodile, and a scorpion. Each tooth was in the form of a tapering spine, two and a quarter inches long, which, when the jaws were closed, stood in alternation from this side and from that. When they were open, the two halves formed a complete circle between two and three feet in diameter, the plate or treading-place in the midst being about a foot square, while from beneath extended in opposite directions the soul of the apparatus, the pair of springs, each one having been in its prime of a stiffness to render necessary a lever or the whole weight of the body when forcing it down, though rust had weakened it somewhat now.

There were men at this time still living at Hintock who remembered when the gin and others like it were in use. Tim Tangs's great-uncle had endured a night of six hours in this very trap, which lamed him for life. Once a keeper of Hintock woods set it on the track of a poacher, and afterwards, coming back that way forgetful of what he had done, walked into it himself. The wound brought on lockjaw, of which he died. This event occurred during the thirties, and by the year 1840 the use of such implements was well nigh discontinued in the neighbourhood. But being made entirely of iron, they by no means disappeared, and in almost every village one could be found in some nook or corner.

The Woodlanders

Ex-poachers and ex-gamekeepers, whom squires had persecuted without a cause, sat elbowing each other – men who in past times had met in fights under the moon, till lapse of sentences on the one part, and loss of favour and expulsion from service on the other, brought them here together to a common level, where they sat calmly discussing old times.

'Dos't mind how you could jerk a trout ashore with a bramble, and not ruffle the stream, Charl?' a deposed keeper was saying. ''Twas at that I caught 'ee once, if you can mind?'

'That can I. But the worst larry for me was that pheasant business at Yalbury Wood. Your wife swore false that time, Joe – O, by Gad, she did – there's no denying it.'

'How was that?' asked Jopp.

'Why – Joe closed wi' me, and we rolled down together, close to his garden hedge. Hearing the noise, out ran his wife with the oven pyle, and it being dark under the trees she couldn't see which was uppermost. "Where beest thee, Joe, under or top?" she screeched. "O – under, by Gad!" says he. She then began to rap down upon my skull, back, and ribs, with the pyle till we'd roll over again. "Where beest now, dear Joe, under or top?" she'd scream again. By George, 'twas through her I was took! And then when we got up in hall she sware that the cock pheasant was one of her rearing, when 'twas not your bird at all, Joe; 'twas Squire Brown's bird – that's whose 'twas – one that we'd picked off as we passed his wood, an hour afore. It did hurt my feelings to be so wronged! . . . Ah well – 'tis over now.'

'I might have had 'ee days afore that,' said the keeper. 'I was within a few yards of 'ee dozens of times, with a sight more of birds than that poor one.'

The Mayor of Casterbridge

In a conversation with William Archer Hardy recalled seeing a man in the stocks at Puddletown –

Mr Hardy. I remember one perfectly – when I was very young. It was in the village I have called Weatherbury. I can see him now, sitting in the blazing sunshine, with not another human being near except me. I can see his blue worsted stockings projecting through the leg-holes, and the shining nails in his boots. He was quite a hero in my eyes. I sidled up to him and said good-day to him, and felt mightily honoured when he nodded to me.

W.A. Do you know what his offence was?

Mr Hardy. 'Drunk and disorderly,' no doubt.

W.A. Then by what authority – by what legal process – was he put in the stocks?

Mr Hardy. I can't say exactly. It used to be understood that the constable could put a man in the stocks, but that only a magistrate could lock them. But perhaps that was only a village superstition.

Real Conversations: William Archer

The firing of the alarm-gun went on at intervals, low and sullenly, and their suspicions became a certainty. The sinister gentleman in cinder-gray roused himself. 'Is there a constable here?' he asked, in thick tones. 'If so, let him step forward.'

The engaged man of fifty stepped quavering out from the wall, his betrothed beginning to sob on the back of the chair.

'You are a sworn constable?'

'I be, sir.'

'Then pursue the criminal at once, with assistance, and bring him back here. He can't have gone far.'

'I will, sir, I will – when I've got my staff. I'll go home and get it, and come sharp here, and start in a body.'

'Staff! – never mind your staff; the man'll be gone!'

'But I can't do nothing without my staff – can I, William, and John, and Charles Jake? No; for there's the king's royal crown a painted on en in yaller and gold, and the lion and the unicorn, so as when I raise en up and hit my prisoner, 'tis made a lawful blow thereby. I wouldn't 'tempt to take up a man without my staff – no, not I. If I hadn't the law to gie me courage, why, instead o' my taking up him he might take up me!'

'The Three Strangers'

17

FAIRS AND CIRCUSES

In Hardy's boyhood such entertainment as was enjoyed by the
village folk was principally of their own making. They sang and
danced, made music and acted the traditional mummers' play, to
the best of their abilities, but the notion of paying to be entertained by
professional performers had no place in everyday life. That was
something of a rare event, a red-letter day in the rural calendar. Each
district had its annual fair which was held primarily for the purposes of
agricultural commerce but served a secondary function by attracting
the itinerant showmen who brought their roundabouts, steam organs,
sideshows and booths to provide an hour or two of fantasy and
amusement. And with them might also come a touring circus or a
company of strolling players. Before the mass mobility that the railway
introduced it was the day of the fair that marked the summit of popular
entertainment. On a lesser scale some villages had their individual
feast or carnival, usually associated with the feast day of the parish's
patron saint. Two notable Wiltshire examples of long-established
tradition that come to mind are Aldbourne Feast and Pewsey Carnival,
events which still attract to themselves 'all the fun of the fair'.

Hardy would have grown up with this sense of special, wonderful
occasions that came round only at rare intervals and acquired an
undeniable glamour from the very fact that they ran counter to all that
was normal and habitual in daily life. His delight in the spectacle of a
circus was frankly expressed. His description of a fit-up performance of
Othello vividly recaptures the atmosphere of such an event, which
clearly stretched the responsive powers of an audience more attuned to

'The Murder in the Red Barn' and 'The Demon Barber of Fleet Street'. Although he had no wish to be regarded as a writer specializing in 'sheepfolds' he took care to celebrate the sheep fair at Woodbury Hill near Bere Regis – 'Greenhill' as he renamed it – with a wealth of detail to justify his claim that it was 'the Nijni Novgorod of south Wessex'. He knew the equally important status of Weyhill Fair in Hampshire – 'Weydon Prior's' in Hardy's nomenclature – and understood the transition from the serious commerce of farming to the popular frivolities. And he was obviously at home with the noise and excitement that fill the market place in Salisbury during the October fair each year – even, at the present day, with a mechanical organ of Hardy's generation belting out *fortissimo* melodies from Italian opera.

In his notebooks and poems he preserved sudden fleeting impressions that came to him in these contexts – an apparently headless woman, a dwarf leading a blind giant, a sale of New Forest ponies, a shooting-gallery attendant. In the larger structures of his novels and stories he drew on his stored resources to portray Troy performing in the circus ring at Greenhill, Henchard attracted to the liquor tent at Weydon, and the young barrister and the maidservant at Melchester Fair, in 'On the Western Circuit', fascinated by 'this most delightful holiday-game of our times' – the steam roundabout.

Characteristically, as a *bonne-bouche*, in the dying moments after the fair, his sense of Time's long perspective animates the shared moments of revelry that link the folk of Casterbridge with their Roman forbears.

'I have loved circuses all my life.'

Letter to John Masefield, 17 June 1923

When I am riding round the ring no longer,
    Tell a tale of me;
Say, no steed-borne woman's nerve was stronger
    Than used mine to be.
  Let your whole soul say it; do:
    O it will be true!

Should I soon no more be mistress found in
    Feats I've made my own,
Trace the tan-laid track you'd whip me round in
    On the cantering road:
  There may cross your eyes again
    My lithe look as then.

Show how I, when clay becomes my cover,
　Took the high-hoop leap
Into your arms, who coaxed and grew my lover, –
　　Ah, to make me weep
　Since those claspings cared for so
　　Ever so long ago!

Though not now as when you freshly knew me,
　But a fading form, 　　　　　　　·
Shape the kiss you'd briskly blow up to me
　　While our love was warm,
　And my cheek unstained by tears,
　　As in these last years!

'Circus-Rider to Ringmaster'

August 14. Strolling players at Dorchester in the market-field. Went to *Othello*. A vermilion sunset fell on the west end of the booth, where, while the audience assembled, Cassio, in supposed Venetian costume, was lounging and smoking in the red light at the bottom of the van-steps behind the theatre: Othello also lounging in the same sunlight on the grass by the stage door, and touching up the black of his face.

The play begins as the dusk comes on, the theatre-lights within throwing the spectators' and the actors' profiles on the canvas, so that they are visible outside, and the immortal words spread through it into the silence around, and to the trees, and stars.

I enter. A woman plays Montano, and her fencing with Cassio leaves much to the imagination. Desdemona's face still retains its anxiety about the supper that she has been cooking a few minutes earlier in the stove without.

Othello is played by the proprietor, and his speeches can be heard as far as to the town-pump. Emilia wears the earrings I saw her wearing when buying family vegetables this morning. The tragedy goes on successfully, till the audience laughs at the beginning of the murder scene. Othello stops, and turning, says sternly to them after an awful pause: 'Is this the Nineteenth Century?' The conscience-stricken audience feel the justice of the reproof, and preserve an abashed silence as he resumes. When he comes to the pillow-scene they applaud with tragic vehemence, to show that their hearts are in the right place after all.

The Life of Thomas Hardy

Greenhill was the Nijni Novgorod of South Wessex; and the busiest, merriest, noisiest day of the whole statute number was the day of the sheep fair. This yearly gathering was upon the summit of a hill which retained in good preservation the remains of an ancient earthwork, consisting of a huge rampart and entrenchment of an oval form encircling the top of the hill, though somewhat broken down here and there. To each of the two chief openings on opposite sides a winding road ascended, and the level green space of ten or fifteen acres enclosed by the bank was the site of the fair. A few permanent erections dotted the spot, but the majority of visitors patronized canvas alone for resting and feeding under during the time of their sojourn here.

Shepherds who attended with their flocks from long distances started from home two or three days, or even a week, before the fair, driving their charges a few miles each day – not more than ten or twelve – and resting them at night in hired fields by the wayside at previously chosen points, where they fed, having fasted since morning. The shepherd of each flock marched behind, a bundle containing his kit for the week strapped upon his shoulders, and in his hand his crook, which he used as the staff of his pilgrimage. Several of the sheep would get worn and lame, and occasionally a lambing occurred on the road. To meet these contingencies, there was frequently provided, to accompany the flocks from the remoter points, a pony and waggon into which the weakly ones were taken for the remainder of the journey.

The Weatherbury Farms, however, were no such long distance from the hill, and those arrangements were not necessary in their case. But the large united flocks of Bathsheba and Farmer Boldwood formed a valuable and imposing multitude which demanded much attention, and on this account Gabriel, in addition to Boldwood's shepherd and Cain Ball, accompanied them along the way, through the decayed town of Kingsbere, and upward to the plateau, – old George the dog of course behind them.

When the autumn sun slanted over Greenhill this morning and lighted the dewy flat upon its crest, nebulous clouds of dust were to be seen floating between the pairs of hedges which streaked the wide prospect around in all directions. These gradually converged upon the base of the hill, and the flocks became individually visible, climbing the serpentine ways which led to the top. Thus, in a slow procession, they entered the opening to which the roads tended, multitude after multitude, horned and hornless – blue flocks and red flocks, buff flocks and brown flocks, even green and salmon-tinted flocks, according to the fancy of the colourist and custom of the farm. Men were shouting, dogs were barking, with greatest animation, but the thronging travellers in so long a journey had grown nearly indifferent to such terrors, though they still bleated piteously at the unwontedness of their experiences, a tall shepherd rising here and there in the midst of them, like a gigantic idol amid a crowd of prostrate devotees.

The great mass of sheep in the fair consisted of South Downs and the old Wessex horned breeds; to the latter class Bathsheba's and Farmer Boldwood's mainly belonged. These filed in about nine o'clock, their vermiculated horns lopping gracefully on each side of their cheeks in geometrically perfect spirals, a small pink and white ear nestling under each horn. Before and behind came other varieties, perfect leopards as to the full rich substance of their coats, and only lacking the spots. There were also a few of the Oxfordshire breed, whose wool was beginning to curl like a child's flaxen hair, though surpassed in this respect by the effeminate Leicesters, which were in turn less curly than the Cotswolds. But the most picturesque by far was a small flock of Exmoors, which chanced to be there this year. Their pied faces and legs, dark and heavy horns, tresses of wool hanging round their swarthy foreheads, quite relieved the monotony of the flocks in that quarter.

All these bleating, panting, and weary thousands had entered and were penned before the morning had far advanced, the dog belonging to each flock being tied to the corner of the pen containing it. Alleys for pedestrians intersected the pens, which soon became crowded with buyers and sellers from far and near.

Far from the Madding Crowd

The trusser and his family proceeded on their way, and soon entered the Fair-field, which showed standing-places and pens where many hundreds of horses and sheep had been exhibited and sold in the forenoon, but were now in great part taken away. At present, as their informant had observed, but little real business remained on hand, the chief being the sale by auction of a few inferior animals, that could not otherwise be disposed of, and had been absolutely refused by the better class of traders, who came and went early. Yet the crowd was denser now than during the morning hours, the frivolous contingent of visitors, including journeymen out for a holiday, a stray soldier or two come on furlough, village shopkeepers, and the like, having latterly flocked in; persons whose activities found a congenial field among the peep-shows, toy-stands, waxworks, inspired monsters, disinterested medical men who travelled for the public good, thimble-riggers, nick-nack vendors, and readers of Fate.

Neither of our pedestrians had much heart for these things, and they looked around for a refreshment tent among the many which dotted the down. Two, which stood nearest to them in the ochreous haze of expiring sunlight, seemed almost equally inviting. One was formed of new, milk-hued canvas, and bore red flags on its summit; it announced 'Good Home-brewed Beer, Ale, and Cyder.' The other was less new; a little iron stove-pipe came out of it at the back, and in front appeared the placard, 'Good Furmity Sold Hear.'

The Mayor of Casterbridge

'At that time women used to run for smocks and gown-pieces at Greenhill
Fair, and my wife that is now, being a long-legged slittering maid, hardly
husband-high, went with the rest of the maidens, for 'a was a good runner
afore she got so heavy. When she came home I said – we were then just
beginning to walk together – "What have ye got, my honey?" "I've won –
well, I've won – a gown-piece," says she, her colours coming up in a
moment. 'Tis a smock for a crown, I thought; and so it turned out. Ay,
when I think what she'll say to me now without a mossel of red in her
face, it do seem strange that 'a wouldn't say such a little thing then. . . .'

The Return of the Native

September 25. Went to Shroton Fair. In a twopenny show saw a woman
beheaded. In another a man whose hair grew on one side of his face.

The Life of Thomas Hardy

At a bygone Western country fair
I saw a giant led by a dwarf
With a red string like a long thin scarf;
How much he was the stronger there
    The giant seemed unaware.

And then I saw that the giant was blind,
And the dwarf a shrewd-eyed little thing;
The giant, mild, timid, obeyed the string
As if he had no independent mind,
    Or will of any kind.

Wherever the dwarf decided to go
At his heels the other trotted meekly,
(Perhaps – I know not – reproaching weakly)
Like one Fate bade that it must be so,
    Whether he wished or no.

Various sights in various climes
I have seen, and more I may see yet,
But that sight never shall I forget,
And have thought it the sorriest of pantomimes,
    If once, a hundred times!

'At a Country Fair'

The man who played the disturbing part in the two quiet feminine lives
hereunder depicted – no great man, in any sense, by the way – first had
knowledge of them on an October evening, in the city of Melchester. He

had been standing in the Close, vainly endeavouring to gain amid the darkness a glimpse of the most homogeneous pile of mediaeval architecture in England, which towered and tapered from the damp and level sward in front of him. While he stood the presence of the Cathedral walls was revealed rather by the ear than by the eyes; he could not see them, but they reflected sharply a roar of sound which entered the Close by a street leading from the city square, and, falling upon the building, was flung back upon him.

He postponed till the morrow his attempt to examine the deserted edifice, and turned his attention to the noise. It was compounded of steam barrel-organs, the clanging of gongs, the ringing of hand-bells, the clack of rattles, and the undistinguishable shouts of men. A lurid light hung in the air in the direction of the tumult. Thitherward he went, passing under the arched gateway, along a straight street, and into the square.

He might have searched Europe over for a greater contrast between juxtaposed scenes. The spectacle was that of the eighth chasm of the Inferno as to colour and flame, and, as to mirth, a development of the Homeric heaven. A smoky glare, of the complexion of brass-filings, ascended from the fiery tongues of innumerable naphtha lamps affixed to booths, stalls, and other temporary erections which crowded the spacious market-square. In front of this irradiation scores of human figures, more or less in profile, were darting athwart and across, up, down, and around, like gnats against a sunset.

Their motions were so rhythmical that they seemed to be moved by machinery. And it presently appeared that they were moved by machinery indeed; the figures being those of the patrons of swings, see-saws, flying-leaps, above all of the three steam roundabouts which occupied the centre of the position. It was from the latter that the din of steam-organs came.

Throbbing humanity in full light was, on second thoughts, better than architecture in the dark. The young man, lighting a short pipe, and putting his hat on one side and one hand in his pocket, to throw himself into harmony with his new environment, drew near to the largest and most patronized of the steam circuses, as the roundabouts were called by their owners. This was one of brilliant finish, and it was now in full revolution. The musical instrument around which and to whose tones the riders revolved, directed its trumpet-mouths of brass upon the young man, and the long plate-glass mirrors set at angles, which revolved with the machine, flashed the gyrating personages and hobby-horses kaleidoscopically into his eyes.

It could now be seen that he was unlike the majority of the crowd. A gentlemanly young fellow, one of the species found in large towns only, and London particularly, built on delicate lines, well, though not

fashionably dressed, he appeared to belong to the professional class; he
had nothing square or practical about his look, much that was curvilinear
and sensuous. Indeed, some would have called him a man not altogether
typical of the middle-class male of a century wherein sordid ambition is
the master-passion that seems to be taking the time-honoured place of
love.

The revolving figures passed before his eyes with an unexpected and
quiet grace in a throng whose natural movements did not suggest
gracefulness or quietude as a rule. By some contrivance there was
imparted to each of the hobby-horses a motion which was really the
triumph and perfection of roundabout inventiveness – a galloping rise
and fall, so timed that, of each pair of steeds, one was on the spring while
the other was on the pitch. The riders were quite fascinated by these
equine undulations in this most delightful holiday-game of our times.

'On the Western Circuit'

The sun is like an open furnace door,
Whose round revealed retort confines the roar
    Of fires beyond terrene;
The moon presents the lustre-lacking face
    Of a brass dial gone green,
    Whose hours no eye can trace.
The unsold heathcroppers are driven home
To the shades of the Great Forest whence they come
By men with long cord-waistcoats in brown monochrome.
The stars break out, and flicker in the breeze,
    It seems, that twitches the trees. –
    From its hot idol soon
The fickle unresting earth has turned to a fresh patroon –
    The cold, now brighter, moon.
The woman in red, at the nut-stall with the gun,
    Lights up, and still goes on:
She's redder in the flare-lamp than the sun
    Showed it ere it was gone.
Her hands are black with loading all the day,
And yet she treats her labour as 'twere play,
Tosses her ear-rings, and talks ribaldry
To the young men around as natural gaiety,
    And not a weary work she'd readily stay,
      And never again nut-shooting see,
      Though crying, 'Fire away!'

'Last Look round St Martin's Fair'

The singers are gone from the Cornmarket-place
    With their broadsheets of rhymes,
The street rings no longer in treble and bass
    With their skits on the times,
And the Cross, lately thronged, is a dim naked space
    That but echoes the stammering chimes.

From Clock-corner steps, as each quarter ding-dongs,
    Away the folk roam
By the 'Hart' and Grey's Bridge into byways and 'drongs'
    Or across the ridged loam;
The younger ones shrilling the lately heard songs,
    The old saying, 'Would we were home.'

The shy-seeming maiden so mute in the fair
    Now rattles and talks,
And that one who looked the most swaggering there
    Grows sad as she walks,
And she who seemed eaten by cankering care
    In statuesque sturdiness stalks.

And midnight clears High Street of all but the ghosts
    Of its buried burghees,
From the latest far back to those old Roman hosts
    Whose remains one yet sees,
Who loved, laughed, and fought, hailed their friends, drank their toasts
    At their meeting-times here, just as these!

                            'After the Fair'

Select Bibliography

HARDY'S OWN WRITINGS

The Collected Letters of Thomas Hardy: ed. Richard Little Purdy and
Michael Millgate, seven volumes (Oxford, 1978–89)
The Collected Short Stories (London, 1988)
The Complete Poems: ed. James Gibson (London, 1976)
The Dynasts: ed. Harold Orel (London, 1978)
The Literary Notes of Thomas Hardy: ed. Lennart A. Bjork, two volumes
(London, 1985)
The novels, available in many editions, deriving from the Wessex
Edition, twenty-four volumes (London, 1912–31)
The Personal Notebooks of Thomas Hardy: ed. Richard H. Taylor
(London, 1978)
Preface to *Select Poems of William Barnes* (Oxford, 1908)
Thomas Hardy's Personal Writings: ed. Harold Orel (Kansas, 1966;
London, 1971)

BIOGRAPHICAL AND CRITICAL SOURCES

A Conversation between Thomas Hardy and William Archer (New York, 1901;
Guernsey, 1979)
Dorset Essays: Llewelyn Powys (London, 1935)
A Hardy Companion: F.B. Pinion (London and New York, 1968)
Hardy, Novelist and Poet: Desmond Hawkins (revised London, 1987)
The Life of Thomas Hardy: Florence Emily Hardy (London, 1962).
Originally published in two volumes as *The Early Life of Thomas
Hardy* (1928) and *The Later Years of Thomas Hardy* (1930).
Young Thomas Hardy: Robert Gittings (London, 1975)
The Older Hardy: Robert Gittings (London, 1978)
Thomas Hardy, A Bibliographical Study: Richard Little Purdy
(Oxford, 1954)
Thomas Hardy, A Biography: Michael Millgate (Oxford, 1982)
A Thomas Hardy Dictionary: the Thomas Hardy Society of Japan
(Tokyo, 1984)